HOW TO THINK ABOUT HOMELAND SECURITY | VOLUME 1

The Imperfect Intersection *of* National Security *and* Public Safety

DAVID H. McINTYRE

BUSH SCHOOL OF GOVERNMENT AND PUBLIC SERVICE AT TEXAS A&M UNIVERSITY

Foreword by Senator Joseph Lieberman

ROWMAN & LITTLEFIELD

Lanham • Boulder • New York • London

Executive Editor: Traci Crowell
Editorial Assistant: Deni Remsberg
Senior Marketing Manager: Amy Whitaker

Credits and acknowledgments for material borrowed from other sources, and reproduced with permission, appear on the appropriate page within the text.

Published by Rowman & Littlefield
An imprint of The Rowman & Littlefield Publishing Group, Inc.
4501 Forbes Boulevard, Suite 200, Lanham, Maryland 20706
www.rowman.com

6 Tinworth Street, London SE11 5AL, United Kingdom

British Library Cataloguing in Publication Information Available

Library of Congress Cataloging-in-Publication Data

Names: McIntyre, David H., 1949– author.
Title: How to think about homeland security. Volume 1, The imperfect intersection of national security and public safety / David H. McIntyre, Bush School of Government and Public Service at Texas A&M University.
Other titles: Imperfect intersection of national security and public safety
Description: Lanham : Rowman & Littlefield, [2019] | Includes bibliographical references and index.
Identifiers: LCCN 2019006402 (print) | LCCN 2019010049 (ebook) | ISBN 9781538125755 (electronic) | ISBN 9781538125731 (v. 1) | ISBN 9781538125748 (v. 1 : pbk.)
Subjects: LCSH: Emergency management—United States. | Public safety—United States. | National security—United States. | Civil defense—United States.
Classification: LCC HV551.3 (ebook) | LCC HV551.3 .M385 2919 (print) | DDC 363.340973—dc23
LC record available at https://lccn.loc.gov/2019006402

This book is dedicated to:

. . . my wife, sons, and daughters-in-law, who have listened to me talk about this stuff for decades while I worked through it in my head. Other husbands have sports and hobbies. I have strategy and security. Other fathers take vacations. We walk battlefields. Other families email and Facebook about grandchildren. We converse about national security issues.

After years as my sounding board, you get my profound thanks and a copy of the book.

We can talk about it at dinner.

There will be a quiz.

Contents

Part III The Emergence of Homeland Security

Part IV Imperfect Intersection

Figures, Tables, and Textboxes

★ ★ ★

Foreword

TODAY, NEARLY A GENERATION AFTER the terrible events of 9/11, it is hard to remember that the US Congress was laying the groundwork for the idea that became homeland security well before the attack. Prompted to some extent by the tragic bombing of the Murrah Federal Building in Oklahoma City in 1995, early efforts included establishing three major commissions to examine issues that would later shape our national response: the Gilmore Commission (US Congressional Advisory Panel to Assess Domestic Response Capabilities for Terrorism Involving Weapons of Mass Destruction, 5 reports, 1999), the Bremer Commission (National Commission on Terrorism, June 2000), and the Hart-Rudman Commission (The US Commission on National Security/21st Century, January 2001). Consequently, although the nation was physically unprepared for the attack of 9/11, we were intellectually prepared to make major changes in government policies, organizations, and operations to try to prevent another such massive tragedy.

This is why, as Chair of the Senate Government Affairs Committee, after 9/11 I immediately began leading a bipartisan effort to establish the new Department of Homeland Security (DHS). We also addressed hundreds of recommendations that came from the three initial commissions and the 9/11 Commission (National Commission on Terrorist Attacks upon the United States). One of the many experts who helped my staff in this effort was the author of this series, Dr. Dave McIntyre. Later, following the national failure of the response to Hurricane Katrina, I worked with Senator Susan Collins to draft legislation that reshaped the Federal Emergency Management Agency to raise its profile in DHS and better prepare it to lead future responses to natural and unnatural catastrophes.

We also worked together on bipartisan efforts to develop countermeasures to Islamist extremism and domestic terrorism—background that helped me in writing a later book with Senator Collins called *Ticking Time Bomb: Counter-Terrorism Lessons from the U.S. Government's Failure to Prevent the Fort Hood Attack*. Since 2015, I have cochaired, with Secretary Tom Ridge, the Bipartisan Commission on Biodefense. I testified before Congress most recently on "Safeguarding American Agriculture in a Globalized World," which reflected my continuing concern about an attack on our critical infrastructure, whether from domestic terrorists like McVeigh, homegrown terrorists like Hassan, international terrorists like al-Qaeda, or from nature in an extreme weather event or an infectious disease pandemic.

Throughout my engagement with homeland security issues, my vision for the nation's domestic defense was strongly influenced by my membership on the Senate Armed Services Committee. Perhaps this is the reason that the premise of this book resonates so much with me. We continue to face threats (some of them international in nature) that could imperil the security of our nation, and we prepare for them using largely domestic public safety resources, approaches, and priorities. In volume 1 of *How to Think about Homeland Security*, Dave McIntyre presents the reason that this imperfect intersection is such a concern. I found his approach to homeland security original, insightful, and worth responding to. I hope it moves you as a citizen to think about how to better secure our nation.

The Honorable Joseph Lieberman
Co-Chair, Bipartisan Commission on Biodefense
Washington, DC

Acknowledgments

THIS BOOK (AND THE FOLLOWING SERIES) is the product of a lifetime of teaching and study. My lifetime and my study—somebody else's teaching. How do you thank a lifetime worth of people who guided you in writing, thinking, questioning, and creating?

I guess I must begin with nineteen people who taught me writing (twenty counting my mother), from Mrs. Painter in the first grade through a phalanx of majors at West Point. It was a generation that demanded precision and eloquence, and never said "Don't worry about correctness— just get your thoughts down in your journal." Thank you for your high standards and dedication to excellence.

Next, I must thank the many senior military officers who taught me to think strategically during a career in the military. That would include MG Joseph (Skip) G. Garrett III in the Army Chief of Staff's Office, Admiral Charles Larsen at the US Pacific Command, LTG Dick Chilcoat at the National Defense University, and many others who trusted and guided a junior officer in writing some pretty important strategic papers that were briefed all the way up to the Office of the President. Thank you for the lessons and the opportunities.

Later I learned that the most important step in getting the right answer in strategy and policy is asking the right question. For that lesson I must thank Ward Allen at Auburn, George Questor and Admiral Stansfield Turner at the University of Maryland, Barry Posen at MIT, and their colleagues who educated me in the great ideas of Western Civilization and the way Security Studies protects them in a world of anarchy. And how can I say enough about my faculty colleagues at the National War College who educated me day in and day out for eight years about the complexities of strategy and policy. I cannot name all of this dedicated group. Please allow me to cite Dave Tretler, Ron Tammen, Cynthia Watson, Bud Cole, and Bard O'Neil as examples of the many others who have taught our brightest military minds the value of inquiry.

I must especially acknowledge the work of those who helped me so much in the struggle to establish Homeland Security as an academic field of study over the last two decades. Many of these scholars and visionaries are identified in chapter 15 in this text. I can mention here only some of those who had the greatest influence on my attempts to think new thoughts at this new intersection of ideas that we call homeland security: Randy Larsen, Ruth David, Phil Anderson, and Elin Gursky (Analytical Services, Inc.); Dick Ewing, Chuck Herman, Jeryl Mumpower, Danny Davis, Walt Peacock, and Jason Moats (Texas A&M and The Bush School); Steve Recca, Stan Supinski, Rich Suttie, and Glen Woodbury (Center for Homeland Defense and Security); James Carafano (Heritage Institute); James Ramsey (University of New Hampshire); Bert Tussing (Army War College); Wendy Walsh (FEMA Higher Education Program); Richard White (University of Colorado, Colorado Springs); William Hancock (US Coast Guard Academy); John Cominskey (Monmouth University); Mike Dunaway (University of Louisiana at Lafayette); Robert Kadlec (Assistant Secretary for Preparedness and Response (ASPR) at the US Department of Health and Human Services); Frank Cilluffo and Bob McCreight (George Washington University); Nadav Morag (Sam Houston State); Paul Thompson (Penn State); Dave McEntire (Utah Valley University); Ed Campbell and Brian Dietzman (US Northern Command); and Paul Stockton (former Assistant Secretary of Defense for Homeland Defense and Americas' Security Affairs).

Others who helped review this text include: Tobias Gibson (Westminster College); Michael Collier (Eastern Kentucky University); Brent Lottman (Penn State); Robert Church (Yavapai College/Northern Arizona University); Richard Paxton (Campbell University); David Williams (Adelphi University).

I am a pretty good writer, but I am slow. I have to really focus on what I am writing about, uninterrupted, for hours at a time. Somebody has to keep the home and the family on track while my mind is elsewhere and act as a sounding board when I return periodically to this world. That is my wife, Cathy. Thanks, Cat.

And finally, if you are going to be published, you need a publisher—someone who believes in you and your work and will see you through until the end. For me, that has been Traci Crowell at Rowman & Littlefield. I cannot thank her enough for her assistance.

Dave McIntyre

Note to the Reader: Why Me?
Why This Book?

The September 11 attacks fell into the void between the foreign and domestic threats. The foreign intelligence agencies were watching overseas, alert to foreign threats to U.S. interests there. The domestic agencies were waiting for evidence of a domestic threat from sleeper cells within the United States. No one was looking for a foreign threat to domestic targets . . .

The terrorists exploited deep institutional failings within our government.

The 9/11 Commission Report

THIS IS A BOOK OF ESSAYS. So it is important for you to know something about the background that shaped the perspectives of the essayist.

The 1993 bombing of the World Trade Center should have been a wake-up call to every public safety and national security official in the United States and to the educational institutions whose graduates fill their ranks. But instead, this failed attempt at mass murder by a nonstate foreign actor on US soil was dismissed as an anomaly by bureaucracies focused on the end of the Cold War and the beginning of a New World Order.

Then the 1995 attack on the Murrah federal building in Oklahoma City by domestic terrorist Timothy McVeigh seemed to take us back to an old pattern that everyone understood—terrorism as criminal activity conceived and carried out within the United States and best addressed by domestic law enforcement. First responders learned some lessons. But nothing about this event required new organizations, new budgets, or new thinking in the established disciplines of academia. The bureaucracies that handle domestic safety and international security as separate issues did not go back to sleep. They went back to business as usual.

However, one small group charged with looking at safety and security issues for the future did see a new problem that required new thinking and new solutions. The 105th Congress, elected in 1996 and convened in 1997, demanded that the Department of Defense examine its alignment of missions and resources in the first of what came to be called the Quadrennial Defense Review (QDR). And to check the work of the first QDR, Congress established the National Defense Panel (NDP). Headed by defense expert Phil Odeen, it released a report in 1997 describing for the first time two important new concepts. The first was that the computer revolution could be leveraged to leap over a whole generation of military modernization, producing a "Transformation" in weapons and war fighting. The second was a warning that foreign terrorism was bound to come to American shores, bringing with it the need for the Department of Defense (and the rest of the government) to decide how they would deal with security at home—that is, with "Homeland Security."

The NDP report, *Transforming Defense*, was released in December 1997. Six months later, after twenty-seven years of Army service and eleven years of writing and teaching national strategy, I assumed duties as Dean of Faculty and Academic Affairs at the National War College (NWC) in Washington, DC. The focus of our curriculum was how to use all elements of national power to develop and promote a national security strategy. Domestic events were not really our concern. But that fall, we arranged for the director of the NDP to speak to our students. Later, a new member of the faculty, Air Force Colonel Randy Larsen (the recently departed commander of DV 1, the flying squadron that owns Air Force One and other VIP aircraft) approached me and said, "I served a fellowship at the Stimson Center and spent a year studying biological warfare. This WMD threat at home is serious business. We are the national experts in teaching *National Security*. We ought to build an elective course in *Homeland Security*."

And so we had several meetings where the two of us laid out on a white board the framework for what we imagined might become a curriculum for Homeland Security. Colonel Larsen went on to become director of the NWC Department of Military Strategy. In the winter of 2000, under his leadership, we organized the first academic conference on homeland security in the United States, in the JCS Chairman's Conference Room at the NWC. Attendees included former FBI Director William Sessions, former Congressman Newt Gingrich, former director of the CIA's Technical Office, Dr. Ruth David, and a dozen other future-oriented security strategists.

Later that year, Col. Larsen retired from the Air Force, and Dr. David (new CEO of Analytical Services, Inc.) hired him to create a think tank (IHS—the Institute for Homeland Security) which became the forerunner of the DHS Homeland Security Studies and Analysis Institute. In early 2001, they partnered with the Center for Strategic and International Studies to create the famous DARK WINTER war game. With former senior leaders of the military, intelligence agencies, and Congress as players, the game postulated a terrorist attack on the homeland by Al Qaeda using a biological weapon. Career security specialists were stunned by the results. A former chair of the Senate Armed Services Committee said, "I didn't even know what questions to ask!" This exercise did much to shape senior-level thinking about international terrorism after the 9/11 attack only eight months later.

In June 2001, I retired from a thirty-year career in the Army and settled in to write a book on National Security. But Randy invited me to join ANSER as his deputy. On September 11, 2001, I was at a conference in DC debating whether Ballistic Missile Defense should be considered part of homeland security, when an office worker rushed in and turned on the television in time for us to see an airplane hit the second tower. I called Colonel Larsen and said, "Randy, it must have been Bin Laden. He really did it." And the world changed.

In the immediate aftermath of 9/11 we became very busy. ANSER owned the URL www.homelandsecurity.org, and had the only electronic publication available on the subject. Within hours we released *A Primer on Homeland Security*, which media and government officials used to come up to speed on the subject.

As director of IHS (and given his background in the subject), Randy became the public face of homeland security. He holds the record for the most consecutive nights on the Larry King show. Because of my credentials in strategy, and my recent background in academia, including expertise in curriculum and faculty development, I gravitated toward research and teaching. With a small grant coordinated by the *Center for the Study of the Presidency and Congress,* I hired a graduate student and built at ANSER the first online library for homeland security documents. When the Naval Postgraduate School received a congressional grant for education, they used this model to develop the excellent Center for Homeland Security and Defense Library—today the gold standard for homeland security research resources worldwide.

Starting in 2002, I taught the first graduate course in homeland security at George Washington University. In 2003, Col. Larsen and I created and taught graduate courses at ANSER under the auspices of The National Graduate School (a business school focused on Quality Systems Management). When my father fell ill, I returned home to College Station, Texas, where I created graduate courses in homeland security, first for the Bush School at Texas A&M University (TAMU), and then at the LBJ School at the University of Texas. Later I joined TAMU full time to redesign and direct *The Integrative Center for Homeland Security*—a partnership between the Vice President for Research and the Bush School for Government and Public Service. With a small permanent staff and several graduate students we created:

- a landmark online graduate certificate program with five courses in homeland security and defense;
- a network of fifteen first-rate homeland security lecturers who went on to populate faculties and universities nationwide;
- an online library with annotated bibliographies of more than five thousand key homeland security documents;
- the first national-level weekly hour-long radio program devoted entirely to homeland security;
- the first university-based YouTube hosted homeland security educational TV program in the nation;
- and one of the first RSS feeds (with podcasts) for homeland security issues, effectively creating an interactive network of experts before social media appeared on the scene.

During this time, I also began working with numerous other agencies and organizations (such as local law enforcement), while struggling to understand the special aspects of what the Department of Defense has come to call Homeland Defense (HD). Taken together, since 9/11 I have taught more than sixty college courses in homeland security, made more than five hundred presentations on the subject, interviewed nine hundred experts for the radio, and made more than eleven hundred media appearances myself. I have learned some difficult lessons.

- Through the FEMA Higher Ed program, I learned that the unity of command I expected based on my military background would never work with state and local responders—but neither would their decentralized "unity of effort" approach work in a mega-disaster that threatened the security of the nation.
- At US Northern Command (NORTHCOM), I found senior officers with vision and a desire to organize and educate their staff and troops for their mission—but keenly disappointed at the resistance they encountered from faculty of major universities who were disinterested in new interdisciplinary education programs unless they came with hefty research grants.
- At conferences and workshops involving hundreds of schools partnered with the Naval Postgraduate School and the Homeland Security and Defense Education Consortium Association, I saw educational program after program with plenty of students in the pipeline, but limited support

from their own tenured faculty and administration, and no cooperation at all from the federal government in trying to align curriculum at civilian schools with job opportunities in the government.

- In the International Association of Emergency Managers and the InfraGard public–private partnership with the FBI, I observed hardworking and well-intentioned professionals struggling to align the differing priorities of bureaucracies, government, and industry.
- At state and local levels, I worked with law enforcement officials, emergency managers, fire crews, CERT teams, and volunteers—all eager to do the right thing, but all constrained by old cultures and small budgets built on one-time grants, making organization, development, and follow-through difficult.
- Finally, and most depressingly, I discovered a yawning intellectual gap between *national security experts*, who often conceptualize strategy and policy based on theory-driven academic concepts, and *public safety practitioners*, who respect solutions-based experience. Caught in between were students at training and educational institutions alike who needed a generalist understanding of homeland security writ large before they could fully apply their specialist background to the problem. They needed to know more about the whole before they could successfully integrate the parts.

After 9/11 many commentators claimed we had all the information we needed to predict the attacks. We just needed a new bureaucratic structure to "connect the dots." But throughout my two decade odyssey in homeland security education I saw a different theme—the inability of existing bureaucratic cultures (especially in academia) to surrender the power, authority, and autonomy required to fully collaborate with others on this subject.

Our problem is not connecting the dots. It is sharing control of the pencil.

I can't fix this problem. But with this series of essays addressing the full range of homeland security issues, perhaps I can clarify the dots—the issues that must be connected if we are to prepare for threats, hazards, and disasters to come and secure the future, without creating an oppressive security state that we will all regret.

That is the purpose of this book and those that follow.

Dave McIntyre
College Station, Texas

REFERENCES

National Commission on Terrorist Attacks upon the United States. 2004. *9/11 Commission Report*. New York: W. W. Norton, 263, 265, 339.
National Defense Panel. 1997. *Transforming Defense*. Washington, DC: Department of Defense. Accessed December 18, 2018. https://www.hsdl.org/?view&did=1834.

How to Use This Book

THE PEOPLE WHO REALLY NEED to understand homeland security (HS)—engaged citizens, medical, fire and law enforcement operators, elected officials, military personnel, students, media personalities, and new teachers—do not have time to wade through dense government documents or complex academic papers to grasp the fundamental issues of this complex topic. What they need is a clear list of issues, a short explanation of each, a coherent framework that shows how they fit together, and a manageable set of additional sources in case they want to explore an issue in greater depth. This book meets those needs.

It is not a heavy academic text, but a set of simple, direct essays (the first of several planned volumes), logically organized to offer a bite-sized approach to what is otherwise an overwhelming subject. Busy people need answers in context, not intellectual debates in an academic vacuum. And as a teacher, I well know the frustration of spending hours picking just the right readings, only to have students bog down in unfamiliar terms and concepts and arrive in class unprepared to participate in discussions. The essays in this volume (and its subsequent companions) are carefully crafted to pack maximum information into minimal packages so students can better focus on just what they need to know to begin analysis and evaluation.

The essays are designed to stand alone. You do not have to read all of them in order to understand the key points. Faculty can pick and choose essays to match individual lessons. And people reading for business or pleasure can skip right to the topics they find most interesting.

But the essays also fit into a larger framework. Too often homeland security looks like a collection of organizations and actions and policies and budgets without a structure. It is all jelly, with no donut. Or alternatively, all muscle and bone with no connective tissue. This first volume,

Imperfect Intersection, provides that connectivity, helping readers explore the nature of homeland security as the jarring collision of national security and public safety in a government system designed to keep those two functions separate.

The book lays out the concepts of nationhood, national security, national power, and national security strategy—to include why the "New Terrorism" presents an unprecedented threat to the United States. It explores the philosophical issue of how we think and what we believe as individuals and as a society, and how this impacts the way we perceive and respond to security challenges. It examines how public safety is different from national security and the challenge of crafting a response to threats that present at the intersection of these two functions. And finally, it explores how the perspectives of those who work in national security differ from those in public safety and private enterprise, and why the challenges of this imperfect intersection require a new approach to training and education. That approach should focus on changing bureaucratic culture and perspective in order to meet the new "Maximum of Maximum" threats that constitute the reason HS was created in the first place.

Subsequent volumes address the major issues of homeland security with a structure that promotes understanding, analysis, and critical thinking. The subjects of these volumes include: Risk and Threats; Vulnerabilities and Consequences; Actors and Drivers; Preparedness and Emergency Management; and Education and Special Topics (like borders, transnational crime, and trafficking). A helpful "Framework for Inquiry" will be provided for examining homeland security issues and dynamics from an educational perspective.

Also uniquely useful in this series are the "Bottom Line Up Front" sections at the beginning of every essay. These serve not only to summarize the individual chapters but to connect them to previous essays and the overall structure of homeland security. Thus, individual chapters may be read or assigned alone to support individual topics or collectively as part of an integrated approach to the overall field of study.[1]

---

[1] Note that in order for all essays to stand alone as individual readings, a considerable amount of repetition is necessary in the "Bottom Line Up Front" sections. Because context is so important to the overall explanation of homeland security and how its parts fit together (or don't), it must be well established in any reading that is examined alone. Readers who peruse all the chapters in order, one after the other, may be occasionally distracted by this frequent repetition of background material. Readers who dip in and out, skipping some chapters in their search for specific issues, will be happy for the additional connective tissue.

Finally, teachers will find that the essays are designed and written to support a broad range of learning outcomes. In my own classes (five dozen at six different colleges), presentations (hundreds on these subjects), and media work (more than nine hundred interviews <u>of</u> others and eleven hundred interviews <u>by</u> others), I tailored my delivery by using the following taxonomy:

1. For a general audience and undergrad level—**Understand** and **Remember** the most important aspects of homeland security as it developed and exists today in the United States.
2. As the bridge between generalist and specialist audiences, and undergrad and graduate students—**Apply** this information to routine and novel cases, researched from other sources.
3. For specialist audiences and graduate-level students—**Analyze** the cause-and-effect relationship between homeland security problems and potential solutions.
4. Also for specialist audiences and graduate level students—**Evaluate** possible solutions in order to determine the best answers with acceptable costs.
5. For select audiences and doctorial-level students—**Synthesize** available information to **Create** new and better solutions with lower costs.

The essays in *How to Think about Homeland Security* support all of these objectives. For readers new to the subject, they provide important background and terms essential to further research. For advanced readers, they provide details required for the analysis and prioritization that are the hallmark of professional discussions and effective graduate seminars. And for experts in the fields and subfields of homeland security, they provide a connectivity that leads to new concepts, constructs, and even theories (something sorely lacking in homeland security studies).

Whatever the level of learning desired, a reader or faculty member can set the stage for a stimulating experience in homeland security by starting with this book and this series.

1

What Is a Nation?

BOTTOM LINE UP FRONT

Thinking clearly about homeland security requires that you begin by understanding national security. To get the right answers in either of these subjects, you must ask the right questions. And to ask the right question, you must use the right language. Unless we use the word "nation" properly, we cannot correctly evaluate the strengths and vulnerabilities of the United States or more complicated formulations like "national security."

*A **nation** is a collection of people, larger and more loosely related than a tribe, who nonetheless feel a bond of close attachment based on common history and beliefs. (This may or may not involve blood kinship.) For this reason, citizens of a nation are willing to work together, sacrifice together, grant legitimacy to national leaders, and protect their common security even at personal cost.*

*A **nation-state** is a political entity that combines the emotional bonds of a **nation** with the physical reality (ability to enforce borders and domestic laws) of a **state**.*

Oranges and grapefruit are both fruits, but we do not use the same word to describe them. The taste is quite different. Depending on the varieties, they may like different soil, different fertilizers, different temperatures, rainfall, and feeding at different times of the year. A customer who buys a bag marked "oranges" and finds it full of grapefruit is likely to be irate. A farmer who contracts to deliver grapefruit and instead delivers oranges is likely to be sued.

Words matter, and so it is with terms that describe political groupings of people such as "tribe," "clan," "state," "nation," "nation-state," and "empire." Unfortunately, security experts (and the media) misuse these terms routinely (especially "state" and "nation"), frequently with confusing results. For example, in some locales, the history and culture are simply not suitable for growing nations, and state-building is the best that an outside entity can hope for, no matter how much they desire otherwise. In fact, even building a unified state may not be possible in a fractured culture.[1]

So, this essay will focus on defining a nation (and related political entities), from both international and domestic perspectives, so that we can figure out how it may be secured.

The protozoa of political organization is the **family**. When individual survival is impossible in a hostile world, people have historically relied on the support of close blood relatives. This generally affords some degree of protection and maybe even prosperity, as long as the individual obeys the family rules—usually designed to protect the family as a whole from both hostile outsiders and misbehaving insiders. For reproduction and resources, families may reach beyond their blood bonds to make alliances with other families. But blood relations remain the most basic political unit of security. Family does not imply the control of territory or the existence of a governing system. It does imply loyalty, frequently above all else.

When extended families are large enough, and the geography is right, they may develop locally dominant political groupings called **clans**.[2] And if their increasing numbers push related members out to create a large geographic footprint, while retaining a form of familial affiliation, the resulting political organization may be called a **tribe**. Because of their common origins, families, clans, and tribes generally develop common customs, beliefs, and practices, which may coalesce into a common culture. Tribes are usually geographically constrained and may defend territory but frequently lack a structure to govern it.

Because they figure into international and domestic security equations, we should include **gangs** and **organized crime syndicates** in our list of political groupings. They share some characteristics with families, as do **cults**, **religious orders**, and even some **communes**. All demand the subordination of the self to the interest of the "family," as well as obedience to family rules and culture. While they do not usually share actual blood kinship, they may share a common sense of origin, resulting in a loyalty that exceeds outside affiliations (like state citizenship). Reformers who assume they will

---

[1] This is a lesson we still seem to be learning in Iraq and Afghanistan . . . again and again.

[2] My definitions and discussions are offered from a security perspective. Anthropologists may offer somewhat different definitions because they approach the subject from a different perspective. For our purposes, we need to know what people want to secure and what they are willing to sacrifice to do so.

easily substitute state loyalty for tribal, religious, or other long-established loyalties are frequently disappointed.[3]

We don't actually have a commonly accepted name to describe groups unified and motivated to action by political beliefs held with religious zealotry. Neither extremism nor fundamentalism works here, because the terms have other applications that often depend entirely on the perspective of one side or the other. A Buddhist may apply the fundamentals of his religion rigorously to his own life without attempting to impose them by force on others. Veganism, defined as adherence to a "plant-based diet avoiding all animal foods such as meat (including fish, shellfish and insects), dairy, eggs and honey," might reasonably be called an extreme version of vegetarianism (The Vegan Society 2017). But no reasonable person would suggest this as a form of "extremism," implying the use of force or violence in any way. So "fundamentalist" and "extremist" are simply too vague to describe Nazis, genocidal racists, and ISIS operatives who are willing to sacrifice their lives, their families, and every element of rational or moral self—as well as the lives of children and other innocents—in pursuit of mixed religious and political ends. We need a new term—perhaps **sacrificial zealots**—to describe what they believe, what they do, and what is required to deter or defeat them.

Moving on, a **nation** is a collection of people, larger and more loosely related than a tribe, who nonetheless feel a bond of close attachment and, for this reason, are willing to work together, recognize each other, and support those bonds even at some personal cost. The origin of this bond may be blood kinship, religious belief, common culture or history, or even allegiance to common values. If a large number of people believe that they are bound together as a nation, and feel those bonds of kinship strongly enough to act on them, then they comprise a nation.[4]

---

[3] The famous nation-building efforts of the Marshall Plan reinforced existing national loyalties built around struggling state organizations. It worked. US efforts in Vietnam, Iraq, and Afghanistan tried to build such loyalties from scratch in places where they did not previously exist, based on offering goods, services, and promises of good governance. Results have been disappointing.

[4] This requires, by the way, a common sense of identity, born of a common culture, history, values, and belief system leading to a common national narrative of who they are and common vision of who they are going to be. This is very difficult to build by design. It requires a dominate culture that can incorporate others into its national mythology without losing its concept of self. And it requires that subordinate cultures within the nation redefine themselves in terms of the dominate culture. Striking this balance is very hard. This is why "state-building" by third parties is sometimes possible, but "nation-building" almost never works. And it is why nations rarely survive the transition to empire—the assimilation of many foreign cultures dilutes the original dominate culture until the nation does not recognize itself any more. Also, nations last only so long as the dominate culture is dominate. Nations may be driven together by a challenge, but they are often fractured by losses that cause the assimilated cultures to question the price of assimilation and reassert their separate identities.

The size of a nation is nowhere set by law or custom, but it must be larger than a clan or a tribe. A nation may be concentrated in a single state, or it may be distributed across several states, which can cause significant friction. The Kurds—distributed across Northern Iraq, Syria, and Eastern Turkey—constitute a nation. Their desire and periodic efforts to establish a separate nation-state upset both the Iraqis (who would lose lucrative oil deposits in Kurdish lands) and the Turks (who do not wish to set the precedent that members of their diverse political entity can simply depart the state when they feel it is to their advantage).

A **state** is different from the previously discussed forms of political organization, in that its participants might not require any form of blood, historical, or cultural affiliation. Families, clans, tribes, and nations are defined by their members. States are defined by the power to enforce external borders and internal laws.

States have real geography and real geographic boundaries. They have the power and organization required to defend those boundaries—else they cease to exist. They can govern the population that resides within those geographic boundaries, although governance may include some negotiated independence for subordinate geographic or demographic groups.

It is not necessary for a State government to be popular, representative, or even kind to its own people. In fact, a state may be ruled by interlopers who have little legitimacy in the eyes of most citizens. But if the ruling elite can defend the boundaries against outsiders and exercise political control over insiders, then the political entity is a state—and is likely to be so recognized by other states in the world. Yugoslavia was an example of a State until it broke apart after the end of the Cold War. The fact that it broke up on its own demonstrates that it was not a nation. It was only a state, held together by external threats and internal security services.

A state may be weaker than it appears, if its people are subject to divided loyalties or if they feel the leadership has no real interest in their well-being.

This is especially true of the special type of state called a **kingdom**. A kingdom has the characteristics of a state (border protection, domestic law enforcement) but is ruled by a king and related or associated aristocracy. A kingdom exists only so long as a king or queen exercises royal power. When the sovereign dies, he or she must be replaced by another sovereign, or the kingdom becomes a state ruled by some other form of power.

Until the early twentieth century, most political entities called kingdoms were ruled by kings, queens, or other "royals." Today some states retain the title "kingdom" as a link to their historic national character but actually employ some different form of government. England was once ruled by royal decree and was in fact a kingdom. Today it retains a king or queen and royal family. They play a role in civil society and even legitimizing the elected government. But for international relations purposes, Great Britain is regarded as a state, not a kingdom. The modern state of Saudi Arabia, however, is clearly a traditional kingdom, with the mechanisms of government established by the King and operating in accordance with the will of the King (and powerful royals within the family).

A **nation-state** is a political entity that combines the emotional bonds of a **nation** with the physical reality of a **state**. This makes it extremely robust and difficult to defeat militarily.

In the early nineteenth century, "Germany" did not appear on any map. Instead, maps showed a patchwork of German States, ranging from Prussia in the north to Bavaria in the south. While they shared Germanic culture and language, they were divided by a variety of factors, including, in some cases, religion. But by the end of the nineteenth century, these independent states and principalities had been welded together into a single political entity, responding to a single head of state and feeling a sense of unifying kinship. By the outbreak of World War I, Germany (like France, Great Britain, and the United States) was a nation-state.

Because a nation-state combines the emotional unity of a nation with the resources and political structure of a state, it can call upon all the power, existing and potential, within its borders. And it can demand sacrifices from its people that might cause open revolt in a mere State. For example, citizens who hide their sons from the military draft of a state might urge the same sons to war in defense of a cherished nation-state.

This voluntary commitment of resources and passions, married with an efficient and effective bureaucratic apparatus, can prove remarkably resilient to the pressures of war. Governments grown used to the collapse of hollow kingdoms and states during the colonial expansion of the nineteenth century were shocked and horrified at the damage inflicted and endured by the clash of robust nation-states in the early twentieth century. Many political parties retain an active fear of nations and nationalism today based on the carnage of twentieth-century nation-state conflict.

External threat is an important factor in maintaining internal allegiance for all of these political organizations. Internal differences, including race, ethnicity, culture, religion, and even outright discrimination or oppression, may be subordinated in the face of external threat. And a clan, tribe, state, or nation can actually be stronger in the face of the challenge than in times of peace and prosperity. Shared hardships unify a nation's citizenry. But prosperity is rarely shared equally. The resentment of underserved, or even oppressed, groups may come as a surprise to elites long accustomed to state or national unity.

For empires the effect of stresses is reversed.

An **empire** is the political organization that results from a state (sometimes embodied in the person of a single monarch or ruling oligarchy) exercising dominion by force over outside states or political groups. Examples include the Roman Empire, the Mongol Empire, and the British Empire. Whether an "American Empire" exists is an important question open for debate.

The formal incorporation of subordinate political bodies is a significant characteristic of empire. Conquering a foreign territory is not the same as ruling it. Ruling is easier if the territory can be governed by local officials in the name of their own people but with the authority of (and in subordination to) a larger empire. The Jewish King Herod, you may recall, ruled Israel with the permission of, and to the benefit of, Rome. Great Britain frequently used local leaders in the same way at the height of its Colonial Empire.

The use of force is an important qualifier. The subordinate parties to an empire are generally forced or intimidated into joining—or at the least, threatened by dominate parties if they fail to join. The Delian League—a "voluntary" confederacy of city-states allied with Athens to fight the Persians—was gradually transformed into the Athenian Empire by threats and aggressive actions. The Melian Dialogue is famous in historical and international relations circles as the exchange between an expansionist Athens and the isolationist island of Melos, whose people simply wished to be left alone. When the Melians refused to join the empire, they were conquered and murdered or sold into slavery. Empires cannot afford to show weakness, lest their far-flung "partners" be encouraged to rebel (Strassler 1996, 351–57 [5.84–116]).

The centralization of leadership is another important feature of empire. Organizations where states or groups cooperate but retain their autonomy are called **alliances**. The Allies of World War II (Britain, France, the United States, Russia, etc.) offer an example; the coordination of military action among these equals was famously difficult. Not so the decisive use by Britain of colonial troops from their empire during the same war.

Because they are larger and more dispersed than a state but lack the integrity and emotional fidelity of a nation, empires frequently appear stronger than they actually are. Although they may have vast resources at their command in theory, in practice, demanding the sacrifice of subordinated people in time of war can be a dicey proposition. And convincing the core of the empire to sacrifice blood and treasure for the periphery can be just as difficult. Thus war and prosperity provide different stresses on empires than on states and nations. Prosperity generally encourages subordinate states and people to bear a gentle yoke of empire in exchange for increased trade and wealth. Threats to the empire that require the raising of local levies and taxes may encourage resistance from locals who no longer see the benefits of empire to be worth the cost.

The core states around which empires are built are also frequently surprised to discover that maintaining an empire is more costly than winning one. Those fighting to gain an empire can generally choose the time, place, and way to concentrate forces for an attack and ultimate victory. Those defending an empire have no such flexibility. They must defend everywhere all the time against both internal and external threats. To ease this burden, rulers of empire frequently turn to local governments and military forces to create local safety, security, and stability. But they also resort to unpopular local taxes to fund this local security. And under some circumstances, forces created to promote domestic stability promote insurrection and revolt instead.[5]

Finally, empires often forget that influence runs two ways. Expecting to change the culture and behavior of "lesser" people, the elite of empires are often shocked to find foreigners emigrating in large numbers, their cultural practices intact, living among them and changing the identity of the home State. That is what happened when Mexico invited Anglo émigrés into Texas to serve as a barrier against the Comanche. That's what happened when Rome offered barbarians land and citizenship to insulate it from other barbarians. That's what is happening in much of Europe today. For better or worse, when a state becomes an empire, it eventually ceases to be a state.[6]

So why does all this matter to Americans (and others) trying to understand the fundamentals of national and homeland security?

It matters because we cannot protect and advance our national security unless we know who we are protecting and advancing interests *for* and *against*. Who are we? Who challenges us? Who might cooperate with us? What motivates them? Attracts them? Deters them? Defeats them? The answer depends to some extent on whether "they" are a family, clan, tribe, zealot, nation, state, nation-state, or empire. Strategies designed to work against cartel families might work differently against gangs or organized crime syndicates whose leaders and soldiers are driven by profit rather

---

[5] As our own King George III discovered.
[6] This is the central story of Alexander the Great.

than blood ties. Nation-building might never work in a location dominated by tribes and tribal hierarchies (or religious beliefs), where each has a one-thousand-year history of fighting to the death against neighbors. State-building, by contrast, might be possible if we find a way to divide geography, resources, and power between existing hierarchies, providing the advantages of security and prosperity to each. Our interaction with foreign enemies and foreign allies might change if we recognize the difficulty of imposing our national values on states fragmented by multiple cultural beliefs.

Also, we cannot craft proper policies for homeland security unless we know what constitutes the homeland. What exactly is it that we are trying to secure and defend? The boundaries of the United States? Our critical infrastructure? Our people? Our economy? Our constitutional rights? Are we securing the resources and governing mechanism of a state? The values and beliefs of a nation? The economic connectivity of an empire?

Perhaps even more importantly, are we still a nation-state? Has encouraging diverse domestic identities strengthened our national bonds by promoting inclusion? Or weakened our body politic so that those national bonds might be strained in a crisis? Should this consideration play a part in our homeland security plans and operations? In our evaluation of risk?

And what of the enemies who threaten us at home? Are they families? Tribes? States? Nations? Sacrificial zealots? What will deter them? Defeat them? Can we regard our enemies as rational actors, as we have in the past? Or are we facing some new phenomena—groups built around blood, ethnic, or religious ties that trump "rational" interests? Do these enemies think in new ways, requiring new thinking from us—new strategies, policies and operations, and maybe organization, processes, and resources—in order to be successful? To achieve victory? To win? What if they don't want a better life or anything else we can give them? What if what they want is revenge? Or to satisfy their god? What strategy will satisfy an enemy driven by blood lust?

We cannot answer any of these questions unless we get the language right.

REFERENCES

Strassler, Robert, ed. 1996. *The Landmark Thucydides: A Comprehensive Guide to the Peloponnesian War*. New York: The Free Press.

The Vegan Society. 2017. "Definition of Veganism." Accessed December 18, 2018. https://www.vegansociety.com/go-vegan/definition-veganism.

2

What Is Security?

BOTTOM LINE UP FRONT

Security in an <u>international</u> sense begins with safety of the state against external attack. It extends to defending and advancing national interests by achieving goals that support those interests. It ultimately includes producing and protecting the power required to achieve those goals, advance those interests, and protect against challenges and attacks.

Security <u>at home</u> is quite different—especially for nations built on a representative government like the United States. For nonrepresentative states, domestic security frequently means protection against internal threats to the state leadership. For the United States, domestic security has traditionally been provided by the citizens' relationship with their government. Threats from overseas actors against US domestic targets have generally taken the form of spying, industrial espionage, counterintelligence, and occasionally sabotage—all countered quite handily by the FBI and other domestic law enforcement agencies.

Normal crime and dangers from technological hazards and natural disasters have been considered public safety matters in the United States, not national or domestic security issues. And even rare attacks against institutions of government (like the attack against the US House of Representatives by Puerto Rican separatists in 1954) have always been managed by standard public safety organizations.

Thinking about internal security against an external threat to the state, its elements of power, or its legitimacy is relatively new to the United States.

Building on our observation that "you can't get the answer right unless you get the question right, and you can't get the question right unless you get the language right," let's look at the condition we are trying to establish: *security* against both internal and external threats.

The "homeland" part of Homeland Security (HS) does not roll easily off of the American tongue. It sounds too much like "fatherland" or "motherland" or some other statist construction that has been hostile to American interests in the past. But everyone pretty much understands what it means.[1] It connotes "domestic" as opposed to "international."

But what is "security"? And how is it different from "safety," which was the focus of most homeland security personnel before the term *homeland security* was coined?

In general use, the difference between terms is clear. *Safety* tends to be personal, specific, and immediate against a specific threat. *Security* tends to be more systemic, more general, and plays out over a longer term, against less well-defined concerns. We employ safety glass, safety boots, work place safety, and fire and police for public safety. But we plan for mall security, executive security, and financial security in retirement. Ballistic missile submarines provide for our national security. Seatbelts promote public safety. We put security systems on our homes, but we make our children wear safety helmets on bikes, not the other way around.

Homeland security seems to mix these concepts. How can we think clearly about the difference?

Dictionary definitions of security generally focus on freedom from risk, physical danger, or psychological fear. From a practical perspective, security suggests confidence or the ability to live free of threat (Kleinedler 2016). A more military perspective, offered by the US Joint Chiefs of Staff, suggests, "Measures taken . . . to protect against all acts designed to, or which may, impair effectiveness" (Joint Chiefs of Staff 2018, 210). However, when combined with "homeland," the term "security" suggests something both larger and smaller than these general definitions.

Homeland Security probably should have been called "Domestic Security," except that term was already "taken" to describe the concern many nondemocratic states have for internal threats to government stability. Dictators especially are always concerned about domestic security. (Alternatively, "state security" is often used in the same context.) In contrast, HS combines concerns over the safety of individuals and their property, the

---

[1] The term "Homeland Security" originated when staff were rushing to conclude the Report of the National Defense Panel (*Transforming Defense—National Security in the 21st Century*) in December 1997. As a (to remain anonymous) staffer who helped write the report told me in a private interview several years ago, "We ran out of time. The report was due for publication and we all knew what we meant. But we couldn't find exactly the right term, and 'domestic security' seemed wrong. So we used 'homeland security' as a stopgap. At the time no one dreamed that the term would take on a life of its own and become a major part of American life."

continued functioning of business and domestic government at all levels, the power and resources of the state writ large, and the national system of governance as a whole—all at the same time. And it overlaps with concerns about international threats.

- As we will discover in later chapters, *national security* (NS) involves the protection of the state and its interests against external threats, by the creation, preservation, and application of power in coordination with or competition against individual members of the international community.
- But the American people expect security in a *domestic context* to provide protection for individuals, private property, key resources and government capabilities, against crime, accidents, and natural disasters, <u>as well as</u> politically motivated attacks—even if these attacks originate overseas. Police, fire, medical services, transportation, energy, and many other components of day-to-day life previously assured under the traditional rubric of public safety are now wrapped into homeland security.
- Security of people at home also includes the security of their business communities, where their jobs reside, and protection of the production of wealth that advances what the Constitution calls "the general welfare."
- Responsibility for government in the United States resides at state and local as well as federal levels. All these government functions, offices, and personnel must be secured against disruption and destruction if the functioning of government is to be assured. That is homeland security as well.
- And finally, beyond the mere functions of government, the system of American *governance* must be secured—that is, the rights and liberties provided by our Constitution and our republican form of government, as exercised through free and fair elections and an independent judiciary, all free from threats and coercion.

Security from international assault on aspects of domestic life is a relatively new requirement in the United States. We are responding to it with some new ideas and structures but mostly traditional bureaucracies, cultures, and language. As a result, the term "security" sometimes has quite different meanings depending upon the context—whether international or domestic. And "who does what" can also be confusing. A police officer responding to a crazed gunman or a traffic accident involving a deadly chemical spill is working a public safety issue. But the same officer is responding to a homeland security event if the gunman is motivated by a foreign ideology or the spill is an intentional attack. Where do we draw the line?

Answering that question requires a clear understanding of the language we use. The next chapter, which expands our inquiry into *national* security, will help.

REFERENCES

Kleinedler, Steven R. ed. 2016. "Security." In *American Heritage Dictionary of the English Language*. Boston: Houghton Mifflin. Accessed December 18, 2018. https://www.ahdictionary.com/word/search.html?q=security.

Joint Chiefs of Staff. 2018. *Department of Defense Dictionary of Military and Associated Terms*. Washington, DC: Department of Defense. Accessed December 18, 2018. http://www.jcs.mil/Portals/36/Documents/Doctrine/pubs/dictionary.pdf?ver=2018-09-28-100314-687.

3

What Is National Security?

National Security—
A collective term encompassing both national defense and foreign relations of the United States. Specifically, the condition provided by: a. a military or defense advantage over any foreign nation or group of nations; b. a favorable foreign relations position; or c. a defense posture capable of successfully resisting hostile or destructive action from within or without, overt or covert. See also security.

Joint Publication 1-02

BOTTOM LINE UP FRONT

Sometimes the words "national security" are used cavalierly to describe issues concerning states or political groups that are not really nations at all. But because of its history and laws, "national security" means a very specific thing in the context of the United States.

For the last seventy years (since the end of World War II), US national security has involved day-to-day <u>physical protection</u> against foreign attack or encroachment upon US territory, its <u>interests</u>, and its <u>elements of national power</u>.

- *By interests, we mean conditions advantageous to the nation's existence, welfare, and ability to shape its own destiny.*
- *By elements of power, we mean capabilities that may be used to protect the nation's interests and advance its goals. These are traditionally described by the acronym DIME (Diplomatic, Informational, Military, Economic).[1]*

---

[1] As will be explained in a later chapter, the initial version of DIME represented Diplomatic, Intelligence, Military and Economic power. The Department of Defense currently substitutes the word "Informational" for "Intelligence."

At another level, of course, national security activities protect the nation's citizens as a whole, their government, and their constitutional rights against external threat.

Interestingly, the safety of <u>individual</u> citizens and their property is not a top national security priority. That role is a function of domestic <u>public safety</u> personnel and organizations.

Because homeland security was born from national security, we must get the national security language and concepts right before we can properly think about the homeland derivative.

But we established a definition for *nation* in chapter 1. We established a definition for *security* in chapter 2. And the Joint Staff offers its professional definition of *national security* in its official doctrine (above). Shouldn't that be enough to serve our needs?

Well, unfortunately, no. Because even international relations experts (actually, especially IR experts), frequently use terms like "country," "state," and "nation" interchangeably, leading to significant confusion. The same is true of *public safety*, *domestic security*, and *international security*. For example,

- In the United States, the concepts of COG and COOP (Continuity of Government and Continuity of Operations—maintaining the structure of government and the functionality of that structure) are regarded as *national security* issues, even if the threat is domestic. We never use the term *state security*, which suggests to the American ear the protection of a perhaps illegitimate power structure against internal dissent.
- When looking overseas, we sometimes use *national security* to describe the protection of states that are not nations and face negligible external threat (Afghanistan), but never nations that are not states, even if they do face outside threats (Kurdistan).

So we frequently confuse ourselves through language and practice. When we talk about the national security of the United States, what exactly do we want to secure? What are we securing it against? And is homeland security a part of the solution?

Let's see if a little history can help us clear things up. Or at least explain the confusion.

A SHORT HISTORY OF STATES, NATIONS, AND SECURITY

Europe of the early 1600s featured a diverse array of kingdoms, principalities, and empires, many of them divided internally along religious, ethnic, cultural, or linguistic lines. "Security" was not a term used to describe government policy of the age, but regimes generally had two major "security" concerns: external threats to the borders and internal threats against the ruling aristocracy.

In 1618, domestic agitation by Protestants became too much for the emperor of the largely Catholic Holy Roman Empire. He set out to suppress Protestantism and its supporters within the political boundaries he controlled. But his Protestant subjects appealed to the citizens and leaders of Protestant states, who began to intervene outside their own borders. Leaders of Catholic states and their subjects responded in kind. The resulting Thirty Years War soon jumped its religious boundaries, and people of both religious persuasions ended up fighting on both sides. The conflict produced three decades of human misery and devastation, perhaps killing as many as a third of Europe's citizens. Domestic security problems created an international security disaster.

The political solution of the day was the Treaty of Westphalia, which, among other provisions, declared the boundaries of states to be inviolable, and the domestic affairs of European states to be nobody's business but their own. The result was an international system in which states (see the definition in chapter 2) were generally safe from external meddling in internal affairs for more than three hundred years. State sovereignty over domestic issues was essentially absolute. And security of the state remained entirely the state's responsibility.[2]

This is an important point, because the divisions within states did not disappear in 1648 with the arrival of the treaty. They were just suppressed—first by the king's army, and later by "state security."

A hundred years later, the concept of nationalism (virtual brotherhood within a state, based on common culture and heritage, even if some significant differences had to be overlooked) shifted the focus of sovereignty in some places from the king and state to the people and the nation. (See the definition of nation in chapter 1.) This shift was evident in the American Revolution, but primarily impacted Europe through the French Revolution. Many of Napoleon's opponents fought for their kings. His soldiers fought largely for their nation and French Revolutionary values.

---

[2] The first major crack in the Westphalian System of absolute respect for international borders followed the assassination of Ferdinand, archduke and heir apparent to the Austro-Hungarian Empire, in 1914. The conspirators sought a domestic objective: the separation of Serbia from the Empire and consolidation into Yugoslavia. But they prompted a threat of cross-border intervention, which triggered a cascade of secret treaties and dragged all of Europe into war. Twenty-four years later, Hitler used the ruse of protecting ethnic Germans from domestic oppression to justify crossing international borders to expand the Third Reich. This flouting of international law based on Westphalian concepts constituted a part of the charges against Nazi leaders in the Nuremberg trials.

Although "state" remained the term of art for diplomacy and international relations during the nineteenth century, the concept of "nation" and nationalism grew steadily, especially in Europe and America. Two of the primary catalysts seem to be the growing sense of self-determination and the growing threat from other nations—especially other colonial powers. States, after all, are limited in the resources (men, material, taxes, etc.) they can coerce from their subjects. Nations can draw deep upon willing contributions from citizens. This power advantage created a growing sense that nationhood was the organizing principle of the modern world and the nation-state its unit of political currency.

Of course, this distinction applied primarily to European colonial powers and not their colonies, many of which won their nationhood through struggle. But that did not stop the visionaries from considering the *nation* rather than the *state* as the basic unit of stable domestic government and peaceful international governance, first in the League of *Nations*, and then the United *Nations*.

Unfortunately, Nazis, Fascists, and the Japanese Military based their concepts of nationalism on bloodlines rather than shared values. And their concept of state sovereignty accepted the law of the jungle as the basis of the international system. Their resulting international aggression and domestic persecution of minorities in World War II culminated in the creation of international tribunals, which established the legal right of the international community to constrain state behavior and intervene in response to extreme domestic human rights violations.[3] The US enthusiasm for postwar "nation-building," which imposed representative government on the defeated powers, further advanced the idea of the nation-state, democratically representing its domestic population and properly respecting the rights of other nations, as the best political model for the world.

FROM NATIONAL SECURITY CONCEPT TO NATIONAL SECURITY COMMUNITY

The detonation of nuclear weapons in 1945, the rise of opposing nuclear-armed camps in the Cold War, and the prospect of nuclear war and annihilation on short notice pushed soldiers, scholars, and the diplomatic community to focus on external threats to the state. In the United States,

---

[3] University-trained elites have been more enthusiastic about the subordination of state sovereignty to supranationalist bureaucracies than have rank-and-file citizens of traditional nations. The British vote to leave the EU and the election of Donald Trump as President of the United States offer examples of this tension.

these concerns crystallized in the passage of the National Security Act of 1947 (and its revision in 1949). The act had three main features:

- It reorganized and consolidated US military forces under a civilian-led the DOD and established the Chairman of the Joint Chiefs of Staff;
- It established a formal National Security Council to coordinate national security information coming into and national security guidance going out of the Office of the President;
- It established the Central Intelligence Agency (CIA) to both coordinate the intelligence being produced by several US agencies focused on international affairs and direct covert security activities in support of the international interests of the nation.

These efforts were soon focused by a national security strategy classified at first (NSC-68) and then published as an unclassified document starting in 1987. Of course, the public version of the National Security Strategy has always been general in nature, while many specific aspects and plans remain routinely classified. But the overall effect was to create a "national security community," soon composed of tens of thousands of government officials, scholars and academic experts, think tanks and contractors, media representatives and weapons manufacturers, teachers, authors, and associations of retired officials. Even chambers of commerce and local community organizations seeking to support the network of military bases that underlay the economy of many small towns spoke in terms of NS. And over time national security plans, parties, and actions spawned a parallel, smaller, but more vociferous "antiwar community" of academicians, think tanks, media specialists, and economic interests of their own.

The point is that within a few years of the identification of national security as a government responsibility, a huge "military–industrial–academic–media" enterprise was beavering away around the world, creating a global security footprint for the United States and consuming annually the largest discretionary part of the federal budget.[4]

---

[4] As Amy Zegart (1999) explains in her book *Flawed by Design*, the existence or absence of previous security bureaucracies played a large hand in shaping the new national security community. The existing military service chiefs, for example, worked hard to weaken the new Chairman of the Joint Chiefs. And the first chairman, General Omar Bradley, a former senior commander himself, assisted in that endeavor. With the new CIA, it was the long-standing Office of Naval intelligence that raised the most serious obstacles, although the opposition by the FBI remains legendary. By contrast, the National Security Council filled a new niche previously unoccupied by any competitor. Zegart credits the success of the fledgling NSC largely, though not entirely, to this fact.

As the National Security concept and community developed, the operating assumption of the United States as a nation was that most *domestic security* concerns (that is, domestic challenges to the state) would be addressed by the representative system of government. The few internal problems that did arise (foreign espionage, domestic crime, and even rudimentary domestic terrorism) could be handled by law enforcement. In fact, parts of the new national security apparatus (CIA, NSA, USAID, etc.) were so completely focused on international concerns that they were forbidden by law from operating within the confines of the United States. Thus the long-standing but newly named concept of national security developed along four "lines of effort."

- *Deter aggression* against US territory, persons, interests, and allies overseas by making any violator think the cost of attack would outweigh the benefit.
- *Defeat aggression* should it occur by using all the power of the nation and its allies to roll back an attack at great cost to the attacker.
- *Support and sustain these efforts* by producing required elements of national power to include: *domestic efforts* like education, ROTC, the industrial base; *international efforts* like treaties, alliances, agreements, and mechanisms for dispute resolution; *pre-war/Cold War preparations,* like raising, training, equipping, and prepositioning forces; *intelligence/ diplomatic* "shaping of the battlefield"; and *funding,* which developed an entirely new industry with specialists in the administration, Congress, academia, and private industry.
- *Develop necessary intellectual concepts* (expressed in law and policy)— both in government and in academia, in order to advance the entire endeavor.

From an operational perspective, until 9/11, national security involved the day-to-day physical protection of the nation, its interests, and its elements of national power (levers that may be used to protect its interests and advance its goals). These elements of power are traditionally described by the acronym DIME.[5] The traditional definitions included:

- **Diplomacy**—"Those overt international public information activities of the United States Government designed to promote United States

---

[5] DOD (together with the Joint Staff) has an exceptionally comprehensive approach to the definition and explanation of terms and doctrine. For example, the DOD Dictionary of Military and Associated Terms (formerly Joint Pub 1–02) is updated *monthly* online, which makes it easy to stay current. But there is no comprehensive archive of past versions that makes it very difficult to track changes in concepts. I first encountered the term "DIME"

foreign policy objectives by seeking to understand, inform, and influence foreign audiences and opinion makers and by broadening the dialogue between American citizens and institutions and their counterparts abroad."

- **Intelligence**—"The collection, processing, integration, evaluation, analysis, and interpretation of available information concerning foreign nations, hostile or potentially hostile forces or elements, or areas of actual or potential operations."
- **Military**—"The destructive and/or disruptive force that a military unit/formation can apply against the opponent at a given time."
- **Economics**—"The combined monetary (active and latent) and production capability of a state that can be applied to protect that state or advance its interests."

From an intellectual perspective, national security strategy came to dominate military and diplomatic activities and frequently the national political scene.

- Eisenhower's 1952 candidacy was boosted largely by the argument that Truman and the Democrats had mishandled national security issues ranging from the establishment of the Iron Curtain, the isolation of Berlin, and the "loss" of China to the stalemate of the Korean War.
- While no single issue ever determines the outcome of a presidential election, Kennedy's argument that Eisenhower and Nixon poorly served the nation's security by allowing a strategic "missile gap" to develop with Russia may well have turned the tide in his favor.
- National security challenges in Vietnam and other Southeast Asian nations paralyzed Johnson's domestic program and drove his decision not to stand for a second term.
- Nixon ran and was elected, largely on the strength of his national security credentials. Carter's election focus was primarily domestic but

---

as a shorthand for the elements of national power at the National War College in the early 1990s. At that time it stood for "Diplomacy, Intelligence, Military, and Economic" power. I collected the definitions used in this section (except for "Economic," which is my own creation as it was not listed in DOD terms) from Joint Pub 1–02 definitions over time and would like to credit the sources. Except they have disappeared from the online library. Also, sometime around 2015, the military began using the term "Instruments of National Power" instead of "Elements." And "Intelligence" was replaced by "Informational" as one of those instruments. As of July 12, 2017, the concise definitions I collected earlier have been supplanted by a multi-page description in the fundamental doctrinal publication of the Armed Forces [Joint Pub 1, 2017], http://www.jcs.mil/Portals/36/Documents/Doctrine/pubs/jp1_ch1.pdf?ver=2017-12-23-160207-587.
Also please note that for the purposes of thinking about securing the elements of national power at home, I expand the traditional DIME to DIIME-D. See chapter 9.

included concerns over perceived national security failures (in Vietnam, with the CIA, etc.).

- Reagan ran on a platform that combined international and domestic issues but emphasized the rebuilding of national security power.
- Bush 41 tried to play on his extensive national security experience in the disorienting aftermath of the collapse of the Soviet Union.
- But Clinton portrayed this as an old vision of times gone by and ran on promises of a peace dividend and national security based on cooperation rather than confrontation. During his eight years as president this concept matured into an argument that America's national security was most threatened by global instability and best served by advancing American values and beliefs. As a result, the part of the national security community that supported Clinton came to emphasize the soft power of influence and example as at least as important as the hard power application of DIME.

Notwithstanding the predictions of some famous academic theorists, history did not end with the death of the Soviet Union.[6] The model of national unity as moderator of domestic tensions, leaving national security to focus on DIME and external threats, was already stressed to the breaking point by Third World conflicts in the 1950s, 1960s, and 1970s. When the discipline of the bilateral Cold War world order collapsed, and technology, travel, communications, and weapons became widely available, the attachments of nationhood proved unequal to the task of holding together restive peoples. At the same time, many political theorists came to regard nationalism itself as a threat to a liberal world order. Hence the push toward globalism of the last two decades.[7]

---

[6] The reference is to the book *The End of History and the Last Man* by Francis Fukuyama (1992). This book and associated articles famously advanced the thesis that with the end of the Cold War, democracy would spread worldwide resulting in popular representation, peace, and prosperity. It turned out to be famously wrong.

[7] Several terms and concepts stressing security emerged as the whole field of International Relations matured. While National Security was conceived as the focus of individual states, it came to overlap with International Security, which suggested that the security of each nation was a function of the security of all nations and the international order that connected them. Global Security has broadened the concept beyond the interests of states to include groups and even individuals who are frequently overlooked by the exclusive focus on states and nations. And Human Security has emerged recently as the study of factors related to the universal safety and security of humankind. This volume does not dismiss any of these additional concepts or concerns. But they are not the focus of this volume or this series. And in accordance with common practice (among the NS community), we will use the terms "national security" and "international security" more or less interchangeably.

NEW NATIONAL SECURITY CHALLENGES AND
THE RISE OF HOMELAND SECURITY

It is now apparent that the three hundred years from 1648 to roughly 1948 might be considered as the great knitting together of nations, and especially democratic nations. The period from the 1950s through today may eventually be viewed as the great unraveling of states and nations alike.

First, the great powers dismembered postwar Germany where nationalism and national socialism combined to create a threat to world order. Then, communist powers began trying to peel apart states and nation-states in order to establish communist regimes in Cyprus, Korea, Vietnam, and elsewhere. At the same time, some Western powers who had been eager at the end of World War I to disassemble the Austro-Hungarian Empire and the Ottoman Empire in order to serve their interests were surprised at the demand for self-determination in their own colonial holdings at the end of World War II. Efforts to shape the resulting political groupings into democratic nations were frequently frustrated by strong family, tribal, ethnic, and religious ties and a general refusal to subordinate those loyalties to some larger and more nebulous concept of national unity. States proliferated; nation-states did not.[8]

Meanwhile **technology exploded and spread—especially weapons technology that made it increasingly easy to oppose central authority and increasingly difficult to enforce it.** By the end of the twentieth century, groups and ideologies were threatening US interests and citizens, both overseas and in the United States, in a variety of new ways, ranging from car bombs to weapons of mass destruction. More recently, cyber weapons have continued the devolution of power to rogue states, criminal organizations, and nonstate actors. International regimes and national security institutions have struggled to adapt.

During the Clinton Administration, several Presidential Decision Directives (PDDs) concerning US domestic security (that is, the protection of the government and the people against domestic and international disasters

---

[8] A June 14, 2018, staff article in *The Economist* suggests that what we see weakening around the world is not so much the glue of nationhood but the essential marriage of liberal norms with democratic structures that makes democratic nations possible. Without norms, autocratic forces use democratic structures for oppression, and without structures to enforce the rule of law, democracy simply becomes the right of the majority to enforce its will on the minority. The article argues that this is a relatively new phenomena as concerns over globalism and immigration stress the marriage. For our purposes (understanding the security challenge to the United States), it is enough to note that new global conditions are presenting new international challenges in a new way—in our domestic space.

and attack) were put in place. But responsibility for countering domestic threats remained with the Department of Justice, while monitoring international terrorism was relegated to international intelligence agencies and the part of the National Security Council that tracked transnational crime.[9] Consequently, the 9/11 domestic attack from foreign soil over foreign issues caught both the US national security community and the public safety community flatfooted.[10] The enemy did not attack at a point of overlap but rather a seam between public safety and national security efforts.[11]

After 9/11, the Bush 43 Administration and Congress struggled to craft new domestic strategies, policies, and organizations in response, but those with a vested interest in the status quo (especially in the public safety community) pushed back hard at the idea of becoming an extension of the national security effort. President Bush 43 attempted with only limited success to clarify the division of responsibilities by formally identifying national policies as either National Security Policy Directives (NSPDs) or Homeland Security Policy Directives (HSPDs).[12]

President Obama took a different approach, eliminating separate national and homeland security designations and unifying strategic efforts under leadership of the national security community. This was matched at the beginning of his term with a general de-emphasis on terrorism and an expanded focus on hazards and natural disasters. By the end of his term, events in Europe and elsewhere had demonstrated that in a world of

---

[9] Shortly after 9/11, two former directors of the White House counterterrorism program, Daniel Benjamin and Steven Simon (2002), voiced their frustrations in *The Age of Sacred Terror*. They argued that while there was plenty of blame to be spread around for being unprepared on 9/11, the core responsibility lay with the FBI: "In an environment saturated with fear of impending attacks, we believed that everyone in the intelligence and law-enforcement community shared the general understanding that al-Qaeda sought to kill large numbers of Americans . . . We were wrong. We were, of course, completely shut out from [FBI] operations." (p. 389)

[10] Not unaware, just unprepared. Benjamin and Simon look back to the Pearl Harbor historian Roberta Wohlstetter for an appropriate description: "The paradox of pessimistic realism of phrase coupled with loose-optimism in practice" (Benjamin and Simon 2002, 387).

[11] The CIA was closely monitoring overseas terrorist threats, including Osama bin Laden. An excellent book explaining this effort and the threat America faced after 9/11, *Through Our Enemies' Eyes: Osama bin Laden, Radical Islam, and the Future of America*, was published anonymously in 2003. The author was later revealed to be Michael Scheuer, Chief of the Osama bin Laden tracking unit at the Counterterrorism Center from 1996–99, and Special Adviser to the chief of the bin Laden unit from September 2001 to November 2004. These books by Benjamin, Simon, Scheuer, and others suggest there was simply no mechanism to convert national security concern into domestic counterterrorism action. We had plenty of intelligence "dots," but we could not connect them.

[12] By popular convention, the forty-first president of the United States, George H. W. Bush, is frequently referred to as Bush 41. George W. Bush (his son and the forty-third president) is referred to as the Bush 43.

diverse populations and global travel, the bonds of nationhood might not be enough to provide domestic security to even the most unified of nations. At home, the growing threats were not just against US interests overseas, or domestic generators of national power, but individual citizens and common activities in an effort to threaten the very legitimacy of the government system. Henceforth, national security will have to include a significant domestic security component. In the United States, that domestic component is called homeland security.

REFERENCES

"After Decades of Triumph, Democracy Is Losing Ground." June 14, 2018. *The Economist.* Accessed December 18, 2018. https://www.economist.com/international/2018/06/16/after-decades-of-triumph-democracy-is-losing-ground.

Anonymous (Michael Scheuer). 2003. *Through Our Enemies' Eyes: Osama bin Laden, Radical Islam, and the Future of America.* Dulles, VA: Brassey's Inc.

Benjamin, Daniel, and Steven Simon. 2002. *The Age of Sacred Terror.* New York: Random House.

Fukuyama, Francis. 1992. *The End of History and the Last Man.* New York: Macmillan Press.

Office of the Chairman of the Joint Chiefs of Staff. July 12, 2017. *Joint Publication 1: Doctrine for the Armed Forces of the United States.* Washington, DC: The Joint Staff. Accessed December 18, 2018. http://www.jcs.mil/Portals/36/Documents/Doctrine/pubs/jp1_ch1.pdf?ver=2017-12-23-160207-587.

———. November 2018. *DOD Dictionary of Military and Associated Terms.* Washington, DC: The Joint Staff. Accessed December 18, 2018. http://www.jcs.mil/Portals/36/Documents/Doctrine/pubs/dictionary.pdf?ver=2017-12-23-160155-320.

Zegart, Amy B. 1999. *Flawed by Design: The Evolution of the CIA, JCS, and NSC.* Stanford, CA: Stanford University Press.

4

National Security Begins with Academics, Theory, and Inquiry

★ ★ ★

BOTTOM LINE UP FRONT

Before 1945, politicians, diplomats, generals, admirals, and other security practitioners crafted the ideas upon which national security was based. They drew their ideas from history and personal experience.

The rise of the global Communist threat, the challenge of exerting national power in a sustained way around the world, and in particular the new realities of the nuclear age, so changed the world that the past experience of military practitioners and political leaders was no longer a reliable guide to the future. National leaders in the United States (and much of the West) turned to academics, with their theories of diplomatic, military, and economic power and academic proofs based on inquiry, research, games, and thought experiments. Since then, theories have come and gone, but the idea that national security begins with intellectual inquiry (usually generated in academia or related "think tanks") remains a mainstay of the national security community.

So while experience remains important to domestic practitioners, a solid academic grounding in security theory remains the price of admission into the senior ranks of the national security community.

Of course, those who study and practice security theory may come to quite different conclusions concerning what to actually <u>do</u> about threats and opportunities, based on their differing perspectives. Those perspectives are frequently influenced by how they think about security and what they believe about the nature of mankind—the subject of the next two chapters.

History is awash with books by famous generals and political leaders (and knowledgeable historians) recounting their experiences as practitioners of security in war and peace. Just a fragmentary list might include:[1]

- **Samuel, Jeremiah, Ezra** (all between 1100 and 440 BC)—Traditional authors of Judges, I and II Kings, and I and II Chronicles, replete with lessons on religion, warfare, and government.
- **Sun Tzu** (544–496 BC . . . perhaps)—Sixth-century BC Chinese general whose traditional portrayal is in question (his work is sometimes conflated with his descendent Sun Bin), but whose book *The Art of War* (if it is his) remains admired in both East and West for his lessons about knowing the enemy and knowing yourself in order to win.
- **Xenophon** (430–354 BC)—Greek historian and author of forty books and a Greek soldier who led *The Ten Thousand*, a Hellenic army, in its retreat from Babylon to the shores of the Black Sea. This epic story, captured in the book *Anabasis*, has served as a model of soldierly leadership and discipline for two millennia.
- **Thucydides** (460–395 BC)—Athenian general and historian whose passion for accuracy in the *History of the Peloponnesian War* set the standard for traditional history. It is regarded as a foundational document for international relations today.
- **Julius Caesar** (100–45 BC)—Roman general and politician responsible for the end of the Roman Republic and the foundation of the Roman Empire, who recorded his own military triumphs (especially in Gaul) in such detail that soldiers still study his work.
- **Marcus Aurelius** (121–180 AD)—The last of Rome's "Five Good Emperors," whose *Meditations* informed senior leaders until the demise of classical studies in the late twentieth century.
- **Niccolò Machiavelli** (1469–1527)—Renaissance historian and survivor of palace intrigue and treachery, sometimes called the "Father of Political Science," for his dispassionate description of state power used for effect without the constraints of ethics and morality.

---

[1] Why the long list? Because it is important to understand the depth, breadth, and richness of the experience we are casting away when we discard the study of history and replace it with the study of theories. If you believe that the nature of man is malleable and we can reason our way past war, then starting with fresh ideas makes sense. If you think the basic nature of man remains unchanged over time, then you see disregarding history as a huge mistake. If you reject both of these absolutes for a middling solution, then you need to explain how and where the balance may be struck. See chapter 6 for a more detailed discussion.

- **Fredrick the Great** (1712–1786)—German monarch more famous for his victories and enlightened reign than personal writings but whose reforms of the Prussian military shaped European land warfare into a force that conquered the world.
- **Antoine-Henri, Baron Jomini** (1779–1869)—Swiss soldier who served both France and Russia during the Napoleonic Wars and later gained fame and influence by extensive writings stressing both the "art" and "geometry" (design and maneuver) of war.
- **Napoleon I of France** (1769–1821)—Soldier, politician, king, and emperor who gained and lost both Egypt and Europe—and whose speeches, writings, and military maxims influenced the Western militaries who conquered the world, until the technical developments of the Industrial Revolution changed the conduct of war.
- **Carl von Clausewitz** (1780–1831)—Prussian general who learned war through loses at the hands of Napoleon, then captured the interaction of war and politics in the most honored Western treatise on the subject of all time: *On War*.
- **Helmuth von Moltke the Elder** (1800–1891)—German career soldier and Chief of German General Staff for thirty years who essentially invented the modern military staff and laid the philosophical ground work for the organization, logistics, command, and control that enabled twentieth-century wars of maneuver.
- **J. F. C. Fuller** (1878–1966)—British career officer, historian, and strategist, he served with the first British tank forces to be employed in World War I. Through his extensive writing, he was instrumental in developing the vision for mobile tank warfare, which the British Army adopted in World War II.
- **B. H. Liddell-Hart** (1895–1970)—Wounded and seriously gassed during wasteful frontal assaults at the Somme and elsewhere in World War I, he envisioned the addition of infantry and artillery to mobile tank warfare. He collaborated with Fuller to advance the theory and ideas of combined arms warfare.
- **Erwin Rommel** (1891–1944)—Innovative German veteran of World War I who recorded his experiences in the book *Infantry Attacks*, then modified those ideas to become arguably the best panzer commander of World War II.
- **George Patton** (1885–1945)—One of several forward-thinking American officers who worked through the concepts of armored warfare in the years between World War I and World War II and implemented them on the battlefield in the liberation of Europe. His major contribution was through articles and arguments (based on his personal experience) rather than the publication of any specific volume.

- **Billy Mitchell** (1879–1936)—Early American proponent of airpower (based on his personal experience) who used the press and public demonstrations (including air races and the sinking of surplus ships by aircraft) to energize public support of expanded funding for aviation. His high-profile arguments with superiors (and subsequent career-ending courts-martial) directly contributed to American ideas and experimentation, setting the stage for aerial dominance in World War II.

- **Hugh Trenchard** (1873–1956)—"Father of the British Royal Air Force" as a separate service and an early advocate of strategic bombing (the use of air attacks deep to destroy enemy logistics, command and control, vs. direct support of tactical efforts on the front lines). Trenchard relied primarily on developing personal expertise in aviation and then advancing its influence through forceful presentation to military and political leaders for years on end. He built capabilities through extensive training programs and developed a reputation for the doctrine of continuous attack by bombers. His work secured separate status and funding for ground-based (vs. naval) aviation, determined the British approach to air organization during World War II, and became the inspiration for the establishment of a separate American Air Force in 1947.

- **Mao Zedong** (1893–1976)—Founding member of the Chinese Communist Party, who became the leader during the Long March—a year-long retreat before the ruling Kuomintang of more than five thousand miles, costing 90 percent of the force—followed by triumph in the civil war and conversion of the most populous nation on earth to a unique version of communism. As a political activist, military strategist, poet, and practitioner of starvation and mass murder, he became one of the most influential revolutionaries in history through both his actions and his writings.

- **Võ Nguyên Giáp** (1911–2018)—Learning Vietnamese nationalism under the shadow of interwar French colonialism, Giáp rose through the ranks to lead the fight against the Japanese, the returning French, the South Vietnamese, the Americans, and their allies (Australia, Thailand, South Korea, and the Philippines). In more than thirty years of fighting, he lost many battles and more than a half million men but won the war, demonstrating in a striking way the superiority of strategy over tactics.[2]

---

[2] I have included General Giáp on this list because of the focus American military education programs have placed on him. Alternatively, many others list Ho Chi Minh as the political master of the war. In their acclaimed documentary *The Vietnam War*, film makers Ken Burns and Lynn Novick name Le Duan (General Secretary of the Communist Party of Vietnam) as the true architect of the victory over the United States, crediting him with fusing both military and political power into a coherent strategy matched with focused operations. If this is correct, then he serves as an example of the main point of this chapter: True national security does not start with power but with sound theory and thinking.

The written records these practitioners left behind were not just exercises in ego or reminiscences of old men past their prime. These were life-and-death lessons in how to think about war and peace, victory and defeat, from those who had seen them all. From the dark emergence of the first infantryman (Cane, who beat his brother to death with a stick) until the bright flash of the first atomic bomb over Hiroshima, the concepts of future war were written largely by those who had experienced past war or studied it in depth. War may be driven by vicious passions and blind chance, but it is also the province of reason and intellect (according to the oft-cited formulation by Clausewitz 1976, 89).

It was the growth of knowledge that caused bronze to give way to iron, and iron to steel. The escalating battle between sword and shield, between long bow and armor, between mounted knight with stirrup and infantryman with pike, all took place inside the heads of practitioners before they played out on the field of battle. The invincible phalanx of pikemen from the seventeenth century was broken by ranks of disciplined musket fire in the eighteenth century. Those ranks were overcome in turn by columns fired with Napoleonic fervor in the early 1800s, only to see similar passionate columns decimated by rifle and rifled cannon fire at Gettysburg and the Somme. The World War I trenches protecting the rifles and machine guns were crushed in turn by artillery and panzers linked by radios in 1939. When entirely new capabilities made their debut—like steam ships and aircraft—it was practitioners and those who studied practitioners (Mahon and Corbett, Hart and Patton, Douhet and Mitchel) who created new ideas and advanced them as practical concepts for winning wars and securing peace. Even the wars of Communist revolution, spawned by theories of economics and politics, were designed and waged according to the ideas of those who had actually practiced revolutionary war. For millennia, changes in technology, tactics, and strategies repeatedly transformed war and security because of the application of intellect to practical experience. Thus, history taught that proper thinking about security was a function of lessons learned.

But in the 1940s and 50s, three things happened that changed the relationship between military experience and security decisions.

First, just as US national leaders expected a respite from the pressures of World War II, **a new enemy emerged with both the will and the capability to wage a long worldwide conflict intended to destroy our system of government.** In February 1946, George Kennan, a diplomat who had served in the American Embassy in Moscow since 1933, sent an exceptionally long cable (the "Long Telegram") to the Department of State. In it he described his understanding of Russia and the Soviet government and his analysis of the challenge that government would pose to US interests worldwide. He described the Soviets as fundamentally paranoid and set on a path to destroy the United States as a rival power. And he outlined their intention to challenge the United States every place in the world where weak states might be subverted by insurgencies sympathetic to communism and the Soviet system. A year later while serving as the first ambassador and second-ranking official at the new National War College in Washington, DC, he penned an article for *Foreign Policy* magazine entitled "The Sources of Soviet Conduct" (Kennan 1947). In it he repeated the idea that the Soviet Union viewed itself as perpetually at war with the capitalist United States and proposed a policy of "containment" of Soviet expansionist tendencies. Later he argued that the "Mr. X" article and his other works were misinterpreted as a call for a more harsh and militant approach than he had intended. But hostile Soviet actions began to stack up, and Kennan's warning set the foundations for a policy of actively opposing the Soviets everywhere in the world.

By that time, Winston Churchill's term "Iron Curtain" had already created a vivid image of the division between the Soviets and the West. In 1948, the Marshall Plan began to rebuild the war-torn economies of Western Europe with the specific intent of countering the Communist message in the West. From June 1948 to May 1949, the Soviets tried to force the Western powers out of Berlin by blockading access to the city on the ground, resulting in the Berlin Airlift. Two months after it ended, the Soviets detonated their first atomic bomb, years ahead of previous intelligence estimates. Two months after that, the Chinese Communists formally took control of China, and less than a year later (June 1950), North Korean Communist troops stormed into South Korea with the clear support of Russia and China, nearly driving American and South Korean forces off the peninsula and into the sea.

At that point, NATO was less than a year old, and the Korean War actually caused a larger deployment of US forces to Europe than to the Korean Peninsula. While the death of Stalin and the end of the Korean War brought temporary hope for the reduction of tensions, the new Soviet Prime Minister, Nikita Khrushchev, exacerbated the situation in 1956 by proclaiming to the West, "We will bury you." In 1957, he announced the successful launch of a nuclear capable intercontinental ballistic missile against which the United States had no defense. A few days after that, the same type of missile launched the first artificial satellite into orbit around the earth. Every night, Americans staring into the night sky could watch that satellite cross the heavens and be reminded that they were now within range of Soviet nuclear weapons. How much of a threat the early Soviet missile force actually posed to the United States remains a matter of debate. But by 1960, the American public believed that a hostile Soviet Union had opened a "missile gap" over America during the Eisenhower–Nixon Administration, and that fear helped tilt the election in President Kennedy's favor.

As tensions rose and the threat of a nuclear exchange became more apparent, military practitioners like US Air Force Generals Ira Eaker and Curtis LeMay concentrated on how to build, protect, and use nuclear forces. Meanwhile, the work of civilian academics like Herman Kahn, Henry Kissinger, Bernard Brodie, and Robert McNamara advanced the discussion of deterrence and preventing escalation in nuclear war. In the competition for senior political attention, theories on how to avoid nuclear war won out over those struggling to describe a vision for winning it. Overturning the tradition of several thousand years of recorded history, those steeped in the theory of politics and war began to take pride of place over those with practical experience in the task.

Second, the size, scale, and duration of a new global Cold War called for expertise and leadership beyond the experience of the most senior military specialists. World War II had required an unprecedented national-level effort in economics, finances, and private industry in order to create the "arsenal of democracy" while supporting simultaneous military operations on six continents and every major ocean in the world. Civilian regional experts, linguists, and specialists in areas from aerial photography to cryptography and mathematics provided essential support to intelligence. Communications and media specialists engaged the domestic population and friendly populations in other nations. Diplomats and those who trained and educated them proved critical to coalition warfare. In short, the global war required a full commitment from every area of national power, including areas where military practitioners had little experience.

The new Soviet threat meant that the United States would have to extend that effort into every corner of the world in a sustained battle for military, diplomatic, intelligence, and economic supremacy while demonstrating the superiority of their system by domestic prosperity. It was a task no nation had ever attempted. And it called for the marshalling of intellectual expertise in every aspect of national security, not just military operations.

Third, in addition to the emergence of a hostile Communist threat and the complex challenge of integrating national power in a sustained global confrontation, **the rapid development of nuclear weapons and long-range delivery systems completed the transformation of the US national security**

situation into something unknown in human history. While President Eisenhower initially seemed to view nuclear weapons as simply larger versions of the bombs he used to destroy the Third Reich and the military services searched for ways to use nuclear weapons across the entire spectrum of conflict, a number of civilian experts with academic backgrounds began to argue that a new, more "scientific" (and theoretical) approach to national security was now required.[3] As Yale University professor Bernard Brodie observed, "Thus far the chief purpose of our military establishment has been to win wars. From now on its chief purpose must be to avert them. It can have almost no other useful purpose" (Brodie 1946, 65–83).[4]

The result was a remarkable shift from generals and diplomats to academics and academia as the primary source of security concepts. No one demonstrated this better than Brodie.

Born in Chicago to Russian immigrants, Bernard Brodie gained his PhD from the University of Chicago in 1940 and taught briefly at Dartmouth College before being employed by the Navy as a military strategist during World War II. A popular, perhaps apocryphal, story holds that Brodie was reading the paper at breakfast when he learned of the nuclear attack on Japan. "Everything I have written is changed," he purportedly said. As a member of the Yale faculty for five years, he focused on international studies before joining the newly established RAND Corporation in 1951. While at Yale, Brodie (1946) authored the groundbreaking book, *The Absolute Weapon: Atomic Power and World Order*, and followed it while at RAND with *Strategy in the Missile Age*. These works shaped the initial debate on nuclear strategy that continues today. In particular, he laid out the concept for nuclear deterrence—the idea that nuclear weapons were of greater utility in preventing war through the threat of annihilation than in fighting or winning such a conflict. His argument shifted somewhat as his thinking matured, as did some of the arguments of those who followed him. Others took nuclear theory in a different direction. Herman Kahn, for example, laid out the concepts for fighting and "winning" a nuclear exchange in his 1960 bombshell, *On Thermonuclear War*. A few of the nuclear security theories and concepts to emerge from the ensuing intellectual battle are listed in the chart below.

---

[3] At one point, for example, the United States Army actually developed a nuclear mortar intended to deliver a tactical nuclear weapon within a few thousand yards of friendly positions.

[4] An excellent article summarizing Brodie's initial thinking and some changes is at Bernard Brodie, "The Development of Nuclear Strategy," *International Security*, vol. 2, no. 4 (Spring, 1978), pp. 65–83, https://people.ucsc.edu/~rlipsch/migrated/pol179/Brodie.pdf (accessed December 18, 2018).

Textbox 4.1 | Nuclear Theories and Concepts and the Practical Capabilities That Support Them

- **Massive Retaliation:** Response to any military provocation with an immediate and overwhelming use of force to include nuclear weapons. Announced by the Eisenhower Administration; abandoned for a more flexible response as the opponent became skilled at pressing right up the edge of provoking action.

- **Mutually Assured Destruction (MAD):** The idea that when both sides were sure to be destroyed by an exchange, then both would be deterred from attack. By extension, any party that attempted to reduce its vulnerability was actually increasing the risk of provoking the other side.

- **First Strike-Second Strike:** A side that builds forces to strike first might prevent an opponent's response but also might miscalculate and precipitate a needless nuclear exchange instead. An alternative is to build forces that could survive an initial strike with certainty (e.g., submarines), thus offering greater deterrence to such an attack.

- **MIRV; Stealth; BMD:** Three technical developments, unrelated except as examples of how theories can be converted to capabilities and impact the strategic balance. Multiple Independently Targetable Reentry Vehicles (MIRVs), allowed the United States to place up to ten warheads on each missile, overwhelming the Russian anti-missile defense designed for Moscow. Stealth protected penetrating bombers from radar detection, allowing them to loiter over the enemy to find and counter mobile missile launchers. Ballistic Missile Defense (BMD) changes the whole strategic calculus by negating the enemy's missile offense . . . if it works.

- **DEFCON Levels:** Five levels of increasing military readiness based on threat—ordered by the National Defense Authority—each directing prespecified security, preparation, and response activities. The system both prepares the military for war and sends a public warning to opponents.

- **Launch-on-Warning:** Should either side be able to mount an overwhelming attack before the opponent could launch his weapons, the initiator might avoid the penalty of MAD. One solution would be the dangerous practice of launching before an attack could be confirmed. The result might be deterrence—or accidental nuclear war.

- **Mobile Launchers:** Weapons (generally missiles) that could displace by road or rail, complicating targeting. This might deter an opponent since he might not know all locations with certainty but might also tempt an opponent into first strike if he could locate and attack the vulnerable launchers. The stealth bomber was designed with this mission in mind.

- **ICBM/SLBM/IRBM:** Three types of nuclear-armed missiles. Their differing capabilities allow them to play different roles in nuclear strategy. **Intercontinental Ballistic Missiles** (ICBMs) are land based—usually in silos protected from nuclear attack—with long range and often carrying up to ten warheads. They follow a high arc making them very hard to defeat. **Submarine Launched Ballistic Missiles** (SLBM) are shorter range and carry a lighter payload (up to three warheads). The launch platform can hide underwater for months at a time and survive a nuclear exchange. **Intermediate Range Ballistic Missiles** (IRBM—no longer in use) had a shorter range (England to Russia). IRBM complicated the Russian defense problem and committed allies to the nuclear fight since they were based in Europe.

- **Game Theory**: Based on economic concepts of rational actors and calculation of costs and benefits, this approach tried to predict how various strategies and actions might encourage an opponent away from conflict and toward cooperation.

- **COG, COOP, Civil Defense**: Three programs to help the US government continue the fight after a nuclear exchange. Continuity of Government allows for the survival of senior officials. Continuity of Operations ensure the functioning of essential (especially defense) operations. Civil Defense is about saving enough of the sinews of national power to win the conflict and ultimately restore the nation as a political unit.

- **Counter Force vs. Counter Value**: Would maximum deterrence and effectiveness come from targeting nuclear strikes against opposing forces or opposing populations/cities/etc.?

- **Warning Shot/Pulse**: Part of a signaling system (escalatory ladder) that would use one or more battlefield nuclear weapons to signal an opponent to stop actions before provoking a general nuclear exchange

- **Offense-Defense Theory**: Concept that building a reliable defense might be seen as an offensive action, since an attack could then be mounted without fear of retaliation. When an opponent sees this taking shape, he might mount a preemptive attack. Thus a strong defense might actually prompt war. This was an argument advanced against IRBMs and missile defense. Remaining vulnerable to Soviet attack was considered stabilizing; developing protection was considered destabilizing and even provocative.

- **Triad:** US concept of maintaining three entirely separate delivery systems (penetrating bombers, land-based ICBMs, SLBM) so that even if one is compromised or a defense developed, delivery of a nuclear strike on the president's order can be assured.

For the purposes of thinking properly about homeland security, the important point is that the arrival of the nuclear age forced a shift from basing national security strategy on military experience to the crafting and testing of theories. Concepts were generated by academic inquiry, not lessons learned from practitioners. Carrier warfare, submarine warfare, armored warfare, air warfare—all of these concepts were developed primarily by military practitioners augmented in some cases by historical analysis. The Cold War changed all that. And even after the Wall came down in 1989 and the Warsaw Pact splintered in 1991, the concepts that drove national security in the Clinton Administration, the Bush 43 Administration, and the Obama Administration all came primarily from academia. As these words are being written, the character of the Trump approach to national security is not entirely clear. But whatever international strategies and policies are developed, the people in the administration who will execute them—the members of the bureaucracy and the Department of Defense, Department of State, Department of the Treasury, National Security Council, and so forth—are all products of a national security education system based primarily in civilian academia. Even the nation's war colleges and military staff colleges draw their readings and teaching materials on national security issues primarily from civilian academic sources.

Thus, the three new challenges of the post–World War II / Cold War era created a new security situation that exceeded the strategic capability of traditional military organizations. Actually it exceeded the capability of any one individual or even single government agency or academic discipline. Sorting out the various challenges, variables, theories, and proofs required a major intellectual effort, first by individuals like Brodie, then by collections of academicians at think tanks like RAND, and finally by Western academia writ large.

To be clear, this proliferation of academic players did not bring about agreement or intellectual coherence concerning what to do about the challenge of creating, protecting, and using the elements of national power in the new era. It did not even bring about agreement on the questions to be asked. In fact, as we shall see in the next two chapters, disagreement over social science processes and beliefs about the nature of man created fundamental differences in intellectual approaches to national security even within academia.

But what did emerge from this turbulent intellectual time was a common conviction that the solutions to our most dangerous and vexing national security challenges lay in the realm of academic theory and inquiry, and not with the practitioners of military art who had dominated strategic discussions since the age of Thucydides.

REFERENCES

Brodie, Bernard, ed. 1946. *The Absolute Weapon: Atomic Power and World Order.* New York: Harcourt, Brace.

Brodie, Bernard. Spring 1978. "The Development of Nuclear Strategy." *International Security* 2 (4): 65–83. Accessed December 18, 2017. https://people.ucsc.edu/~rlipsch/migrated/pol179/Brodie.pdf.

Kennan, George. July 1947. "The Sources of Soviet Conduct." *Foreign Policy*. Accessed December 18, 2018. http://www.historyguide.org/europe/kennan.html

Von Clausewitz, Carl. 1976. *On War.* Edited and translated by Michael Howard and Peter Pared. Princeton, NJ: Princeton University Press.

5

Conflicting Ways to Think about Security

★   ★   ★

BOTTOM LINE UP FRONT

Obviously, <u>what</u> we think will influence our perceptions of threats and opportunities in national security, and, by extension, in homeland security. Less obvious is the fact that <u>how</u> we think influences our perspectives as well. By this I mean quite literally, the way in which we order our thinking process, especially as we inquire into cause and effect.

For centuries in the West, thinking and reasoning were built on Inductive Logic: the creation of general laws or principles by collecting many specific examples as data points and connecting them to determine general rules of cause and effect. Practitioners, who frequently see the same pattern of events over and over, tend to think this way. If the last twenty homicides in a given area were drug deals gone wrong, investigators are prone to look first to the same cause as the source of the next such event. But since the eighteenth century, science and academia (the primary source of security thinking today) have been increasingly influenced by Deductive Logic: arriving at specific conclusions based on generalizations, expressed as theories. Tests are then conducted to validate, invalidate, or modify those theories.

Today, national security specialists are generally educated using theory-based deductive reasoning. Training for homeland security practitioners tends to be more inductive and based on lessons learned—like security education before the advent of nuclear weapons. The overall effect is to put inductively inclined practitioners of public safety who reside in homeland security organizations intellectually at odds with the deductively inclined national security practitioners who occupy senior federal security positions.

Understanding public safety, homeland security, national security, and most other aspects of politics and government requires us to understand how we think. And that requires us to come to grips with two opposing concepts of knowledge. The first is that we know things through experience. The second is that we know what we know through a process of creating and testing theories. Many (perhaps most) of us hold both of these approaches in our heads at the same time. And therein lies a conflict at the heart of homeland security and its struggle to be established, respected, and implemented today.

When the Greeks set the foundations of Western science, they did so primarily by drawing conclusions from serial observations. Archimedes's famous discovery that the volume of his body could be established by measuring how much water he displaced in the bath (resulting in his exclamation "Eureka!") was made by observation, not exploration of a theory. He went on to conduct additional observations where an object of known volume (say a box of known dimensions) was immersed in water and displaced the same volume of liquid. From repeated observations, he crafted a general theory that came to be recognized as a scientific truth. With many such repetitious observations in math, physics, biology, and philosophy, *inductive science* (deriving general principles from specific observations) was born. Today's homeland security operators would call this "lessons learned."

But among the Greek philosophers (and what passed for scientists), the concept of *deductive science* was also born. This approach starts from a premise or theory and examines it by controlled tests, throwing out concepts that are disproved along the way, until only the truth is left. This is a more rigorous but abstract (and time-consuming) approach.

For obvious reasons, the more linear, event based, inductive ("lessons learned") approach is a comfortable fit with the practical needs of police, fire, emergency responders, military personnel, and indeed, the popular mind of the citizenry as a whole. For people who face the reality of criminal attack, hazardous events and natural disasters, it is a short step from inductive truths, lessons learned and principles of action, to training, doctrine, tactics, techniques, and procedures. In a moment of crisis, there is not much patience with theory.

But in the latter half of the twentieth century, champions of deductive logic won the high ground in American academia. For example, in the 1950s, we had no historical experiences upon which to draw inductive conclusions about nuclear strategy. So nuclear war fighting concepts (including deterrence, Mutually Assured Destruction, Ballistic Missile

Textbox 5.1 | **How We Think Shapes Perspective**

Inductive reasoning is the creation of general laws or principles by collecting many examples as data points and connecting them to determine general rules of cause and effect. Using the study of military history to infer "Principles of War" is an example of inductive reasoning. Anticipating the next attack from a terrorist cell by analyzing attacks in the past is another.

Deductive reasoning arrives at specific conclusions based on generalizations, expressed as theories. Tests are then conducted to validate, invalidate, or modify those theories. These tests may be conducted by properly controlled historical analysis. Democratic Peace Theory (the idea that building democracies leads to peace because rational voters do not choose war) is an example of deductive logic. So are many of the concepts underlying community actions designed to counter violent extremism.

Defense, nonproliferation, etc.) were developed by gaming and deductive theorizing, mostly by academics using "thought experiments." Today, political science, economics, international relations, public administration, sociology, and similar studies, which now constitute major contributors to the field of national security, are based on deductive reasoning.

The overall effect here is to put the practitioners of public service who have been captured by homeland security organizations (people inclined to think in inductive terms) in conflict with the deductively inclined academics who generally provide education for their policy-focused masters in government. The people doing and training homeland security tasks are inclined to be dismissive of the theory-focused academics who provide the intellectual grounding for almost every other public and private function from business to government administration. And academics who judge themselves and their peers by how well they craft and test theories tend to be dismissive of inductive-based homeland security practitioners. As a result, homeland security is both an academic discipline still struggling for a home and a profession still searching for its theoretical underpinning.

A further complication is that the social sciences are generally grounded on "positivism" and its intellectual descendants. This philosophy of science suggests that all authoritative knowledge comes from *measurable sensory experience* expressed through laws which may be used to guide future actions (like the development of strategies and policies). This concept firmly rejects, for example, the inclusion of religion or other belief systems as a source of truth, or even something to be considered, as it cannot be measured. The effect is to restrict and focus knowledge to the realm of what may be proven by deductive inquiry.

This simplified national security issues in the past. For example, in World War II, the United States did not concern itself with the motivation of the individual Japanese infantryman. He was raised, trained, equipped, and deployed by an opposing government system that was the legitimate focus of military and diplomatic action. But terrorists may fight for a variety of reasons, ranging from religion, to vengeance, to perceived injustice, to pay, or even bloodlust—the enjoyment of murdering civilians and taking slaves. Such motivations frequently defy measurement. This makes traditional comparative analysis, using a deductive approach, very difficult. Perhaps impossible. As a result, our Western experts have a hard time even thinking about the most fundamental problem of homeland security (the terrorist threat), much less crafting a solution.

Thus the theory-based patterns of thought that catapulted the West to the leadership of the world on the back of academic education in business, national security, and government are unconvincing to those who grapple with the day-to-day issues of homeland security. And the experience-based "lessons learned" that drive practitioner thinking are often dismissed as naïve by university-educated policymakers. The result is a conflict in the way we think about some of the most basic concepts of homeland security.

6

Conflicting Beliefs about Security and the Nature of Man

★ ★ ★

"What worries you masters you."

John Locke (1632–1704)

BOTTOM LINE UP FRONT

It would be rational for how we think about security to determine what we believe about security. That is, for our strategies, policies, operations, and so on to be based on inductive or deductive logic.

But, in truth, it frequently works the other way around—what we believe about the nature of man exerts a strong influence on the way we interpret "facts," and thus our theories and perceptions of security. Although the West is home to thousands of political philosophies, three schools of belief in particular have strongly influenced traditional American security concepts.

- *In the late seventeenth century (following the English Revolution), Thomas Hobbes concluded that the natural inclination of fallen Adam was to violence. The only alternative to anarchy, he argued, was power and an aristocracy (today we might say an elite) to wield it. Security he regarded as a matter of getting power and keeping it.*
- *In the late eighteenth century (roughly coinciding with the French Revolution—and the rise of Romanticism in literature), Jean-Jacques Rousseau sought security in rule by the naturally virtuous common man. Humans, he asserted, were endowed with value and rights by birth—by virtue of their existence. Destroy the old system that produced inequality*

(church, king, family, private ownership, and even history itself), and replace them with the natural rights of man, and you would naturally enter an era of peace and prosperity.

- *Between these two in time (and helping to set the stage for the American Revolution), John Locke advanced the Judeo-Christian concept of the dual nature of man. That is, man has values and rights granted by God but must learn to govern himself wisely by balancing power and look to his own security because not all others are inclined to "Right Reason."*

In the United States, "reasoning" about security generally takes place within a framework built on some combination of these beliefs.

Until the mid-seventeenth century, the nature of man did not pose much of a political mystery for Western Civilization. God ruled through His representative the Pope and theocratic emissaries under the color of the Roman Catholic Church. Order was maintained through an anointed king and an aristocracy determined by birth. The role of the common people was to shut up, work hard, and do as they were told. Had there been a term for "national security" at the time, it would probably have been something like "sovereign security," as the security of the king and the security of the kingdom were pretty much one and the same.

Almost alone in all of Europe, England, because of its geographic isolation and historical development, offered an expanded role for the individual citizen. The tradition of the Magna Carta (which first saw the power of the king constrained by the rights of nobility in 1215), and the training regime of the longbow (which offered enormous military advantage at the cost of allowing citizens to keep this powerful weapon at home and practice with it), combined to infuse Englishmen with a sense of civic value not generally enjoyed by the serfs on the continent.

This made for a fertile political soil, into which dropped the seeds of the Protestant Reformation. This new vision held that each man was ennobled by the fact that Jesus died for him individually and emboldened by the idea that each man could read and interpret his Bible as he saw fit, with guidance but not direction, from the clergy. In Luther's words, "Each man his own bishop." In the mid-1600s, Cromwell's Protestant "Roundheads" (so named for the shape of their helmets), poured through this political opening. They declared the House of Commons the only legitimate source of political power and executed King Charles I for treason against the people. Although the old order returned with Charles II a mere eleven years later, the principle had been established that the common man had a role in the political security of the nation. The nature of that common man was suddenly a matter of important debate.

First into the intellectual fray was **Thomas Hobbes**. After two decades of disorder in the English Civil War, he concluded that the natural inclination of fallen Adam was to violence. Left to his own devices without benefit of political order, man would degenerate into a state marked by "the warre of man against all men," where life was "nasty, brutish, and short." The only alternative to such anarchy, Hobbes argued, was a system of moral aristocracy. It was incumbent upon these leaders, he further proposed, to be constantly prepared against challenges to state security, both internal and external, posed by the natural anarchy of the universe in which each state existed.

Almost exactly a hundred years later, **Rousseau** acted as a similar apologist but for the revolution of the common man in France. Here the excesses of both the aristocracy and the clergy were far greater and washed away Hobbes's argument that an enlightened elite deserved dominance as they were necessary in order to save the common man from the anarchy of his own rule. In fact, Rousseau stood Hobbes on his head, arguing that mankind was naturally virtuous (like children born into innocence) and inclined to peace. Evil, inequality, war, and violence were learned from the existing institutions and their culture. Destroy those institutions (church, king, family, economic system, and even history itself), and because man was naturally virtuous, you would naturally enter an era of peace and prosperity (guided by the elite thinkers of the revolution, of course). Rights were not granted by God or maintained by an educated elite. They were "natural" to Man's birth. And because Man had the *authority* to change corrupt moral institutions, he also had the *responsibility* to do so.

Our political language today springs from the collision of these two views of human nature. As the French parliament debated the new order of things, those supportive of a traditional structure to control fallen man sat on the right. Those who saw salvation in return to the moral purity of the Noble Savage sat on the left. There were no seats for "moderates." There seemed no middle ground between these two visions.

But about half way through the century between Hobbes and Rousseau, a figure with a political vision somewhere between them gained the attention of the American colonists who would become rebels and then the Founding Fathers of the United States.

John Locke put forth a political solution based on the religious concept of the dual nature of man. That is, man has the capability to be devil or angel, depending on his embrace of reason, his own choices, and the moral education he receives. To be sure, Locke was a British political philosopher and not an American religious theologian. But the concept that "All men are created equal" and "endowed by their Creator with certain unalienable rights" evolved directly from his teachings. In another example, Locke argued that the right to own property is the most fundamental and unalienable right of all. Just as God owns man, because He created him, man owns what he creates by the sweat of his own brow, and no one may take the product of his work without compensation—not even the king or state. (Hence the importance of Christianity to the movement for abolition. If slaves were wholly men, then their rights were granted by God. If not, then the rights of property owners predominated.) Concerning security, Locke's views advanced the idea that man can learn to govern himself wisely but must prepare for war because not all others are inclined to what a previous generation called "Right Reason."

A fourth Western political tradition emerged in the late 1800s, captured under the mantle of **Fredrick Nietzsche**. In brief, it argued that man has rights only because he seizes them from others and protects them against all comers. Man has rights because he asserts them—and those who assert most strongly have the greatest claim. It was a Darwinian argument for a Darwinian age.

And finally, over the last several decades, various political visions have emerged to suggest that the nature of man is not fixed at all. Nurture trumps Nature. For lack of a better term, the word **"constructivist"** may be applied, because these theorists suggest that our approach to reality is "constructed" and can be changed. Some feminists, for example, see children as a blank slate. Boys become "men" because we give them tool sets and toy guns as children; girls become "women" because we give them Barbie dolls and Easy-Bake Ovens. Change the mental construct—the "narrative"—they argue, and you can change reality.

Of course, these brief paragraphs cannot adequately capture a lifetime of writing by Hobbes, Rousseau, Locke, or other authors of that age or this. But this approximation can adequately set the context for our study of how to think about National and Homeland Security.

Strategy, as we will see in chapter 8, depends upon fundamental concepts of cause and effect. And those concepts are driven by beliefs about the nature of man. Is your opponent like you or different? How? Is he inclined toward war or peace? What will provoke him? What will deter him? What will cause him to choose death before surrender? What will make him decide the game is not worth the candle? Is he driven by punishment or incentive? Is he inclined to negotiate or fight to the death?

Obviously, no one holds to just one of these world views to the exclusion of all others. The most politically tolerant liberal may turn Hobbesian when an older boy first arrives to date his young daughter. And even a closet supporter of Nietzsche's power politics is likely to doubt her vision when she encounters the starving children of the Third World. In the United States in particular, most political perspectives are neither absolutist nor written in stone.

But all that said, people do tend to perceive and act within certain habits of thought. Understanding those habits, and your own perceptions, is key to understanding how to think about safety, security, and strategy both at home and abroad.

7

From Thought and Belief to Security Theory and Practice

★ ★ ★

BOTTOM LINE UP FRONT

Despite our best efforts at objectivity, the way we think and the beliefs we hold about the nature of man tend to shape the way we approach security issues.

From an <u>international security perspective</u>, these approaches are generally divided into some variation of Realist (I prefer Neoclassic) theory and Liberal (I prefer Romantic) theory. From an American political perspective, the Realist or Neoclassic approach has been advanced (at least until recently) by many on the Right who identify as Neocons. The Liberal or Romantic approach is preferred by those on the Left who identify as Progressives.

Lockean theory, born of a crisis in domestic political legitimacy (challenges to King George III) and adapted to the isolated context of early American geography, favors solving international dilemmas by staying out of them. The Monroe Doctrine, promulgated 119 years after Locke's death, captures this aspect of Lockean Theory. Today neither major American political party embraces Lockean Theory, and some deride it as "isolationist." Proponents (and President's Trump's election shows that there are many among the electorate) argue that their views are actually more nuanced that that.

Regardless of the international viewpoint adopted by the president, he or she pretty much has the power to incorporate it into the national security strategy and the political philosophy of his administration. Subject, of course, to congressional constraints on making war, treaties, and budgets.

But the application of Realist theory to domestic security issues is prevented (or at least impeded) by the Constitution. Collecting all domestic political power in a "Leviathan" (a strong central government) as Hobbes recommended, is not possible. Too many powers are reserved to the states.

So our domestic conflict over security cause and effect is between Progressive/Romantic and traditional Lockean ideas—between using government to advance values-driven solutions and constraining government to ensure a balance of powers.

This conflict over ideas and beliefs is played out in politics at every level of elective office. It shapes policies, operations, organizations, resources and perspectives regarding domestic security and other national issues.

Thus, while both national security and homeland security are grounded on some of the fundamental intellectual constructs of Western politics, they play out in quite different ways.

In previous essays, we learned that the modern approach of academia requires that thinking be expressed as theories, with facts collected and hypotheses tested to confirm the application of those theories to government, business, education, and so on. This conflicts with an older approach based on practical experience, which is still popular with public safety practitioners.

And modern Western political beliefs fall somewhere on the spectrum between:

- Neoclassic reason-based man in a world of anarchy;
- Romantic values-based man, struggling to free the inherent goodness of all peoples;
- Lockean "dual-natured man," seeking to balance freedom and responsibility between the two; and
- With the "constructivist" version of romanticism seeking to remake man (ok, "humankind") by remaking his (their) environment.

Now what?

How are these beliefs and habits of thought pressed into service to understand and shape the challenges around us, and in particular the challenge of securing the nation, inside and out?

For the last eighty years, external security has been the purview of international relations. From a Western perspective, the challenges and solutions are shaped primarily by two schools of thought, known as Realism and Liberalism.

Textbox 7.1	Realism as a Concept of National Security Theory

There are many variations on the concept of **realism**, but at its simplest, it combines the following ideas and beliefs into theories:

1. The most important actors on the world stage are states;
2. States exist to secure and advance their own interests;
3. States exist in an environment where anarchy reigns—they can only save themselves through power (mostly "hard power" in the form of DIME, used to compel behavior from others);
4. States are rational actors who understand their own best interests;
5. Because of that, all states pursue power and can negotiate with other states who rationally pursue power themselves.

To make use of a construct from the previous chapter, Realism views the world in a way similar to Thomas Hobbes—where the natural state of things is "the warre of man against all men." This does not necessarily mean that Realism produces a state of constant war. Realists can negotiate. But as Thucydides captured the Athenians telling the Melians, "The strong do what they will, and the weak suffer what they must" (Strassler 1996, 352/5.89). Thus, the Realist (Neoclassic) prescription for any state is to gain power, use it rationally, and strive to keep it. In international relations parlance this is called "securing and advancing national interests."

Again, to refer to the concepts of the last chapter, Liberalism reflects Jean-Jacques Rousseau's romantic vision of the nature of man. Great power is based on "Soft Power"—Liberal (Romantic) ideals and values, which can best influence the behavior of others. Of late, the term Liberalism has given way to Progressivism, which (depending on the user) may incorporate the idea of basing all actions on values that will promote proper social evolution.

These two intellectual constructs for understanding international relations are in direct opposition—each believes that the other actually promotes war, one by inviting aggression, the other by threatening it. You might think that the use of deductive inquiry and the scientific method would resolve the issue, but as generations of academics have struggled to produce testable, reproducible, and falsifiable evidence to support their security theories, they have been more successful at hardening the divide than convincing anyone from the other side.

So our theories, thoughts and beliefs have <u>not</u> provided a universally approved solution to the "security dilemma"—how to prevent war without encouraging it. But they <u>do</u> provide an excellent departure point

Textbox 7.2	Liberalism as a Concept of National Security Theory

Liberalism also exists in many variants. At its simplest, it combines the following ideas and beliefs into theories:

1. Individuals are basically good—born into goodness with rights based on their common humanity.
2. Evil exists because a few individuals, ideas, and conditions pervert the natural good nature of people.
3. Government exists to advance the dignity and rights of good individuals. Government that does not advance that dignity is illegitimate. Governments and people have the right and responsibility not just to protect themselves but to overthrow illegitimate rules and rulers.
4. That dignity is codified in democratic values. To the extent that democratic values are protected and advanced, the peace, prosperity, and security of the world (and the United States) are advanced.
5. The best way for legitimate government to do that internationally is in collaboration with other governments. It is therefore in our best interests to create and maintain an international order of cooperative and power-sharing institutions.
6. This cooperation may require that larger states accept compromise on some of their interests (especially economic interests) in order to advance the broader interests of all.

for research and discussion and a perspective from which to consider homeland security. A good way to see these concepts in action is to consider "Presidential Doctrines" from various administrations.

Presidential Doctrines are simple, direct statements of intended goals and actions in foreign affairs (which is to say national security). Obviously, not every foreign issue can be addressed by a single statement. And sometimes the doctrines are not stated by the administration at all but represent an interpretation of intent as loosely agreed upon by scholars.[1] But it is informative to see how what Presidents think and believe has been reflected by positions on major issues.

- The **Truman Doctrine** ("It is the policy of the United States to support free peoples who are resisting attempted subjugation by armed minorities

---

[1] An essay requires reduction. But summarizing nearly seventy years of doctrines and the history that produced them in a few sentences is more than challenging. It risks inaccuracy just because of brevity. For a longer but more nuanced explanation, see Joseph Siracusa and Aiden Warren's *Presidential Doctrines* (New York: Rowman & Littlefield, 2016). For another excellent attempt at a short summary, see History News Network http://historynewsnetwork.org/article/377.

or by outside pressures") expressed the willingness of the US to contain Communist expansion by providing military, technical, and economic support, first to Greece and Turkey during the Greek Civil War, and subsequently to other nations in Europe. This early Cold War doctrine actively combined the promise of Realist hard power projection with Liberal soft power support of democratic values.[2]

- The **Eisenhower Doctrine** expanded the Truman Doctrine to support Mid-Eastern governments under pressure from communism. These governments were not democratic in nature, so the doctrine represents a movement away from Liberalism and toward Realism.

- The **Kennedy Doctrine** was focused primarily on Latin America, where the Soviet Union was expanding, not where it was already entrenched (as in Eastern Europe). Consequently, Kennedy had a freer hand on his southern flank than Eisenhower did in Hungary (1954). Kennedy's support for opposing communism and reversing its progress anywhere in the Western Hemisphere reflected both Realist and Liberal thinking at the time.

- Despite the association of Lyndon Johnson's name with the Vietnam War, the **Johnson Doctrine** as it came to be called was also promulgated in response to Communist activity in the Western Hemisphere. Specifically, after his intervention in the Dominican Republic in 1965, he stated that revolutionary politics would not be considered a local matter when they sought to replace a non-Communist government with a Communist one. Again both Left and Right generally supported this idea of using Realist politics to support Liberal values (at least near our shores).

- Nixon's case somewhat reverses Johnson's experience. While his name is today increasingly associated with a longer term strategic focus on issues like China and detente with the Soviets, the **Nixon Doctrine** was connected to the Vietnam War. Announced in Guam in 1969, it sought to reassure allies that the American nuclear umbrella still covered them

---

[2] The Cold War was a power struggle forced on the United States by an opponent determined to demonstrate the superiority of its values and threatened by the existence of any other successful model of government. Thus all US doctrines during the Cold War had to contain responses to both the physical and moral/political challenges of Communism and the Soviet Union. The differences between administrations were largely a matter of degree and focus: Were our security policies based on power supported by values, or values supported by power? Both sides of the Realism/Liberalism debate could find something to support, so "national politics stopped at the water's edge." Once the Cold War ended, this bipartisan approach to security broke down. Realists wanted to use hard power to expand hard power. Liberals wanted to constrain our hard power as a means of soft power. The divide continues today.

but also encouraged them to handle their own conventional defense. It prepared the way for the policy of "Vietnamization" announced two months later, and the eventual withdrawal of US combat troops from that Southeast Asian nation.

- Following the shock of the Soviet invasion of Afghanistan in 1979, the **Carter Doctrine** specifically extended American hard power assistance against Communist expansion to states of the Persian Gulf. This Realist expression of support to states led by monarchies and strong men was especially noteworthy, since President Carter himself was primarily supportive of expanding US Liberal values, even at the expense of some former partners.

- The **Weinberger Doctrine** (named for President Reagan's Secretary of Defense) was a Realist attempt to increase the effectiveness of hard power by decreasing its diversion to pursue Liberal goals. It stated that US military power would be used only in support of US vital interests.[3]

- The **Clinton Doctrine** (never stated as such but outlined repeatedly in presidential documents and in a series of speeches by Secretary of State Albright in late 1996 and early 1997) turned the Weinberger Doctrine on its head by using Realist language to advance Liberal ideals. As the first fully post–Cold War doctrine, it argued that instability anywhere was a threat to US interests everywhere, since it could pull us into a wider conflict. And the greatest cause of instability was a lack of democratic values. Thus, advancing Liberal (democratic) values constitutes a survival interest of the United States, and early use of hard and soft power to address regional or ethnic conflicts is justified. It is therefore in our interest that democracy be at once the foundation and the purpose of the international structures we build through constructive diplomacy: the foundation, because the institutions will be a reflection of shared values and norms; the purpose, because if democratic institutions are secure, instability will be reduced and free markets will flourish.[4]

- The Bush 43 Administration entered office ready to demonstrate its Neocon/Realist rejection of the Clinton Doctrine by initiatives around

---

[3] During the formative (early Cold War) years of the US approach to national security, interests were generally identified as Survival, Vital, Important, or Peripheral. These terms will be explained in greater detail in chapter 9.

[4] Per the Introduction of the 1996 Clinton *National Security Strategy*, "Our national security strategy is therefore based on enlarging the community of market democracies while deterring and limiting a range of threats to our nation, our allies and our interests. The more that democracy and political and economic liberalization take hold in the world, particularly in countries of strategic importance to us, the safer our nation is likely to be and the more our people are likely to prosper."

the world but found itself focused on the Global War on Terror. Some critics have claimed that President's statement "You are either with us or against us," constitutes the **Bush 43 Doctrine** . . . except that it was not enforced against anybody except the Taliban in Afghanistan and Saddam in Iraq. Bush's statement that the United States would rather work with allies to pursue its interests, but would go it alone if necessary, probably comes closer to capturing the spirit of the administration. That idea was clearly grounded in Realism.[5]

- As with Bush 43, the Obama Doctrine defies easy description in a single sentence.[6] But also like Bush 43, it rejected the previous administration's world view outright, as well as its cooperation with illiberal states for the purpose of securing power for use against a terrorist enemy. While pundits have derided "leading from behind" as a "bumper sticker," it might, if fully considered, actually qualify as an **Obama Doctrine**. It essentially argued that international safety and security are advanced when no party or state dominates, and everyone's interests are considered. This means that the United States might have to lead by restraint, forgoing its own advantage in some negotiations in order to advance collaboration by all. The sweeping invocation of this principle in situations from the Arab Spring to the Iranian missile program to the South China Sea helped to push the transformation of traditional Liberalism in international affairs toward what might now be called Progressivism.

Of course, this short exposition on Realism and Liberalism policy only scratches the surface of International Relations theory. One of the standard textbooks in the field contains more than a dozen chapters of theories subdivided into micro and macro causes; economic and environmental considerations; concepts of cooperation, integration, and deterrence; ideas on gaming and decision-making; and theories of deterrence, to name only

---

[5] Interestingly, this is not much different from President Clinton's statement in his 1996 NSS: "When our national security interests are threatened, we will, as America always has, use diplomacy when we can, but force if we must. We will act with others when we can, but alone when we must" (Clinton 1996, Preface). And yet many Democrats objected strongly to the Bush 43 formulation—just as many Republicans found the Clinton approach too internationalist. The difference was in the context. Clinton was speaking post-Bosnia, when force was deployed to support democratic values. Bush was speaking about entry into Afghanistan to destroy physical threats to the United States. Similar language but Liberal vs. Realist objectives. Also, Clinton never mentioned "preemption" or "regime change," both of which eventually came to symbolize the strategic vision of 43's "Neo-Cons."

[6] President Obama famously told the press on Air Force One (perhaps in jest) that his doctrine was "Don't do stupid sh*t." That's actually a great policy for every administration to follow. If only it were the case . . .

a few (Dougherty 2000). A similar text highlighting only theories for the more narrowly focused program of security studies also contains a dozen chapters written from entirely different perspectives (Schultz 1997).

So, despite our best efforts at scientific objectivity, the way we think and the beliefs we hold about the nature of man tend to shape the way we approach <u>international security</u> issues. In academia, these approaches are generally divided into some variation of Realist theory and Liberal theory. And in government, they can be applied by central control of foreign policy, trade policy, military policy, and so on.

★   ★   ★

But the application of Realist theory to <u>domestic security</u> issues is prevented (or at least impeded) by the Constitution. At one point in our history, we had a centralized authority that maximized power and controlled all domestic government actions through federal officers, governors, and local officials. That authority was King George III, and we replaced him with a philosophy and a system that feared centralized power more than domestic threats.

In short, traditional American Lockean government will pursue Realist power but for limited objectives, while advancing Liberal values, but by opportunity and example rather than force. This might seem a middle approach, ripe for agreement. Nothing could be further from the truth.

Timing is important here. While Realism developed over several thousand years of history beginning with Thucydides, and Liberalism began to emerge from the Romantic Movement in the late eighteenth century, they did not really develop into academic theories, rise to prominence, and begin to do battle for dominance in the field of national security until the beginning of the Cold War. Lockeanism, however, sank its roots deep into the American psyche during the colonial period. Conflicts over the nature of man and the role of government played out not in academic theory, but in "the Great Awakening," the development of the Constitution, the maturing of the courts, early political arguments about the role of government, the debate over slavery, and even the American Civil War.

<u>Lockeanism is not a term you will find in textbooks; you will not find its ideas reflected in modern national strategies or government policy papers.</u> The religious aspect of the arguments (God as author of man's liberties, and man's adherence to God's laws as the primary basis of the nation's security) was rejected by Positivism and associated scientific approaches early in the twentieth century. So these ideas don't appear anywhere in the intertwining of academic arguments and government policies

Textbox 7.3	Lockean View as a Concept of National Security Theory

The Lockean view, held by most of America's Founding Fathers, suggests a different road from either Realism or Liberalism:

1. Individuals have a "dual nature"—they contain the impulse for both good and bad. To be good they require moral education and rules to help maintain self-control. To be bad, they need only be left to their own devices.
2. Nonetheless, every individual has intrinsic worth, demonstrated by the fact the Jesus died for his/ her sins.
3. That worth is confirmed in the rights to life, liberty, and property granted by God.
4. Government exists to secure and ensure those rights. Democratic government is the protector of individuals. But because of the nature of man, consolidated power, even in a democracy, will inevitably lead to abuse.
5. So the best government is democratic in shape, and large enough to do its job, but too small and diffuse to dominate the lives of citizens.

that has produced our Realist versus Liberal divide in national security thinking today.

But in domestic politics, Lockeanism has never really gone away. It just put its head down and went to work, internalized by the millions of citizens who do their jobs, raise their families, attend their churches, watch their ballgames, and respond to defend their nation when called. They are not usually generals or ambassadors, captains of industry or presidents of nonprofits. They don't write academic papers or opine in the media. They are mostly practical people—farmers and construction workers, full-time homemakers and small business people, union members, and the self-employed. They don't even have a unified vision of what constitutes a threat, what problems the government should fix, and how much consolidated government power is too much. It is easy for the elite to imagine that this practical view of life died out about the time game theory was born.

However, every once in a while, when the Realists and the Liberals seem to lose control of the world order, the Lockeans step to the ballot box and remind the elite of their presence. The elite would like to think of them as ignorant, narrow-minded, and easily led. The people President Obama described as "clinging to their God and their guns." But they are frequently less doctrinaire and more unpredictable than the media and the elite imagine. They are dairy farmers who don't like socialism but voted for FDR. They are union members who don't like right to work laws but voted for Ronald Reagan. They are southern churchgoers who voted for a New York developer who mispronounces the books of the Bible.

Lockeans tend to take a dim view of overseas adventures (where the nature of man is not moderated by their religious vision of self-control) and so are generally left out of the international security debate until a foreign power threatens, by which time the intellectual arguments for response are well established by Realists or Liberals. At home, Lockeans favor breaking up domestic security powers among hundreds of law enforcement agencies rather than constructing a national police. The Lockean focus, starting in 1776, was on building a working domestic government that operated within self-limiting constraints—"A machine that would go of itself," some have called it (Kammen 2006). This approach means Lockeans do not often appear on the register of theorists for international relations or security. But they fill the ranks of police, fire, medical services, and emergency responders—practical people who think local problems are best solved at the local level (but best funded by the feds or somebody else).

Partly because Realist power of various types can be easily concentrated for international adventures (even if applied for Liberal ends), academics have flocked to security studies but remain largely disinterested in domestic security issues. Perhaps because Lockeans made it so hard to collect domestic power and authority to address domestic issues, academic study of what might be called domestic security (or homeland security) has lagged. Those studies that do exist are frequently fragmented along disciplinary or jurisdictional lines. And the large number of jurisdictions engaged and academic fields involved in domestic government makes it nearly impossible to create unified homeland security theories (which is just fine with the practical men and women who populate public safety and security jobs).

The security challenge of 9/11—a domestic attack by foreign forces—struck precisely along this unprotected boundary. The Realist and Liberal debate over beliefs and theories of international security did not help at home. The Lockean vision of domestic government was unprepared to respond to the international threat. Thus, while both national security and homeland security are grounded on some of the most fundamental intellectual constructs of Western politics, our well-established thoughts and beliefs have not promoted a perspective that serves us well in advancing domestic security. We have not yet figured out how to think about homeland security.

REFERENCES

Clinton, William J. 1996. *A National Security Strategy of Engagement and Enlargement.* Washington, DC: The White House. Accessed December 18, 2017. https://fas.org/spp/military/docops/national/1996stra.htm.

Dougherty, J. E., and Robert Pfaltzgraph. 2000. *Contending Theories in International Relations: A Comprehensive Survey (5th edition).* London: Pearson.

Kammen, Michael. 2006. *A Machine That Would Go of Itself: The Constitution and American Culture.* New York: Routledge.

"Presidential Doctrines." *History News Network.* Columbian College of Arts and Sciences, The George Washington University. Accessed December 18, 2018. http://historynewsnetwork.org/article/377.

Schultz, Richard A., and Roy Godson. 1997. *Security Studies for the 21st Century.* Edited by George H. Quester. Lincoln, NE: Potomac Books.

Siracusa, Joseph, and Aiden Warren. 2016. *Presidential Doctrines.* New York: Rowman & Littlefield.

Strassler, Robert, ed. 1996. *The Landmark Thucydides: A Comprehensive Guide to the Peloponnesian War.* New York: The Free Press.

8

What Is Strategy?

BOTTOM LINE UP FRONT

The first step in moving from thoughts, beliefs, and theories (whether inductive or deductive) to action is crafting a strategy.

"Strategy" is a concept of cause and effect, applied in context, to achieve victory against a thinking enemy over time. It is a desired end state with an associated forcing function.

"Victory" (the goal of strategy) means getting what you will settle for at a price you are willing to pay.

Many other definitions of strategy are available. They tend to be context or situation dependent—like the military definition that argues strategy is only conducted at the highest level of government. The definition put forward in this chapter is simple, clear, and applicable in virtually every context. It works for foreign and domestic issues, in government, business, or individual settings. It suggests that everyone at every level designs and implements strategy, which then influences policy, plans and operations, organizations, bureaucracies, and budgets, at every level.

First, a really, really important point. Everybody does strategy. Everybody at every level.

The US Army, and by dent of their influence, most of the Department of Defense (DOD), talks about the "strategic level of war." By this they mean "the highest decision making level of government during war." This concept is derived from the German General Staff in the nineteenth century and works fine for military operations. But unfortunately, it leaves the impression that the word always carries this specific military meaning, even though "strategy" is widely used in almost every endeavor. This makes it very difficult for people with a military or national security background to communicate clearly about homeland security strategies.

However, nonmilitary people tend to use the term in an undisciplined way that also impedes communication. Business people have business strategies, and kindergarten teachers have learning strategies. Pop stars have media strategies. Self-help books offer strategies for raising a healthy child. And because homeland security was born by collecting together mostly operators who focus on one event at a time (a flood, a fire, an arrest, a periodic intelligence report), the term barely resonates in the HS field at all. And yet without strategic direction (and periodic redirection) by leaders, homeland security operations become the bureaucratic repetition of tactics, techniques, and procedures, without clear strategic purpose.

This chapter offers a holistic definition of strategy. It can be used at the national security level, and actually applies better than the traditional "balancing ends and means," which has struggled for relevance in the nearly two-decade-long War on Terror. And it can be used by fire chiefs seeking to design a focus and plan for their department or emergency managers looking to prepare their communities for disaster. It works especially well in conjunction with the Framework for Inquiry recommended in a subsequent volume focused on the Study of Homeland Security. But it also works for anyone trying to provide structure and coherence and a sense of cause and effect to an activity over time.

However, one warning is in order. People who use strategies (especially in homeland security) rarely use the word "strategic" to describe what they are thinking and doing. In fact, they may back into a strategy—meeting a problem by creating an organization, beginning operations first, and only later giving thought to the real underlying goals and how to do them most efficiently and effectively over time. This is the case with homeland security. Don't expect to find a list of homeland security strategies that you can simply analyze and implement. That list has not yet been created. You will have to do the hard thinking about homeland security strategies for yourself.

STRATEGY IS ABOUT CAUSE AND EFFECT

Many authors and organizations offer definitions of strategy unique to their discipline: security strategy, military strategy, grand strategy, political strategy, economic strategy, business strategy, learning strategy, test-taking strategy . . . the lists goes on. But for more than four decades—until well after 9/11—military and civilian academicians defined strategy as "The balancing of Ways, Means, and Ends." This sufficed in a national security context throughout the Cold War because the actual strategy ("Containment"), set in place by NSC-68 in 1950, remained the underlying blueprint for US strategic policy for four decades. Thus from the 1950s until the 1990s, the overall national security strategy was fixed. The primary national strategic questions involved the balancing of forces, diplomacy, action, reaction, and so on rather than the more fundamental strategic questions of cause and effect.[1] Balancing was a way of implementing strategy, not creating it.

Once the wars in Afghanistan and Iraq were joined, it became clear that the old definition of strategy did not fit the new situation. The *DOD Dictionary of Military Terms* was changed to define strategy as, "A prudent idea or set of ideas for employing the instruments of national power in a synchronized and integrated fashion to achieve theater, national, and/or multinational objectives" (DOD Dictionary 2018, 223). But again, implementing means employing. That is not the essence of strategy. How do you come up with the prudent set of ideas in the first place?

After twenty-five years of pondering this question and examining examples of successful and unsuccessful strategies in history, I have concluded that strategy is, at its core, a concept of cause and effect—a concept applied at specific times and under specific conditions.

Strategy is a concept of cause and effect, applied in context, to achieve victory against a thinking enemy over time.

Strategy is not a plan, or a prioritization, or a vision, or the use of means to achieve ends, or even "balancing." Those may be components of a strategy, or products of a strategy, or approaches to operationalizing a strategy—all important in their own right.

But a strategy in its most basic form is **an idea that establishes a cause-and-effect relationship**—an end state with an associated forcing function.

Forcing functions work differently in different contexts. History, culture, religion, geography, demographic makeup, composition of fighting forces, bureaucratic organization, leadership, technological sophistication (and dependence), economic system, resources available, and so on—all influence how the forcing function works. Change one aspect of the strategic context and the utility of the cause-effect concept may change as well.

The purpose of a strategy is "victory" —which itself requires a definition, since getting it wrong early on is the single most common strategic

---

[1] In brief, *Containment* postulated that the Communist collectivist system could not prevail, or even survive, if constrained to using its own resources in its inherently inefficient ways. It certainly could not compete with the self-initiating and self-sustaining drive and energy of democratic/republican capitalism. It could only compete by consuming resources from outside its boundaries. Cutting off access to outside people and other resources would ultimately spell its doom. Alternative strategies considered, but rejected, included *Isolationism, Detente,* and *Roll-back.*

failure.[2] **"Victory" means getting what you will settle for at a price you are willing to pay.**

- Victory is NOT getting everything you want because what you want is the enemy's complete abdication without cost. What you want is for your enemy to slap his forehead and say, "Geez, what was I thinking? The other side has been right all along! Where do I sign up?" Political and military fantasies aside, it is difficult to find a single example of such a victory in history.
- No, in truth you must always settle for something short of perfect victory. And even imperfect victory will come at a cost. The cost might be blood, or treasure, or time, or effort, or emotional, or psychological pain. But there will be a cost to forcing (or convincing) an opponent to give you what you want. This is the most important and most overlooked aspect of crafting a strategy. Strategists repeatedly launch off on adventures where the cost turns out to be higher and the benefit lower than initially thought.
- Even worse, this misestimation becomes a slippery slope. "But we have already invested so much! We can't allow these lives (or dollars) to have been spent in vain!" So the overconfident and self-focused strategist is drawn into a larger and larger investment that produces less and less in the final analysis.
- This is the origin of the term Pyrrhic Victory—or as King Pyrrhus said of his temporary victory over a Roman force, "Another such victory and we shall be lost" (Dupuy 1977, 58). Contemporary history offers many examples.

The reason that strategists (and more precisely, generals, officials, and politicians who fancy themselves to be strategists) get this aspect of victory so wrong so often is that they so often miss the next aspect of strategy entirely. Any strategy must consider the opponent—a **thinking enemy.**

- Remember that your opponent is working just as hard as you are to prevent your cause-effect relationship from succeeding while trying to gain his own victory over you.
- It is astonishing how often "strategists" denigrate or even disregard their opponent, assuming that their own force or technology or logic (or mandate from God) is simply irresistible.

---

[2] "Wars must vary with the nature of their motives and of the situations which give rise to them. The first, the supreme, the most far-reaching act of judgement that the statesman and commander have to make is to establish by that test the kind of war on which they are embarking, neither mistaking it for, nor trying to turn it into, something that is alien to its nature. This is the first of all strategic questions, and the most comprehensive" (Clausewitz 1976, 89).

- This is why the most important question for any strategist to ask is this: "Once I take action to implement this strategy, what will happen next?" What intended and unintended consequences might follow?

Put another way, if my opponent were to use my strategy against me, what would I do? After making adjustments for history, culture, religion, and other aspects of context, this is a good way to check the logic of the forcing function at the core of your strategy. If the strategy would not illicit a surrender from you, why do you think it will produce a surrender from him?

And finally, the aspect of strategy which makes it strategic is that it plays out **over time**. Military officers generally try to distinguish between tactics (how to win a battle), operations (the stringing together of several battles), and strategy (a plan to bring about a desirable end state). Politicians distinguish between political tactics and political strategy. Business leaders talk about short-term strategies and long-term strategies. All of these distinctions from various disciplines have one thing in common: strategies are accomplished over time.

Why? Because the objectives set for strategies are generally so large that they cannot be accomplished by a single blow, a single action, or a single step. It would be a very unusual situation to achieve a major, lasting change over a thinking enemy in a single leap. Big changes generally require lots of resources—one of those resources is time.

So to repeat: **"Strategy is a concept of cause and effect, applied in context, to achieve victory against a thinking enemy, over time."**

This is almost always the case. But why "almost"? Because it is possible to create a strategy to deal with a force of nature, like a strategy for flood mitigation, or response to an earthquake, or even a hazard that results from human or technical error (like a major chemical spill). Hurricanes do require a strategy worked out over time—response may take days; recovery may take years. But the next hurricane will be no smarter than the last. So sometimes you need a strategy even in the absence of a thinking enemy. (This is very important in a homeland security context where some threats are from human adversaries, some from human accidents, and some from natural disasters.)

Caveats aside, the above definition of strategy may be adapted to any discipline, context, or situation. But whatever else you may add to a strategy, it must at its irreducible core contain:

- A forcing function (cause and effect)
- Considered in the current setting (context)

- To achieve an objective (victory)
- While considering the actions of the opponent (against a thinking enemy)
- Over time

All strategies are not equal of course, and the following four traditional tests would apply to any strategy conceived under this rubric. Is the strategy:

- **Adequate**—will it achieve the end state you desire?
- **Feasible**—can you actually pull it off?
- **Acceptable**—does it violate any moral, ethical, or legal boundaries?
- **Sustainable**—do you have the resources to carry it out despite the actions of your thinking enemy?

★   ★   ★

Perhaps it would be appropriate at this point to offer an example of the utility of seeing strategy as a concept of cause and effect as opposed to the more traditional balancing of ways and means.

The "Indian Wars" between American settlers and Native Americans lasted from the earliest colonial days until the surrender of the last Apache Renegades in 1924. One of the most active periods was the fight for the Great Plains from the Dakota War of 1862 until the Great Sioux War, which ended in 1877. So many presidents and generals struggled with so many Indian leaders using so many different techniques (forts, raids, patrols, etc.) in so many places that we cannot speak of a single strategy as the solution to "the Indian problem." But one extremely successful strategy hit upon by Generals Sherman and Sheridan was the hunting of the buffalo to near extension.

Having tested their concept of resource denial on the unprotected women and children of the South (and in particular Georgia), they understood that the buffalo was the key to the independent existence of Indians on the Plains (Weston 2016). Destroying the huge herds of the animals deprived the Sioux and other tribes of food, clothing, and shelter in a single stroke, forcing them to return to the reservations to survive. The thinking enemy tried many counterstrategies, including targeting settlers, patrols, forts, railroads, and so on, but could neither end the slaughter nor do without the resource. Their own strategy of living off the land was defeated. Taking on this task would have prevented the undermanned army from attending to its many other duties, but encouraging and supporting civilian hunters got the job done at no additional cost. And since the hunters cost the army nothing, the pressure could be maintained for years.

To put the strategy for securing the West against the Apache Indians in our format:

- **Cause and Effect:** <u>If</u> the buffalo were eliminated, <u>then</u> the Indians would be forced to return to the reservations to survive.
- **In context:** The Indians depended on the buffalo for most of their survival needs (the approach might not have worked at another place and another time against another enemy).
- **To achieve victory:** Defined as elimination of the threat to American expansion westward.
- **Against a thinking enemy:** The Apache would be unable to develop a viable alternative.
- **Over time:** By using free civilian hunters, the army could sustain the operation until the Indians had to choose between starvation and surrender.

A quick check shows that the strategy was:

- **Adequate:** It would work.
- **Feasible:** It could be accomplished.
- **Acceptable:** It crossed no moral or legal boundaries (of that time—it would be totally unacceptable today, of course).
- **Sustainable:** It could be continued until it was effective.

And by the way, the strategy was clearly NOT designed "at the highest level of government" nor did it link other hunts or other battles together as a series of operations. It did not "employ the elements of national power in a synchronized and integrated fashion." And it was more than just a case of "balancing ways, ends, and means."

So the concept of causing the Indians to cease threatening the Great Plains and move back to reservations by using civilian hunters to kill the buffalo does satisfy our definition of a strategy. Applying this analysis provides insights and perspectives not achieved by a simple discussion of ways and means.

REFERENCES

DOD Dictionary of Military and Associated Terms. 2018. "Strategy." Accessed December 18, 2018. http://www.jcs.mil/Portals/36/Documents/Doctrine/pubs/dictionary.pdf?ver=2017-12-23-160155-320.

Dupuy, R. Ernest, and Trevor N. Dupuy. 1977. *The Encyclopedia of Military History.* New York: Harper & Row.

Phippen, J. Weston. May 13, 2016. "Kill Every Buffalo You Can! Every Buffalo Dead Is an Indian Gone." *The Atlantic.* Accessed December 18, 2018. https://www.theatlantic.com/national/archive/2016/05/the-buffalo-killers/482349/.

Von Clausewitz, Carl. 1976. *On War.* Edited by Peter Paret, Michael Howard, and Bernard Brodie. Princeton, NJ: Princeton University Press.

9

What Is *A* National Security Strategy?

★ ★ ★

BOTTOM LINE UP FRONT

I define a national security strategy (NSS) as: a strategy that will secure a nation-state, its people, its interests, and its power against a specific external threat or set of threats.

The Peloponnesian Wars provide an excellent beginners case study in the use and limits of a national security strategy. During the Cold War, it was used to think through the US strategic situation.

The Cold War national security strategy of Containment is perhaps the most successful NSS of all time. It postulated: if the Soviet Union's expansion and external influence could be contained, then its threat would be reduced, and it might even adopt internal changes more benign toward US interests.

In fact, Containment produced the intellectual collapse of the opponent followed by its collapse as an empire. Given this amazing outcome in a global conflict, the cost of Containment was relatively low in blood. But it was high in treasure. And some would add, high in missed opportunities and discarded values. It offers at least five lessons for our current national security situation:

1. *Crafting and executing a successful national security strategy with a global reach is possible.*
2. *But the national strategy that ended the Soviet Union did not end all threats to the United States.*
3. *The unfortunate truth is that even a good national security strategy does not provide perfect security.*
4. *No single security strategy can account for all security issues a nation may face.*
5. *Even more sobering is the fact that the integration of national security and public safety during the Cold War was relatively easy compared to some of the challenges we face today.*

From 1947–1989 the importance of the challenge, scale of the solution, and the need for national consensus was clear. Things are not so clear at the current intersection of national security and public safety threats, which we call homeland security.

Having read this far in Volume 1, you know that:

- **Security** in an international sense includes safety against external attack, defending and advancing national interests and goals, and producing and protecting the power required to achieve those interests and goals.
- A **nation-state** (our real subject here) is a political entity that combines the emotional bonds of a **nation** with the physical reality (ability to enforce borders and domestic laws) of a **state**.
- The **elements of power** required to protect and advance national security interests and goals include DIME—Diplomatic, Informational, Military and Economic. (I add two more: another "I" for Intelligence and a "D" at the end for Domestic power, which includes the legitimacy of the state in the eyes of its citizens. So my acronym for national power is DIIME-D.)
- **Strategy** is a concept of cause and effect, in context, that produces victory against a thinking enemy over time.

So a national security strategy would be . . . well, perhaps an example would be useful at this point.

In the early days of the Cold War, academics trying to conceptualize and war game the conflict between the United States and the Soviet Union sometimes turned to the Peloponnesian War for inspiration. This might seem a curious choice as the twenty-seven-year war between the Athenian Empire and Sparta's Peloponnesian League ended nearly twenty-four hundred years before the Cold War began. The Peloponnesian Wars featured spears, shields, and triremes. The Cold War featured intercontinental ballistic missiles and nuclear weapons. What could the two conflicts possibly have in common?

Well as we will see below, a lot. And for many of the same reasons, it's an excellent case for understanding the concept of a national security strategy.

In the Western classical age, the Peloponnesian War called for the integration of all elements of power in the way we speak of national security strategy today. The war was fought by relatively homogeneous populations over clear issues and large swaths of geography. Military power alone was simply not enough to deliver victory to either side. **Athens** was a sea power, depending on sea lanes into the Black Sea for enough food to support a city-state surrounded by a seventeen-mile wall. It used trade, diplomacy, intelligence, and economic leverage to build military power and encourage allied city-states to join its navy and defend its coasts. **Sparta** was a land power, with its strength dependent on slave labor and a highly militarized citizenry for its military prowess. It leaned heavily on hoplites (trained cadres into which all males were drafted) and allies (or vassals) to flesh out its ground forces and used all elements of statecraft to accomplish this.

Interestingly, Sparta and Athens worked well together as allies against the Persian Empire in wars a half-century earlier (as did the United States and the USSR against Hitler's Nazis in the Second World War). According to the general and historian Thucydides, it was Sparta's fear of rising Athenian wealth and power that sparked the three-decade-long, civilization-destroying war beginning in 431 BC. That is, Athens' grand strategy of using trade, wealth, and alliances to grow its power sparked fear and then a clamor for war in their chief rival, even though their growing power presented no immediate threat to the Spartan state. As mentioned in chapter 4, George Kennan's analysis of the Soviet perspective on the United States came to a similar conclusion. Also, in both the Peloponnesian War and the Cold War, the actual clash of arms was sparked by conflicts between lesser allies into which the major powers were drawn. It was not the first time that increasing defense by one state looked like preparation for aggression to another. Or that allies cultivated to deter conflict actually dragged principals into war. It would not be the last.

Throughout these early Western wars, both with Persia and between Greek city-states, military, political, and economic strategies were all developed by a relatively small group of leaders at the top, even if they had to be ratified by allies or popular vote (as in Athens . . . and the United States). For example, in the first year of the war, the Athenian general and statesman Pericles implemented a military and economic strategy of attrition and a diplomatic strategy of allied unity. Knowing that Sparta exerted tenuous control over its many slaves and reasoning that the more robust Athens could protect its allies and its food supplies from the sea, while bleeding Sparta economically and militarily with a campaign of raids along the coast, Pericles built an integrated "Periclean Strategy." It secured his city-state inside its walls, while his enemy grew weaker with every day that its army was deployed. It was a wonderful example of an integrated national security strategy at war.[1]

---

[1] Pericles had long promoted the unity of Athenian citizens and the legitimacy of Athenian government in their eyes with a program that shared the burdens of citizenship and the benefits of wealth, culture, and security more broadly than other cities and states of the time. If you consider that the greatest domestic threat to many cities was unrest and revolt,

But it was a hard strategy for many in the populace to swallow. In particular, some property owners had to wait impotently in Athens while Spartan soldiers pillaged their homes and farms outside the walls. But it saved Athens both blood and treasure. It saved them the emotional exhaustion that comes from losing sons in battle. It saved the government the risk of lost legitimacy that comes with every tactical defeat. And it was a cleverly calculated use of time against an enemy without a strategy for homeland security, whose vulnerability to slave revolt grew as long as the Spartan army was away from home.

Unfortunately, we will never know if Pericles's innovative strategy, which leveraged both the external elements of international power and the domestic elements of legitimacy, would have worked. He died of the plague the year his strategy was implemented. In his absence, proponents of seeking out the enemy for decisive combat won the day, and strategies on both sides degenerated into a question of who could bear the greatest losses. Sparta built a navy to go after Athenian interests at sea, and Athens built an army to overcome Sparta's great strength on land. Allies who tried to leave their respective alliances were compelled to stay. Diplomacy gave way to force. Strategic logic surrendered to the brutal tactic of exhaustion. Ultimately, Athens lost but nobody won. All Greek states were permanently weakened, Greek learning and culture were stifled, and disorder eventually invited the invasion of Philip of Macedon and his son Alexander—followed by the subjugation of Greece by Rome.

While these examples of successful and unsuccessful city-state security strategies seem clear, the language which the Greeks left behind to describe such events was not always so helpful. In one of the many Spartan wars that followed the conquest of Athens, King Epaminondas of Thebes (371 BC) intentionally weakened his flank to draw in a Spartan army, break its front, and then envelop it from the side. This brilliant tactic was promptly called a stratagem (Lendering 2017). But was not a strategy as we use the term today.[2] It was a tactic. This and similar misnomers have confused the language of strategy and security for nearly two and a half millennia. This remains a problem today, so let us be clear about definitions.

---

especially in response to the cost of foreign threats, Pericles conscious efforts to promote legitimacy at the intersection of foreign and domestic affairs might be considered one of the earliest successful homeland security strategies.

[2] The changing use of the term "strategy" or "stratagem" is clearly demonstrated by a 1793 text for British officers entitled *Polyænus's Stratagems of War*, as translated by R. Shepherd and published by George Nicol of London. Throughout this text (and especially in chapter 3 referring to Epaminondas), stratagem means "clever devices," or even "tricks," whether of grand maneuver, battlefield tactics, or simple deception.

With the Peloponnesian example as background, I define a national security strategy as: **a strategy that will secure a nation-state, its people, its interests, its structure, and its power against a specific threat or set of threats and opponents.**[3]

If this were a book about strategy, we would spend the next several hundred pages talking about the development of states, nations, and their strategies over the last two thousand years. But the essays in this series are trying to promote thinking about homeland security. We are working our way through the subject of national security so we can set the proper context for understanding security at home. And so we are going to leap over the Roman Empire, the Dark Ages, the Middle Ages, Machiavelli, Frederick the Great, Napoleon, Clausewitz (the greatest martial philosopher of them all), and the mother of all national strategies—the two-part global war of the first half of the twentieth century (that's World Wars I and II). We are also going to skip past Washington's strategy for defeating the British, the Monroe Doctrine of 1823, General Winfield Scott's Anaconda Plan to defeat the Confederacy, Manifest Destiny and the Indian Wars, Theodore Roosevelt's Great White Fleet, Woodrow Wilson's 14 Points and the League of Nations, and FDR's demand for unconditional surrender— as well as his astonishing domestic preparation of the nation to achieve that goal.

We're going to skip right to the greatest national security strategy in the history of the world. We are going to look at a strategy that faced down a massive opposing empire, combat tested and armed to the teeth, capable of destroying any enemy, anywhere in the world, in a matter of minutes with a single blow. A strategy that caused that enemy to lose legitimacy in his own mind, collapse back within its own borders, free its vassal states, and change its entire system of government—all without a single direct clash of arms between major belligerents. That strategy, conceived in the late 1940s and signed by President Truman in 1950, was known formally as NSC-68. Politicians, generals, academics, and citizens called it "Containment."

The strategy began with two core beliefs about the United States (and the Western world) and the Soviet Union (and its Warsaw Pact minions).

1. Communism and international socialism were fundamentally at odds with human nature. People would not work hard and do their

---

[3] This definition implies that since there might be more than one national-level threat or set of threats, there could be more than one national security strategy. Of necessity, these would be prioritized. When people use the term "national security strategy," they are usually focusing on vital and survival threats. *The National Security Strategy of the United States* is an entirely different thing, as we will discuss in chapter 10.

best for a state that confiscated the products of their labor and redistributed them to everyone regardless of their contribution.

2. Republicanism, Liberalism, and capitalist economies were fundamentally in alignment with human nature. People would be creative, innovative, and exceptionally productive if allowed to select their political leaders, make their own laws, and benefit from their own hard work.

This two-part vision of the context in which national strategic issues would play out led to a concept of cause and effect: Because of the statist bureaucracy and inefficient economy, the Soviet Union and its satellites would not be able to make good use of its domestic resources. It could only grow its international power by pulling in resources (people and materials) from outside its boundaries.

This logic led to the strategy of **Containment**: *IF the Soviet Union's expansion and external influence could be contained, THEN its threat would be reduced, and it might even adopt internal changes more aligned with US interests.*

Other strategies were available but rejected.

- The United States might have adopted a more *aggressive* posture, attacking the Soviet Union directly, or attempting to peel off Communist allies whenever possible. President Eisenhower rejected such an approach when he decided not to intervene in the Hungarian Revolution in 1954.

- The United States might have adopted a more *passive* posture, seeking to appease the Soviet Union, allowing advances in places like Greece, South Korea, the Middle East, Southeast Asia, and elsewhere to go unchallenged.

Instead the Secretary of State made a speech in 1950 in which he essentially drew a line around existing Communist influence and announced that the United States would meet any attempts to expand outside that line as though it were an attack on its own soil.[4]

The strategy demanded a costly and expensive commitment that lasted forty years. The United States built a massive peacetime military,

---

[4] Whether by accident or by design, the "Red Line" famously failed to include South Korea inside its arc of defense. Less than six months after the Secretary of State's speech, the North Koreans launched a full-scale attack precisely into a location the United States had left off its very public list of vital interests.

ready to respond quickly to Communist provocation across the spectrum of conflict, from a local insurgency to interstate nuclear war. It deployed that military in a global footprint that matched the perimeter described in the Containment strategy, expanded to include South Korea. It built a global network of alliances to house overseas bases, committed additional forces to common defense, and reinforced governments that might have found themselves challenged internally if not for the presence of the clear American commitment to their stability.

The military component of the strategy was matched and frequently led by an exercise of diplomatic power that blunted Soviet initiatives and reinforced liberal principles and values worldwide. Both of these efforts were informed by a massive global intelligence effort that eventually consisted of fifteen (now seventeen) independent but coordinated agencies keeping a constant eye on threats to US international interests. And the entire enterprise was supported by a broad range of formal and informal economic efforts to support and sustain a stable economic system worldwide. This last component of the national Containment strategy was not always visible since (unlike the Soviet Union) the United States did not have a command economy that could simply be ordered about. Thus, US influence was often exercised through international organizations and cooperative efforts like the Bretton Woods agreement, the International Monetary Fund, and the establishment of the US dollar as the reserve currency for the world.

It is difficult to describe the scale of this massive undertaking in a short essay. Policies on everything from interaction with allied states to retirement rules for soldiers had to be established, constantly reviewed, and revised as necessary. A complex set of thousands of operations had to be planned, executed, and coordinated, from the training and placement of a single Peace Corps officer in a remote village in Africa, to continuous patrols by ballistic nuclear submarines. Whole bureaucracies involving millions of people had to be created, housed, trained, educated, and managed. The entire endeavor had to be funded by budgets that competed for funds with domestic priorities. And leaders had to constantly review the plans and actions of every agency as a thinking enemy responded to our strategy with a national security strategy of its own.

In the end, Containment proved more effective than even its strongest proponents could have imagined. Communism was delegitimized as a political theory, the Soviet Union ceased to exist, and its proxies ceased to disrupt and threaten peoples and governments around the world. A global thermonuclear war, which many once thought inevitable, was prevented.

The number of nuclear weapons stockpiled by belligerents was significantly reduced. The direct threat to the United States largely evaporated. The strategy worked.

Five strategic lessons stand out from this remarkable case.

1. Crafting and executing a successful national security strategy with a global reach is possible. Early in the Cold War the list of national security challenges seemed impossible to meet in light of the scale of operations and competing domestic concerns. The demand for resources was too great. The likelihood of domestic and international political cooperation too small. Many of the essential components, like ballistic missile submarines and a successful space program, had to be invented. And it was clearly easier and less expensive for the Soviet Union to stir up trouble abroad than it was for the United States to counter the resulting conflicts and ensure stability. Like today, the strategic framework often appeared too frail for the weight of the world's problems. But the framework did survive; the strategy did work; the struggle for the survival of the United States was resolved to our advantage. Despite other issues, our domestic situation and our international position are today envied by every other major power on earth.

2. But the national strategy that ended the Soviet Union did not end all threats to the United States. The forces arrayed and aligned in the bipolar global confrontation actually had the effect of tamping down many local disputes and confrontations. When every competition in the world was a potential matter of superpower conflict, local opponents learned to tread softly lest they trigger a superpower intervention. Once the bipolar tension was relieved, all the hidden grievances were free to break into the open. Also, the world evolves. So do threats. Cyber, climate, immigration, transnational crime, global trafficking, Weapons of Mass Destruction proliferation, natural pandemics, apocalyptic terrorism—all these new threats and more challenge our national security in ways that Containment could never address. New threats will require that new strategies be conceived, evaluated, implemented, and managed in a never-ending cycle.

3. The unfortunate truth is that even a good national security strategy does not provide perfect security. Containment saved the world from global war and the United States from communism, but it had many unintended consequences. Nuclear deterrence put the world on a hair-trigger for nuclear war—a situation not entirely resolved today, nearly thirty years after the fall of the Berlin Wall. The debt incurred for military buildups and deployments will remain on our national books for another generation or more. Overt challenges to Soviet expansionism prompted US interventions in Europe, Korea, the Dominican Republic, Vietnam, Grenada, and else-where. Covert activities led to a reputation for nefarious dealings around the world. Promotion of stability caused us to back many unsavory leaders because of their promise to maintain the status quo. And some of our most successful efforts to undermine communism have morphed into challenges to our interests long after communism left the field of battle. One example is our assistance to the Afghan resistance fighters who broke the confidence of the Soviet military only to metastasize into the Taliban, Al Qaeda, ISIS, and other current threats. Even successful strategies have unintended con-sequences. The bigger the stakes, the bigger the efforts, and the bigger the consequences.

4. No single security strategy can account for all security issues a nation may face. Despite the fact that the Cold War demanded the full attention of the national security community, leaders had to find time to deal with other serious but unrelated threats. Many of these were domestic in origin, even if they took place at the intersection of international and domestic affairs—a space we now call homeland security. For example:

- Truman faced the problem of employing soldiers returning from war, a national housing crisis, civil rights issues, the desegregation of the Armed Forces, and a paralyzing steel strike during the Korean War.
- Eisenhower was confronted by serious economic problems, a new challenge from immigration, domestic clashes over civil rights, disrup-tive unrest from labor unions, and the challenge of funding both a space race and his dream of an interstate highway system.
- Kennedy entered office during the second of two recessions in three years and presided over a steady decline in the stock market throughout his tenure. Civil liberties and civil rights issues dominated the domestic news, as did nationwide conflicts between industry and unions.

What all presidents know is that domestic issues generally determine the outcome of presidential elections. Even at a time when vital national security issues are at stake, they must be prioritized against other pressing concerns. A president with a winning national security strategy cannot implement it if he loses the election over domestic issues.

5. Even more sobering is the fact that the integration of national security and public safety during the Cold War was relatively easy compared to some of the challenges we face today. As complex as the Cold War challenge was, the new world, the new threats, and the new opponents we face are more challenging because they (and we) are more diverse. A clear sense of the challenge, a clear explanation of the solution, a clear understanding of the context, and a clear consensus on what constitutes victory at the nexus of national security and public safety—the place occupied by homeland security—are simply not available to today's strategists, bureaucrats, and citizens, as they were during the Cold War.

Learning to think about these challenges is the purpose of these essays. Solving these challenges is the purpose of your reading and deliberating upon them.

REFERENCES

Lendering, Jona. June 9, 2017. "Epaminondas." *Livius*. Accessed December 18, 2018. http://www.livius.org/articles/person/epaminondas/.

Shepherd, R., trans. 1793. "Epaminondas." *Polyænus's Stratagems of War*. London: George Nicol. (Facsimile by University Microfilms International, 1981), 65–70. Accessed December 18, 2018. https://babel.hathitrust.org/cgi/pt?id=uc1.c008112906;view=1up;seq=6.

10

What Is *THE* National Security Strategy of the United States?

(And what does that have to do with Homeland Security?)

★ ★ ★

BOTTOM LINE UP FRONT

"The National Security Strategy of the United States" DOES NOT MEAN "the one and only security strategy of the United States." Because there are multiple threats to US security, there must be multiple strategies to address those different threats. Some of those threats reside within the area of homeland security. Logic would suggest that homeland security strategies might be developed and expressed in the same way as national security strategies. But despite numerous efforts over the last several years, that has not been the case.

The National Security Strategy (NSS) of the United States is a document, not a strategy. It probably should be entitled, "The US National Security Strategy Report." This is the president's opportunity (mandated by Congress) to explain to foreign and domestic audiences his perspective on US interests and goals worldwide, threats to those interests, and his administration's priorities and ideas for dealing with those threats.

One problem, for the administration and the nation, is that the strategic cascade—the huge array of policies, plans, procedures, operations, and budgets that support the nation's priorities and strategies—is not generated anew after every release of the NSS. Most of these subordinate documents and programs are cyclical in nature—they are reviewed and revised on a set schedule. It would be impossible, for example, to relet contracts, change personnel policies, and modify multiyear acquisition programs every time an annual strategy report is released. So there will

*always be a certain amount of overlap, underlap, and perhaps even contra-
diction and confusion, as government bureaucracies struggle to align their
long-term programs and perspectives with evolving the NSS.*

*This constant realignment of presidential guidance and bureaucratic
action is especially challenging in the field of homeland security.*

- *Given the unique geographic situation of the United States, national
  security threats are usually expressed against overseas interests or our
  international borders.*
- *Given the unique constitutional configuration of our government, the
  United States does not generally use the term NSS to describe the protection of people and property <u>within</u> the nation against <u>domestic</u> threats.
  The United States calls this Public Safety (PS).*
- *At the intersection of these two sets of responsibilities—national security
  and public safety—a new set of threats has emerged, requiring a new
  form of protection we call homeland security.*
- *But the vision of what to do about this new intersection of threats and
  responsibilities changed significantly between the Bush 43 Administration
  and the Obama Administration. It appears to be changing again in the
  Trump Administration.*

*In truth, our entire system is still working out what homeland security
means and what should be done about it. The problem is largely one
of bureaucratic perspective. Almost everyone at this new intersection of
threats and responsibilities has some other full-time job. As the NSS and
many other government documents demonstrate, neither the national
security nor the public safety community sees homeland security as a primary responsibility. And those who do work homeland security full time
have little authority—especially across jurisdictions—and relatively few
resources.*

*This is not just an issue of organization or resources. Solving this
problem will require a new understanding of, and new way to think about,
homeland security.*

If you are reading this essay because you think from the title that I am going
to reveal "the one and only" current NSS of the United States, then you
are about to be sorely disappointed. THERE IS NO "ONE AND ONLY"
NATIONAL SECURITY STRATEGY FOR THE UNITED STATES—
because there is no one and only threat, and consequently, no one and only
solution to that threat.

The National Security Strategy of the United States is a document, not a strategy. It probably should be entitled *The US National Security Strategy Report*.

For the first 210 years of our nation's history, there was no requirement or mechanism for the president to place before the public on a routine basis a formal statement of the external challenges we face as a nation or the administration's plans and philosophy for dealing with them.[1] This changed with the Goldwater–Nichols Department of Defense Reorganization Act of 1986—the largest single set of changes to our national security apparatus since the National Security Act of 1947 (Public Law 99-433-Oct. 1, 1986).

This act was a bipartisan (it passed 95–0 in the Senate) response to a number of political pressures, including

- the failure of the Iranian hostage rescue attempt in 1980; and
- concern among Democrats about the strategic appropriateness of military expenditures during the Reagan era military buildup.[2]

The primary focus of the act was the restructuring of elements within the Department of Defense (DOD) to improve civilian control over the military and promote joint collaboration between the military services as a counter to service parochialism. In order to promote a unified perspective across DOD and provide an external window into that perspective, the law requires an annual report from the president, submitted with the budget, detailing how the administration will meet global challenges and secure national-level interests and goals. New administrations are to submit a report within 150 days of taking office.

In practice, the reports have been somewhat uneven in both publication and focus. Reagan produced two reports in two years. Bush 41 produced three reports in four years. Clinton produced seven reports in eight years. Bush 43 and Obama produced two reports each in their respective eight-year tenures. Reagan's reports were short and crisp and focused on meeting the challenge of the Soviet Union. Delayed by the Gulf War, Bush

---

[1] Of course, the president has always been able to address strategic issues through public speeches or executive orders anytime he wants, as with President Roosevelt's famous request for a declaration of war against Japan on December 8, 1941. And he can use the annual State of the Union address to highlight any issues he desires. But neither of these approaches provides for routine, cyclical presentation of a NSS.

[2] This is similar to the way Republican concerns over the national security focus of the Clinton Administration created the requirement for the Quadrennial Defense Review, which led to the National Defense Panel, which created the term "homeland security." Sometimes our system of checks and balances actually works.

41's last report continued to focus on the relationship with Russia but also "broadened the definition of national security, making a concerted effort to expand the concept of national security to include economic health . . . [while shifting] the focus of military preparedness from direct confrontation with the Soviet Union to regional conflict" (National Archives 1991). Clinton's later reports captured the philosophy of the administration by providing a catalog of strategic accomplishments. Not surprisingly, Bush 43's reports provided a justification and direction for the Global War on Terror. Obama's reports added some new dimensions to global threats, such as climate change, and some new priorities, such as an emphasis on promoting American values worldwide.

Operators looking for a short, succinct mission statement tend to be dismissive of these strategic reports as being too general and too "high-level" to be of practical use. However, this criticism misses several important points.

The NSS is the single unified source of information about the president's top international concerns and priorities. Outside of this document, the president's messages on international affairs are scattered across many speeches, presentations, interviews, and soundbites. Sometimes these are impromptu or unscripted. Sometimes they are tweets. By contrast, the national security report is months (sometimes years) in the drafting and carefully coordinated across every major element of the administration. And it provides as much time and space as the president desires to make his points. This report, even more than the State of the Union Address, is the president's definitive statement on what his administration is concerned about from a security perspective and what they plan to do about those concerns.

The NSS communicates that perspective to key audiences. Ambassadors, generals, admirals, and government representatives may communicate with foreign leaders in private. But what friend and foe alike know about this document is that the president has committed to it in public before the American people—and the press. He will have a hard time walking back or making quick changes to a fully coordinated position months in the making and published for the record. So we can look to these reports to track how different presidents have perceived the threats and actions that comprise homeland security today.

BUT BEFORE WE BEGIN, let's pause to include **Presidential Doctrines** prior to 9/11.[3]

---

[3] In chapter 7, we talked about presidential doctrines from a different perspective and for a different purpose. There we were examining examples of the Realist–Liberal divide in thinking about national security. Here we are using presidential doctrines as examples to clarify strategic intent. I am offering the same reference source as in chapter 7:

The study of National Security Strategies is frustrating because they are official statements of strategic interests, goals, and priorities for action but expressed in vague generalities. They express concerns, priorities, and intent. They may even commit to action. But they do not generally meet the definition of a strategy offered in chapter 8 because they rarely offer a cause–effect argument leading to some sort of specific achievement in security, whether international or domestic.[4]

Presidential doctrines are more specific and help to clarify strategic intent. They are generally crisp, focused statements of US action on major issues previously identified in national strategies. Strategies present the (sometimes ambiguous) "why" of national security plans and actions. Doctrines provide the clear "what" we are going to do in specific situations.

Unfortunately, doctrines are frequently best expressed by media or historians after the fact based on a variety of presidential statements and actions.

* **The Truman Doctrine** is an exception since the president said in a direct fashion, "It is the policy of the United States to support free peoples who are resisting attempted subjugation by armed minorities or by outside pressures."
* **The Eisenhower Doctrine** said that the United States would provide military forces to nations threatened by armed aggression from another state. It was stated less crisply but reinforced by US actions in the Mid-East.
* **The Kennedy Doctrine** restated the US commitment to Containment and emphasized its application in the Western Hemisphere.
* **The Johnson Doctrine** reinforced this policy and its application to Latin America.
* **The Nixon Doctrine** assured the "nuclear shield" for allies but (with Vietnam in mind) reduced the global commitment to some extent by calling on others to take primary responsibility for their own defense.
* **The Carter Doctrine** restated the US commitment of force to defend nations in the Persian Gulf.

Joseph Siracusa and Aiden Warren (2016), *Presidential Doctrines*. But I also offer a good source at: https://en.wikipedia.org/wiki/United_States_presidential_doctrines (accessed November 30, 2017). Like all serious graduate faculty, I tell my students to never include Wikipedia as a research source. But it is always a good place to start a search. And the references at the end of the entries are frequently quite useful.

[4] As we shall see, Ronald Reagan's approach to national security strategies was an exception to this rule. His reports addressed many issues but were clearly focused primarily on securing the United States from Soviet aggression and rolling back Soviet influence wherever possible.

It is telling that none of these doctrines addressed any aspect of public safety or homeland security. Short of global thermonuclear war, international threats were simply not expected to manifest themselves as domestic dangers.

PRESIDENT RONALD REAGAN, NSS, AND HOMELAND SECURITY

The **first** *National Security Strategy* ever published, **Ronald Reagan's 1987 version,** identified the Soviet Union's actions (and existence) as the primary threat to the United States and proposed a strategy of active opposition everywhere that communism sought to expand. The corresponding **Reagan Doctrine** was a policy to reverse Soviet expansionism by supporting anticommunist guerrillas in Soviet client states. Underlying both was a concept of cause and effect advanced by Secretary of Defense Casper Weinberger under the title "competitive strategies." The idea was to leverage the robust resources of capitalism by expanding Containment to the point of reversing communism where it was vulnerable and bankrupting the Soviet Union in the process. It worked.

The 1987 strategy report lists terrorism (and Low-Intensity Conflict) last among potential threats and sees it primarily as a means of subverting weak governments overseas. It prescribes security assistance to friendly military forces as the solution (Reagan 1987). It does not mention security at home.

PRESIDENT GEORGE H. W. BUSH (41), NSS, AND HOMELAND SECURITY

George H. W. Bush (Bush 41) inherited a disoriented post–Cold War world where the United States was the only superpower left standing. The **1990 NSS** reflected the uncertainty of an administration working its way through a dramatically new strategic situation, with the goal of advancing what Bush 41 called a "New World Order" (Bush [41] 1990).[5] Global trends were identified as a combination of "Opportunities and Uncertainties,"

---

[5] Analysts have made much of this phase over the last three decades. Republicans, and especially neocons, have argued it indicates a new collection of power by free market democracies led by the United States. Democrats, and especially progressives, argue it describes a collection of global citizens and states who subordinate their interests for the common good. Conspiracy theorists have postulated a secret cabal of wealthy puppet masters. My own take is that Bush 41 sought to create a common post–Cold War understanding that some worldwide challenges would require formal international cooperation rather than solutions pursued by single sovereign nations. This is the concept President Trump takes on directly in his 2017 NSS.

with a single sentence devoted to terrorism and a half page on illicit drugs. This apportionment captures the entire thinking about homeland security at the time. The general approach was to prioritize US strategic attention by region—an approach reinforced by the US response to the subsequent Iraqi invasion of the Kuwaiti oil fields, a perceived threat to the lifeblood of the American economy.

From this experience, the president's key advisers (led by Secretary of Defense Dick Cheney) advanced the concept of the United States in the lead globally as a "benign hegemon," using the elements of national power (DIME) to promote international trade and stability in ways that benefitted the United States first and the entire world by extension. These ideas were best captured in the DOD *Regional Defense Strategy,* released the last day of the Bush 41 Administration (Cheney 1993). It suggested that while collective defense was preferred, both advanced military technology and regime change would be used as required to prevent regional crises from threatening the interests of the United States. As part of this general line of thought, the Chairman of the Joint Chiefs of Staff, General Colin Powell, developed both a pathway for the use of military force and a brake on that use through guidelines that came to be called the **Powell Doctrine.** Essentially, it argued that the military is to be used as a last resort, but when required, used with overwhelming force.

Absent from these explanations of US interests, goals, and priorities is any mention of domestic safety and security. In response to the dramatic changes shaking the world in the aftermath of the Soviet collapse, Bush 41's NSS begins by repeating the "Enduring Elements" of US strategy, including contributing to international peace, a commitment to an alliance strategy built on shared values, support for a free and open economic system, maintaining a capability for global power projection, and preventing any hostile power from dominating the Eurasian landmass. In keeping with the traditional separation of domestic and international issues, the only discussion of domestic concerns involves the DOD and the Department of State (DOS) contribution to countering the trafficking of narcotics outside our borders (Bush [41] 1990, 28–29). Low-intensity conflict is again addressed as an overseas issue, and there is no mention of terrorism.

PRESIDENT WILLIAM J. CLINTON, NSS, AND HOMELAND SECURITY

Benefiting from both the end of the Cold War and the overwhelming victory in the Persian Gulf War, **President Clinton's 1994 NSS** shifted the focus from threats to opportunities for overseas engagement and enlargement of democratic values (and markets).[6] At a time when critics in the president's own party were calling for a "Peace Dividend," the report not only emphasizes efforts to maintain "military forces that are ready to fight" but also highlights using them for diplomatic outreach (Clinton 1994, i) It addresses only the international aspect of terrorism. Although it does mention the 1993 bombing of the World Trade Center, it focuses on the international nature of the attackers, not the domestic impact. (The 1995 Oklahoma City Bombing would change this vision of national security priorities.) Furthermore, terrorism is collected under a larger heading that includes Drug Trafficking and "Other Missions," to be addressed by intelligence agencies and specialized units (Clinton 1994, 8). The traditional focus on international security without mention of public safety is maintained.

Six years later, the **NSS of 2000** shows big changes. It begins with a new way to look at national interests (Clinton 2000, 9). Gone is the traditional division into survival, vital, important, and peripheral. Instead, "We divide our national interests into three categories: vital, important, and humanitarian." The categories (and conditions for using the military) are much broader than before, including regions where America holds a significant economic or political stake, issues with significant global environmental impact, crises that could cause destabilizing economic turmoil or humanitarian movement, acting to halt gross violations of human rights, and encouraging adherence to the rule of law (Clinton 2000, 9).

And for the first time, vital interests are defined to include not just "the survival, safety, and vitality of our nation [and] economic well-being of our society" but also "the protection of our critical infrastructures—including energy, banking and finance, telecommunications, transportation, water systems, vital human services, and government services—from disruption intended to cripple their operation" (Clinton, 2000, 9).

What is most remarkable for our purposes is *the first mention of Protecting the Homeland as an element of the NSS*. And it is not just a passing reference. A significant part of the report (nine pages—more than 10 percent of the document) is devoted to National Missile Defense, Countering Foreign Intelligence, Combatting Terrorism (to include the FBI's work on domestic terrorism), Domestic Preparedness Against

---

[6] The Clinton Administration intended the title of the strategy, "Engagement and Enlargement," to suggest their interest in open diplomatic relations with all nations, while convincing others to embrace the advantages of democratic principles and values. The DC rumor mill (quoting "informed sources") suggested that Chinese translators initially assigned military meanings to the title terms, so the US NSS was portrayed as something like "Combat and Aggression." The confusion was quickly remedied, but this miscommunication stands as an example of the challenge of communicating strategy and diplomacy across languages and cultures.

Weapons of Mass Destruction (WMD), Critical Infrastructure Protection, National Security Emergency Preparedness, and Fighting Drug Trafficking and Other International Crime (Clinton 2000, 26–34). This is not just lip service. The actions highlighted reflect real efforts to create new initiatives (like Presidential Decision Directive 69 on Critical Infrastructure Protection) and energize existing organizations with new working groups and direction (as with the WMD Preparedness Interagency Working Group). On 9/11 these efforts proved inadequate, but largely because their proponents underestimated the internal resistance of existing practitioners and organizations to new ways of thinking. The overall effort was quite remarkable for its time.[7]

Taken together, the Clinton strategies mark a significant departure from past philosophies, focusing as they do on promoting democratic values as a high-level strategic interest and preparing for international threats on our own shores as a strategic concern.

PRESIDENT GEORGE W. BUSH (43), NSS, AND HOMELAND SECURITY

Published twelve months after 9/11, the George W. Bush 2002 NSS clearly reflected the impact that event had on thinking about national security. In the foreword he wrote,

> Defending our Nation against its enemies is the first and fundamental commitment of the Federal Government. Today, that task has changed dramatically. Enemies in the past needed great armies and great industrial capabilities to endanger America. Now, shadowy networks of individuals can bring great chaos and suffering to our shores for less than it costs to purchase a single tank. *[As a result]* . . . The gravest danger our Nation faces lies at the crossroads of radicalism and technology. (Bush [43] 2002, 3–4)

But while terrorism did assume a role of central concern in the strategy document, homeland security did not. Terrorism was addressed in some depth, along with concerns over regional conflicts and a resurgent Russia.

---

[7] Scholars have not agreed on a specific **Clinton Doctrine**. My own opinion is that the single greatest change President Clinton made in national security during his administration began in speeches and the 1996 NSS and was sealed by Secretary Albright in several sets of remarks when she came into office in 1997. The cumulative message was that henceforth defending and advancing American democratic values (however the administration defined them) would be considered a survival issue. This change, more than any other factor, has politicized US foreign policy to the detriment of the nation for the last twenty years. While consensus over prioritizing interests across party lines was previously possible ("politics stops at the water's edge"), consensus over spending blood and treasure to advance values on foreign shores has proven impossible to achieve.

And the culminating argument of the document was for transformation of national security institutions.[8] But homeland security was not addressed—primarily because the issue was separated from national security and addressed by a separate *National Strategy for Homeland Security 2002*, issued three months earlier (Homeland Security Council 2002). Its express purpose was to answer four questions:

- What is "homeland security," and what missions does it entail?
- What do we seek to accomplish, and what are the most important goals of homeland security?
- What is the federal executive branch doing now to accomplish these goals and what should it do in the future?
- What should nonfederal governments, the private sector, and citizens do to help secure the homeland?

That was an important set of questions to answer at a moment when the entire nation was searching for explanations and guidance. Those who labored long and hard to place a clear explanation before the public deserve recognition for their efforts. But answering those questions provided **policy guidance—*what* the Administration wanted Americans to do. It did not provide a *why*—it did not frame the cause-and-effect relationship required of a true strategy.**

This gap between strategy and policy—between convincing state, local, and industry officials and simply directing them—continues to haunt us today. Pushback became especially heated as it became clear that the Bush Administration expected many first responders to change their operations to comply with a centrally designed National Response Plan—and nonfederal governments and private enterprise were called on to pay about two-thirds of the quickly accumulating homeland security bill.[9] (Needless to say, this policy did not last.)

---

[8] The Bush 43 NSS is no help to understanding the role of homeland security, as it focused entirely on international relations. Some find the fundamental expression of the doctrine in the president's warning, "You are either with us or you are against us." Other's look to the continuation of *Preemption* (from the Cheney *Regional Strategy* from 1993) as a way to deal with developing threats. Neither provided any guidance for security in the domestic context.

[9] To be clear, in later essays I will suggest that it may not be possible to craft a strategy for homeland security along the model of national security. National security generally deals with states or at least major actors who can be addressed with a rational model. The number of players—both friends and opponents—is limited. Everyone working the issue for the United States works for the president. And international politics can sometimes be held at arm's length. The stakes may be high (war or peace), but the game is manageable. Homeland security is far more complex. Opponents may be domestic, international, or home grown (from organizations or lone wolfs) or accidents or nature itself. Tens of thousands of jurisdictions may be involved and even more businesses. Few of them work

The key element in addressing the strategy–policy gap tuned out to the gradual professionalization of the Department of Homeland Security (DHS). As the department gained experience and confidence (sometimes the hard way, as through the Hurricane Katrina debacle), its tone improved from "here is what you should do" to "here are some ideas that might help." FEMA's transition from the directive Nation Response Plan to the suggestive National Response Framework is one such success. That (easier to stomach) model was later replicated by the Obama Administration with a series of other documents (National Prevention Framework, National Protection Framework, National Disaster Recovery Framework, CPG 101 Developing and Maintaining Emergency Operations Plans, etc.). And the fact that use of national standards like the Incident Command System and the National Incident Management System became prerequisites for federal grants helped answer the "why" question posed by the missing strategy.

Interestingly, "common framework" is the way DHS describes the **2007 NSHS**, noting that with the benefit of several years of experience the Bush Administration was now able to focus on four goals vice answer four questions as in 2002 (Homeland Security Council 2007). Those goals were:

- Prevent and disrupt terrorist attacks;
- Protect the American people, our critical infrastructure, and key resources;
- Respond to and recover from incidents that do occur; and
- Continue to strengthen the foundation to ensure our long-term success.

Overall, the document displays a clear sense that the concept of Homeland Security has evolved. Terrorism remains the focus, but the impact of Katrina is reflected in a determination to strengthen "our Nation's preparedness for both natural and man-made disasters" (Homeland Security Council 2007, 5). The organizing construct of "Prevention, Protection, Response and Recovery" has been adopted from FEMA and applied to the department as a whole (although Mitigation is curiously missing). The DHS itself was to be restructured along less theoretical and more functional lines, in accordance with practical experience with real and potential terrorists, hazards, and natural disasters. The approach to Critical Infrastructure and Key Resources has been refined (central guidance provided, federal sponsors identified, and coordination between public–private partnerships initiated). The importance of local Resilience to Recovery is highlighted along with a

---

for the president. And every decision is subject to domestic political influence. Under the circumstances, the first *National Strategy for Homeland Security* (NSHS) was a fine effort. But the thinking about HS was understandably incomplete.

new sense of federal aggressiveness in pushing support forward even before it is requested. Overall, it is a more nuanced view of the issue than any of the previous efforts, reflecting many lessons learned from five years of concentrated effort.

But there is still a problem with the concept of strategy as expressed in the document. The intent of the administration is clear:

> The United States will use all instruments of national power and influence—diplomatic, information, military, economic, financial, intelligence, and law enforcement—to achieve our goals to prevent and disrupt terrorist attacks; protect the American people, critical infrastructure, and key resources; and respond to and recover from incidents that do occur. We also will continue to create, strengthen, and transform the principles, systems, structures, and institutions we need to secure our Nation over the long term.
>
> "This is our strategy for homeland security." (Homeland Security Council 2007, 13)

Except, of course, that is *not* a strategy because there is no forcing function—*no sense of cause and effect*. The passage explains what the administration intends to use (elements of power, principles, structures, institutions, and what it intends to achieve ("a secure Homeland that sustains our way of life as a free, prosperous, and welcoming America") (Homeland Security Council 2007, 13). But that is a statement of policy—"we will . . ." That's not strategy (if X then Y).

If General MacArthur, as Commander of Allied Forces in the South Pacific, had said in 1944, "We intend to use all our national power and all our ships and planes and solders to defeat Japan," no one would have called that a strategy. And yet administrations seem to take that approach time and again—they marshal forces for action and call it a strategy. Something is wrong with their thinking on this subject.

PRESIDENT BARACK OBAMA, NSS, AND HOMELAND SECURITY

Because of events, the Bush 43 Administration had to revise its strategic thinking several times from its pre-9/11 worldview, to a post-9/11 Global-War-on-Terrorism perspective. The differences between their early strategic documents and their final versions demonstrate some significant changes.

The Obama Administration faced no such reality-altering events. So their public documents reflect a refinement of initial views over time, not a significant change in those views. We will focus here on the final NSS released in 2015, as it represents the culmination of their thought.

My next observation will come as a shock: just as a matter of intellectual structure, Obama's overall security approach actually looks more like Reagan's than any of the three presidents between them. The similarity is not in intellectual substance, mind you, but in intellectual structure.

Reagan's strategy acknowledged a variety of threats but really focused on one: global instability encouraged by the Soviet Union. His solution was American leadership using American national power. Obama also presents threats ranging from violent extremism to cybersecurity to Russia to climate change. But the central danger is instability stemming from the absence of human rights and the failure to advance democratic values. His solution is American leadership, in support of American values (Obama 2015, i).[10]

And like Reagan 1987 NSS, **Obama's 2015 NSS** presents his solution in a cause-and-effect structure. If the United States will do the following, it will lead the world to greater peace and prosperity:

- **Secure the United States and its allies against major threats** (maintain a strong military; confront terrorism; engage local partners; transition to sustainable energy; work against the spread of nuclear weapons; collaborate against bio dangers; address climate change; expand free trade; etc.);
- **Reinforce our homeland security to keep the American people safe from terrorist attacks and natural hazards while strengthening our national resilience.**
- **Advance <u>universal values</u> at home and around the world** (maintain high US standards; promote democracy, human rights, and equality; confront corruption; support transparent governance; prevent and respond to human rights abuses and mass atrocities as well as gender-based violence and discrimination against LGBT persons);
- **Advance an <u>international order</u> that promotes peace, security, and opportunity** (promote stronger collaboration; update the rules, norms, and institutions that are foundational to order and human dignity in the twenty-first century; strengthen global alliances, partnerships, diverse coalitions; advance multilateral organizations and stability in critical regions including Asia-Pacific, Europe, Middle East, and Africa) (Office of the Press Secretary 2015).

This is of course a list of generalities (the stock-in-trade of NSS reports) presented as forcing functions. But imprecise as the forcing functions might

---

[10] In intellectual substance, Obama's NSS is a refinement and extension of Clinton's concepts. It is the structure of clearly articulated forcing functions that I find similar to Reagan's approach.

be, I regard the construct of such an argument as the distinguishing characteristic of a strategy.

In the area of homeland security, the Clinton Administration showed foresight in addressing an emerging problem but dealt with it through intergovernmental cooperation by existing players. The Bush 43 Administration met a dramatically increased threat with a dramatic government restructuring, actually separating homeland security efforts from national security efforts in order to give them additional emphasis. **The Obama Administration reversed this approach, reincorporating homeland security as one of many elements supporting national security.** There are two ways to think about this decision.

- One is that this better integrated domestic security into the national security framework.
- The other is that it reduced—some would say minimized—its importance.

In practice, Obama shifted homeland security out of the national security realm and almost completely into the public safety domain. Federal homeland security entities performed their functions at the intersection of national security and public safety, and in many cases refined their focus (as with risk management and critical infrastructure, for example) but with a much reduced profile. DHS and FEMA fully implemented *Presidential Decision Directive 8: Preparedness*, using federal frameworks to dramatically improve the structure and integration of prevention, protection, response, recovery, and mitigation right down to the local level. The *Strategic National Risk Assessment* was established, recognizing the risk of terrorist attack but establishing an equivalence with hazards and natural disasters. Intelligence fusion centers were established under state and local control with federal assistance but minimum federal control. Guidance for business continuity and public–private partnerships improved with minimum federal oversight . . . and minimum federal funding.

In short, the 2015 NSS provides a clear guide to President Obama's attitude toward homeland security: important to his vision of a peaceful and prosperous world but (unlike the Bush 43 approach) not a top priority in response to a perceived existential threat to the nation's existence.

PRESIDENT DONALD TRUMP, NSS, AND HOMELAND SECURITY

As we come to the close of this long essay, it is worth repeating Patrick Porter's caution that "the National Security Strategy as a ritual of state is more a signaling than a strategic device" (Porter 2017). The NSS reflects presidential vision, perspectives, and priorities—a codified explanation before the American public, and the world, of the way the administration sees the global strategic context, the way it prioritizes concerns, and its approach to addressing them. From this perspective, the NSS released by President Trump in December 2017 is unique in at least three ways (Trump 2017).

First, no other NSS in American history, either formal or informal, received such a blistering rejection from the media and academic and foreign policy communities.[11] Proponents of other perspectives have often disagreed with presidential strategies in the past. Indeed, as previously mentioned, the legal requirement for a formal NSS document arose from Democratic objections to Republican Ronald Reagan's strategic priorities and expenditures. But mainstream critics have never before challenged a president's right to craft a strategic vision for the nation or his competence to advance that vision or condemned his NSS as "un-American." The reasons for this vociferous response from critics offer fodder for a great classroom seminar but are irrelevant to our purposes here. So I will note the objections and move on.

Second, Trump's NSS is grounded in neither traditional neoclassic realism nor romantic progressive liberalism but a sort of hybrid, which the Introduction calls "principled realism."

> It is realist because it acknowledges the central role of power in international politics, affirms that sovereign states are the best hope for a peaceful world, and clearly defines our national interests. It is principled because it is grounded in the knowledge that advancing American principles spreads peace and prosperity around the globe. We are guided by our values and disciplined by our interests. (Trump 2017, 55)

But although the document borrows traditional language from the two IR camps, the actual underlying theme is a term adopted from business that I don't ever remember seeing in a NSS: "competition." The world is described not as a power driven "warre of man against all men" or a romantic domain of global citizens steadily evolving toward democratic values. Instead, the world is described as "competitive" (Trump 2017, 2). The chief challengers to the United States (China, Russia, North Korea, Iran, jihadist terrorists, and transnational criminal organizations) are not

---

[11] For example, the *New York Times* White House correspondent Mark Lander wrote, "Mr. Trump has transformed the world's view of the United States from a reliable anchor of the liberal, rules-based international order into something more inward-looking and unpredictable" (Lander 2017).

called threats but competitors. And competitors can include friends and allies. In fact, "Competition does not always mean hostility, nor does it inevitably lead to conflict" (Trump 2017, 3). Competitors, the NSS argues, can cooperate, and their interests are best served when they do so as sovereign states. This leads to the interesting (and again, unique) conclusion that the primary role of the US government is to be a successful competitor for US vital interests laid out as:

- PILLAR I: Protect the American people, the homeland, and the American way of life;
- PILLAR II: Promote American prosperity;
- PILLAR III: Preserve peace through strength;
- PILLAR IV: Advance American influence. (Trump 2017, 3)

Third, and *most importantly for our purposes*, this NSS presents protection of the homeland as the departure point for national security (see Pillar I above). As this essay has previously explained, all presidential strategies since Clinton's in 2000 have addressed safety and security at home in some way, ranging from Clinton's first mention of critical infrastructure, to Bush 43's publication of a separate National Strategy for Homeland Security, to Obama's incorporation of homeland security as one of many elements supporting national security. But Trump's NSS is the only one to list protecting the homeland as a vital interest. In doing so, it moves well beyond Clinton's early focus on preparedness, terrorism, and critical infrastructure, forcefully reintegrates the Bush 43 vision that separated national security and public safety, and inverts Obama's concept that homeland security supports national security.

Thus, the Trump NSS presents an entirely new way of thinking about HS.

Furthermore, it narrows the focus of protecting the American People, Homeland, and Way of Life to a focus on:

- Securing US Borders and Territory (against WMD, Biothreats and Pandemics, and Immigration issues);
- Pursuing threats (from Jihadi Terrorists and Transnational Criminal Organizations);
- Promoting Cyber Security; and
- Reaching beyond preparedness to Promote Resilience.

This is not to suggest that the NSS calls for a reduction in the size or activities of DHS or any of the other agencies, federal, state, local or private, that conduct homeland security activities. It does not. Nor does it reduce the American commitment to a strong military with a global reach or aggressive diplomacy in pursuit of American interests and values. But the shift from traditional focus on the ways and means of employing the elements of statecraft according to the theories of the national security elite to advancing domestic safety, security, and prosperity (per PILLARS I and II) *as the central vital interest of the nation* is truly striking.

The implications for this new perspective at the intersection of national security and public safety remain to be fully developed.

CONCLUSION: SO WHAT'S THE POINT?

During the first year of the Trump presidency, the nation suffered five major events that might in the past have changed the course of homeland security: three massive hurricanes in Texas (Harvey), Florida (Irma), Puerto Rico (Maria); the largest mass shooting in American history (Las Vegas 2017); and the murder of twenty-six people in an attack on a church (Sutherland Springs, Texas). None resulted in demands for major adjustments to the organization or functioning of homeland security. As long as costs do not rise and effectiveness does not fall, both the public and the administration seem satisfied with the status quo. This by itself is a remarkable change from the experience of the previous four administrations which, over twenty-eight years, found themselves frequently whipsawed by changes in threats, organization, funding, and requirements. This moment of serendipity will not last.

Somewhere overseas an international challenge that will play out as a matter of public safety is gathering. At some point, a major domestic safety event with implications for the power and security of the nation will take place. When that happens, the fault lines between public safety and national security will again appear in bold relief. The differing perspectives between some public servants focused on the security of the nation and others focused on the safety of its citizens will emerge as a serious, perhaps life threatening, disconnect. A full understanding of competing strategic and policy perspectives, and an ability to apply new considerations, evaluate the results, and craft innovative solutions will be critical to our survival as individuals and as a nation.

In order to properly prepare for that moment, we need to train and educate the leaders, theorists, and practitioners who serve at the imperfect intersection of national security and public safety. We need to think hard about the nature of HS. And that is the subject of the next chapter.

REFERENCES

Bush, George H. W. (41). September 11, 1990. *Address before a Joint Session of the Congress on the Persian Gulf Crisis and the Federal Budget Deficit.* Washington, DC: The White House. Accessed December 18, 2018. https://en.wikisource.org/wiki/Address_Before_a_Joint_Session_of_the_Congress_on_the_Persian_Gulf_Crisis_and_the_Federal_Budget_Deficit.

———. 1991. *National Security of the United States.* Washington, DC: The White House.

Bush, George W. (43). 2002. *The National Security Strategy of the United States of America.* Washington, DC: The White House.

Cheney, Dick. 1993. *Defense Strategy for the 1990s: Regional Defense* Strategy. Washington, DC: Department of Defense. Accessed December 18, 2018. https://nsarchive2.gwu.edu/nukevault/ebb245/doc15.pdf.

Clinton, William J. 1994. *The National Security of the United States.* Washington, DC: The White House.

———. 2000. The *National Security of the United States.* Washington, DC: The White House.

Homeland Security Council. 2002. *The National Strategy for Homeland Security.* Washington, DC: The White House.

———. 2007. *The National Strategy for Homeland Security.* Washington, DC: The White House.

Lander, Mark. December 28, 2017. "Trump, the Insurgent, Breaks with 70 Years of American Foreign Policy." *The New York Times.* Accessed December 18, 2018. https://www.nytimes.com/2017/12/28/us/politics/trump-world-diplomacy.html.

Lieberman, Senator Joseph. December 13, 2017. "Safeguarding American Agriculture in a Globalized World." Hearing of the Senate Committee on Agriculture, Nutrition, and Forestry: Washington, DC: US Senate. Accessed December 18, 2018. https://www.agriculture.senate.gov/imo/media/doc/Testimony_Lieberman.pdf.

National Archives staff comment. 1991.*The National Security Strategy of the United States.* Washington, DC: The National Archives. Accessed December 18, 2018. http://nssarchive.us/national-security-strategy-1991/.

Obama, Barack. 2015. *National Security Strategy.* Washington, DC: The White House.

Office of Homeland Security. 2002. *The National Strategy for Homeland Security.* Washington, DC: The White House.

Office of the Press Secretary. February 6, 2015. "White House Fact Sheet: The 2015 National Security Strategy." Accessed December 18, 2018. https://obamawhitehouse.archives.gov/the-press-office/2015/02/06/fact-sheet-2015-national-security-strategy.

Porter, Patrick. December 22, 2017. "Tradition's Quiet Victories: Trump's National Security Strategy." *War on the Rocks.* Accessed December 18, 2018. https://warontherocks.com/2017/12/traditions-quiet-victories-trumps-national-security-strategy/.

Public Law 99–433. October 1, 1986. "Goldwater–Nichols Department of Defense Reorganization Act of 1986." Washington, DC: United States Congress. Accessed December 18, 2018. http://history.defense.gov/Portals/70/Documents/dod_reforms/Goldwater-NicholsDoDReordAct1986.pdf.

Reagan, Ronald. 1987. The *National Security of the United States.* Washington, DC: The White House.

Siracusa, Joseph, and Aiden Warren. 2016. *Presidential Doctrines.* New York: Rowman & Littlefield.

Trump, Donald J. 2017. *National Security Strategy.* Washington, DC: The White House.

"United States Presidential Doctrines." *Wikipedia.* Accessed December 18, 2018. https://en.wikipedia.org/wiki/United_States_presidential_doctrines.

11

So What Is Homeland Security, and Why Does It Exist?

★ ★ ★

BOTTOM LINE UP FRONT

The purpose of Volume 1 in this series is to conceptualize homeland security (HS) in the context of national security (NS). The first ten chapters lay out why national security experts think the way they do. Logic would suggest that homeland security specialists think in a similar way. This chapter begins the explanation of why this is not the case.

National Security is focused on threats to national interests and power overseas. Congress provides funding and some specific legal guidance for overseas activities. And federal courts have jurisdiction over some aspects of overseas activities. But beyond that, the administration has a pretty free hand in collecting and using national power while applying some combination of Realist and Liberal (Neoclassic and Romantic) strategies, policies, and so on.

Public safety is a different matter entirely. Here responsibility, authority, and power are divided across levels of government—federal, state, and local. And the rights of citizens and corporations (treated under some laws as citizens) must not be abridged.

Homeland security is the set of national-level issues that falls where national security and public safety intersect. It begins with an overseas threat but is manifested as a public safety problem. Mixing these two challenges causes both conceptual and practical problems.

As you will learn in a later chapter on Emergency Management, Public Safety has been a concern in the United States since the first Indian raids and the first local health epidemics in the early colonies. Local militia units

Figure 11.1 What Is Homeland Security?

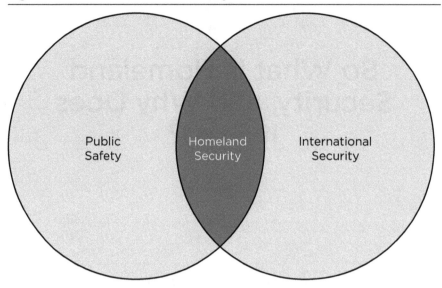

were formed at least as early as 1690 (Wright 1986). Ben Franklin organized the first public volunteer fire company in Philadelphia in 1738 (private companies were in operation earlier). Police forces were operating in major cities well before the American Civil War (Potter 2013).

While the potential scope and scale of disasters has grown with population and density, citizens have long been subject to major hazards and natural disasters. The Peshtigo Firestorm killed at least 1,555 in Wisconsin in 1871. The Johnstown Flood in Pennsylvania killed more than two thousand in 1889. And the Galveston Hurricane of 1900 killed perhaps as many as twelve thousand (Wikipedia, "Disaster List") Yet given the nation's vast size and its political heritage, its citizens regarded public safety as largely a local matter until recently.

True, federal domestic law enforcement has played a significant role in our history. The first Secretary of the Treasury, Alexander Hamilton, saw customs duties as the primary source of funding for the new US government and oversaw the establishment of the US Customs Service on July 31, 1789 (US Department of the Treasury 2010). The US Marshalls Service was established as the first federal law enforcement organization (LEO) in September of that same year—only two years after the Constitution was adopted (US Marshals Service 2018). Federal LEOs have grown in number as Federal laws have grown, and today number more than fifty (Federal Law Enforcement 2018).

But for the first 214 years after the signing of the Constitution, America improved its federal domestic security efforts mostly in response to specific domestic events. For example, federal law enforcement focused on sedition and sabotage during World War I, shifted to interstate criminal activity in the 1920s and 1930s, and then returned to domestic threats from international actors in World War II and the Cold War. The United States did not establish a single organization responsible for criminal challenges at home, the way the Department of Defense (DOD) is responsible for all military challenges overseas.

Public safety from accidents and disasters also remained primarily a state and local responsibility until the twentieth century, when the federal role gradually expanded in response to the increasing scale of natural disasters. Civil Defense was established as a national-level safety *and* security program in the 1950s but was de-emphasized as the possibility of surviving a nuclear war declined. This nationwide structure might have been adapted to address potential biological pandemics, but that threat was left to local health departments, and the framework for national coordination withered. By the time the Berlin Wall fell (1989), national security was the largest discretionary part of the federal budget. Expenditures for public safety and domestic security were small and fragmented by comparison.

In fact, homeland security in its current form—multiple federal agencies consolidated under one department, working to coordinate activities nationwide across the entire homeland security enterprise—was not even discussed until the mid-1990s. Then, in late 2002, with the creation of the Department of Homeland Security (DHS), HS suddenly appeared as a major, stand-alone function of the federal government. After more than two centuries, why the sudden change?

Homeland Security was NOT created simply in response to a large number of American deaths on September 11, 2001. Two hundred fifty people were killed, hundreds of thousands displaced, twenty-three thousand square miles of land submerged, and the national economy disrupted during the Mississippi Flood of 1927. Yet the nation did not respond by creating a major new government department employing hundreds of thousands of people to coordinate public safety at the national level.

And Homeland Security was NOT created solely because of a single spectacular terrorist event. The United States has experienced major domestic attacks before: when Puerto Rican Separatists opened fire inside the Capitol building; when Timothy McVey destroyed a major government building and killed 168 people in Oklahoma City; when assassins killed the President of the United States (on four occasions); and in other cases. Yet the nation did not respond by creating a major new government department to address terrorism.

So why did Congress and the President act, creating initial concepts in the 1990s, passing the initial Act of Congress in November 2002 and opening the Department of HS in 2003? **Answer: because of changes in warfare, the development of weapons of mass destruction, and their growing availability to small, nonstate actors. Homeland Security was a response to a new national security situation.**

In addition to hazards and natural disasters, states (the word is used in the international sense) may be faced with three types of violence:

- Crime. Cases of law breaking may be large (as with organized crime) or small (as with a single local assault). Certainly crimes matter. But as a rule, crime does not rise to a level that threatens the existence and continuity of the state.
- War. Such events come in many flavors, but what all traditional wars have in common is that they are (by definition) attempts by legitimate states to use violence to advance political interests, guided (somewhat) by rules agreed upon by the international community. Wars are more dangerous than traditional crime because they can threaten the existence of the state. Of course, not every action in war plays out according to the Geneva Conventions. But the concept of rules and boundaries in war is important because it influences how a state prepares for and wages war and helps clarify the danger to the state.
- Criminal War. Like war, this is an attempt to advance political interests through violence, but it is waged outside the traditional bounds of war BY DESIGN. This distinction is extremely important. We are not talking here about close calls, one-time events, or even a "tit-for-tat" response to an enemy's violation of the rules of war. Criminal war is a premeditated breaking of the rules to gain additional advantage. It poses a special danger because BY DEFINITION criminal war strikes a weak spot in the armor of the state—too threatening to the state for traditional law enforcement solutions yet not amenable to traditional military solutions. Terrorism is an example of criminal war.[1] It is uniquely dangerous

---

[1] In one of the bestselling books on the subject before 9/11, author Bard O'Neill (1990) explains that the real challenge we face is insurgency. He identifies seven types including anarchist, egalitarian, secessionist, etc. He explains that terrorism is just one means of war used by insurgent groups. The fundamental question he raises (which we do not seem to have addressed with any success) is not why they are using terrorism, but why they are waging war at all? This issue is explored in greater depth in Volume 2 of this series.

because it threatens the legitimacy of the state and its ability to defend its citizens, even as states operating under rule of law (domestic and international) are structurally unprepared to combat it. Terrorism targets not just the safety of citizens or the interests of the nation but what might be called the *civil security* of the state—its ability to govern.

In the first 225 years of its existence, the United States developed significant resources to address both domestic crime and international war. But it was neither organized nor prepared to wage a war for the survival of the nation against criminal elements employing criminal means. The Homeland Security Act of 2002 took significant steps to address this situation, including establishing a new DHS.

However, it was not just the terrorist nature of the 9/11 attack that drove the creation of DHS. It was also the fact that the growing availability of Weapons of Mass Destruction (WMD) meant the outcome of a criminal attack could be much worse than the collapse of buildings on 9/11.

The concept of WMD was not new. In fact, concerns were so wide spread that both military and civilian organizations (like FEMA and the Department of Justice) already used an acronym to discuss them: CBRNE.

- **Chemical:** A 1984 chemical incident in Bhopal, India, killed more than ten thousand people and sickened thousands more. An attack on a chemical plant in the United States might have a similar impact.
- **Biological:** Bio had long been a major military concern. Yet in the panicky review of major threats after 9/11, the United States discovered it was unprepared for large-scale attacks by even well-known naturally occurring diseases like smallpox and anthrax.
- **Radiological:** Incidents at Three Mile Island (1979) and Chernobyl (1986) demonstrated that even low levels of radiation could cause major disruptions by contaminating people, places, and things in ways that would last for decades. Thousands of readily available sources of radiation used in everyday life (from hospitals to construction sites) could cause local disruption.
- **Nuclear:** The destructive power of a small nuclear weapon was old news by the end of the Cold War. What emerged in the 1990s was the new effort to create such weapons by rogue states (like North Korea and Iran) coupled with the possibility that they might share or sell the weapons to terrorist groups who would deliver them in ways that made traditional defense obsolete.
- **Explosive:** The long-running terrorism campaign against Israel showed how vulnerable a modern state was to small-scale suicide bombers

and larger attacks. The Marine barracks in Lebanon (1983), the first attack on the World Trade Center (1993), and the attack on the Murrah Federal Building in Oklahoma City (1995), showed the growing power and sophistication of car and truck bombs.

Concerns about these dangers arose in the 1990s after the end of the Cold War, as small groups and regimes were freed of the controls previously applied by a bi-polar world, and thousands of highly skilled experts in CBRNE found themselves jobless and available to the highest bidder. Additionally, as the computer revolution began to take off, science raced forward developing techniques that allowed even small labs with a few people to develop powerful new weapons.

The marrying of these three developments—the rise of terrorism/criminal war, the growing power of WMD, and advances in technology that were making big weapons available to small groups—aggravated concerns over national security at home during the 1990s. And on a parallel track, because of the growing population density in vulnerable locations, it became clear that state, local, and federal efforts in preparation for and response to major hazards and natural disasters were inadequate. A better, more centrally directed effort was required.

In 1997, the National Defense Panel (1997) voiced these concerns by coining the term "homeland security" in their report "Transforming Defense."[2] Within three years, congressional commissions began issuing reports making the challenges of homeland security clear and offering suggestions concerning what to do. These included the Hart–Rudman Commission (1998–2001), the Gilmore Commission (1999–2003), and Bremer Commission (2000). Cyber concerns also began to emerge, causing experts in that field to create the concept of "critical infrastructure" (Marsh 1997). These concerns were highlighted in the short-lived hubbub over computer disruption called Y2K.

The Clinton Administration responded to this rising chorus of concerns with a series of Presidential Decision Directives (PDDs) including:

- PDD 39 US Policy on Counterterrorism (PDD-39);
- PDD 42 International Organized Crime (PDD-42);
- PDD 56 Managing Complex Contingency Operations (PDD-56); and
- PDD 63 Critical Infrastructure (PDD-63).

---

[2] Interestingly, the central concern was that terrorism would be coming to America, and unless a way was found to address the security of the homeland, then in time of crisis, DoD resources, required for national security overseas, would be diverted for domestic use.

At the same time (and partly as a result), fledgling efforts to lead and coordinate responses to new, more dangerous domestic events began to take shape in the Department of Justice, FEMA, the DOD, and elsewhere.

But most people, including most national security experts, missed the game-changing significance of these developments. So when the attacks on 9/11 shocked the nation, international security experts, public safety personnel, and the general public were surprised to discover that they lived in a new world where:

- State and nonstate groups were willing to use a new form of criminal war against which traditional techniques of crime fighting and war waging were less effective;
- Rogue nations and small groups now had access to big weapons;
- And the United States as a whole was unprepared to coordinate protection and response efforts against major events that crossed jurisdictions between federal, state, local, and private levels of ownership and operation.

Taken together, these developments during the Clinton Administration and the 9/11 attack in the early days of the Bush 43 Administration, resulted in a strong push to consolidate domestic security efforts—at least at the federal level—under a single organization. The result was the DHS created by the Homeland Security Act of 2002 and formally established in 2003.

DHS <u>does not</u> consolidate <u>all</u> domestic security responsibilities, assets, and authorities under a single roof. But it does act as a national focal point for such efforts. And given the threats it faces, it should clearly be regarded as an extension of our national security efforts.

Unfortunately, neither government security officials nor national security academics see it that way.

So the concept of contributing to the traditional security of the nation is missing from official definitions of homeland security. Moreover, just as the rationale for homeland security has changed over time, so has the definition. Early (post-9/11) definitions focused almost entirely on countering terrorism. More recently, this focus has changed to address a broader range of public safety concerns.

For example, in the 2007 *National Strategy for Homeland Security*, written by the Bush 43 Administration and published by the Office of the President, homeland security was defined as, *"A concerted national effort to prevent terrorist attacks within the United States, reduce America's vulnerability to terrorism, and minimize the damage and recover from attacks that do occur"* (Homeland Security Council 2007, 3).

In 2010, the Obama Administration issued a revised definition in the *2010 Quadrennial Homeland Security Review (QHSR)* defining homeland security as*: "A concerted national effort to ensure a homeland that is safe, secure, and resilient against terrorism and other hazards where American interests, aspirations, and ways of life can thrive"* (US Department of Homeland Security 2010, 13). (Note the shift from an exclusive focus on terrorism to include broader issues.) The 2010 definition was repeated in the 2014 QHSR, and, although other versions emerge in different government documents from time to time, it remains (as of 2018) the definition most frequently quoted from DHS (US Department of Homeland Security 2014).[3]

In the Trump Administration, DHS dropped a definition of HS from its website and instead presents a "Vision" of homeland security: "to ensure a homeland that is safe, secure, and resilient against terrorism and other hazards" (US Department of Homeland Security Vision 2018). The site goes on to list its "core concepts" as Security, Resilience, and Customs and Exchange—without further definition.[4]

Meanwhile the most current DOD definition of HS continues to focus on specific threats:

> A concerted national effort to prevent terrorist attacks within the United States; reduce America's vulnerability to terrorism, major disasters, and other emergencies; and minimize the damage and recover from attacks, major disasters, and other emergencies that occur. Also called HS." (DOD Dictionary 2018)

This leaves a question hanging in the air: *Do we need a new community-wide definition of homeland security that better integrates the elements of public safety, national security, and domestic national interests?*

REFERENCES

DOD Dictionary of Military and Associated Terms. November 2018. Washington, DC: DOD. Accessed December 18, 2018. http://www.jcs.mil/Portals/36/Documents/Doctrine/pubs/dictionary.pdf?ver=2017-12-23-160155-320.

---

[3] For a good summary of the various homeland security definitions in government use and their changes, see Shawn Reese, *Defining Homeland Security: Analysis and Congressional Considerations* (Washington, DC: Congressional Research Service, 2013), https://fas.org/sgp/crs/homesec/R42462.pdf (accessed November 30, 2017).

[4] However, the Trump Administration's *National Security Strategy of the United States* (December 2017) is the only NSS ever to include protection of the homeland as the departure point for national security (US Department of Homeland Security 2018, 3)

Federal Law Enforcement. "The Scope and Mission of Federal Law Enforcement." Accessed December 18, 2018. https://www.federallawenforcement.org/what-is-federal-law-enforcement/.

Gilmore Commission. 1999–2003. *U.S. Congressional Advisory Panel to Assess Domestic Response Capabilities for Terrorism Involving Weapons of Mass Destruction.* 5 reports. Accessed December 18, 2018. https://www.rand.org/nsrd/terrpanel.html.

Hart-Rudman Commission. 1998–2001. The U.S. Commission on National Security/21st Century. The U.S. Commission on National Security. Accessed December 18, 2018. http://www.au.af.mil/au/awc/awcgate/nssg.

Homeland Security Council. 2007. *The National Homeland Security Strategy.* Washington, DC: Office of the President. Accessed December 18, 2018. https://www.dhs.gov/xlibrary/assets/nat_strat_homelandsecurity_2007.pdf.

Marsh, Robert, et al. October 1997. *Critical Foundations: Protecting America's Infrastructures, The Report of the President's Commission on Critical Infrastructure Protection.* Washington, DC. Accessed December 18, 2018. https://www.nist.gov/sites/default/files/documents/2017/04/26/keyes_part2_032613.pdf.

National Defense Panel (NDP). 1997. *Transforming Defense.* Washington, DC: Department of Defense. Accessed December 18, 2018. https://www.hsdl.org/?view&did=1834.

O'Neill, Bard. 1990. "The Nature of Insurgency." In *Insurgency & Terrorism.* New York: Brassey's, Inc.

Potter, Gary. June 25, 2013. "The History of Policing in the United States, Part 1." Accessed December 18, 2017. http://plsonline.eku.edu/insidelook/history-policing-united-states-part-1.

Reese, Shawn. 2013. *Defining Homeland Security: Analysis and Congressional Considerations.* Washington, DC: Congressional Research Service. Accessed December 18, 2018. https://fas.org/sgp/crs/homesec/R42462.pdf.

US Congress. Senate. Select Committee on Intelligence. (Bremer Commission). 2000. Report of the National Commission on Terrorism. 106th Cong., 2d sess., Sr. Hrg. 106–864. Accessed December 18, 2018. https://fas.org/irp/threat/commission.html.

US Customs and Border Protection. October 5, 2010. "First Officers of the U.S. Customs Service." Accessed December 18, 2018. https://www.cbp.gov/document/history/first-officers-us-customs-service-0.

US Department of Homeland Security. "Our Vision." Accessed December 18, 2018. https://www.dhs.gov/our-mission.

US Department of Homeland Security. 2010. *Quadrennial Homeland Security Review* (QHSR 2010). Washington, DC: Department of Homeland Security, 13. Accessed December 18, 2018. https://www.dhs.gov/xlibrary/assets/qhsr_report.pdf.

US Department of Homeland Security. 2014. *Quadrennial Homeland Security* Review (QHSR 2014). Washington, DC: Department of Homeland Security. Accessed December 18, 2018. https://www.dhs.gov/sites/default/files/publications/2014-qhsr-final-508.pdf.

US Department of the Treasury. December 1, 2010. "History of the Treasury." Accessed December 18, 2018. https://home.treasury.gov/about/history.

US Marshals Service. "Historical Timeline." Accessed December 18, 2018. https://www.usmarshals.gov/.

The White House. June 21, 1995. *PDD-39, U.S. Policy on Counterterrorism.* Washington, DC: The White House. Accessed December 18, 2018. https://fas.org/irp/offdocs/pdd39.htm.

The White House. October 21, 1995. *PDD-42 International Organized Crime.* Washington, DC: The White House. Accessed December 18, 2018. https://fas.org/irp/offdocs/pdd/pdd-42.pdf.

The White House. May 1997. *PDD 56 Managing Complex Contingency Operations.* The White House. Accessed December 18, 2018. https://fas.org/irp/offdocs/pdd56.htm.

The White House. May 22, 1998. *PDD 63 Critical Infrastructure.* Washington, DC: The White House. Accessed December 18, 2018. https://fas.org/irp/offdocs/pdd/pdd-63.htm.

Wikipedia. n.d. "List of Natural Disasters in the United States." Accessed December 18, 2018. https://en.wikipedia.org/wiki/List_of_natural_disasters_in_the_United_States.

Wright, Robert K. Jr. July 19, 1986. "Massachusetts Militia Roots: A Bibliographic Study." Washington, DC: Departments of the Army and the Air Force Historical Services Branch Office of Public Affairs, National Guard Bureau. Accessed December 18, 2018. http://www.history.army.mil/reference/mamil/MAMIL.HTM.

12

Building a Systemic Solution for a New Domestic Defense

BOTTOM LINE UP FRONT

The good news is that despite the unique nature of homeland security and the initial shock of the attack on 9/11, the United States has done a solid job of creating a systematic solution to the new domestic challenges to national security—the condition many now call the New Normal.

The range of potential threats is intimidating. The vulnerabilities of our elements of power to those threats are numerous. The consequences of those threats could be so expensive in blood and treasure as to undermine the legitimacy of the national government. And the political pressure to focus on high probability–low consequence problems rather than more dangerous low probability–high consequence events is significant.

Despite these challenges, government and private organizations have adapted old solutions and adopted new ones in some quite effective ways. Existing organizations like the FBI and the Department of Defense (DOD) have made important changes in the ways they are organized and the ways they do business in order to address homeland security. The Department of Homeland Security (DHS) has expanded the focus of some subordinate agencies, like FEMA, and created others entirely new, like Transportation Security Administration (TSA). These changes extend down to the state level as evidenced by the fact that operation centers have much improved the ways they deal with natural disasters, while new fusion centers share important information and intelligence at state and even local level.

Most (not all) of these efforts have benefited from new thinking that includes a new approach to risk management, a new structure for preparedness nationally, and new emphasis on capabilities required to meet these needs. In particular, responses to cyber security are moving so quickly that this page would need to be printed with erasable ink to keep up.

A robust family of concepts and documents has been developed to promote protection of critical infrastructure, and preparedness for organizations and individuals alike. While the guidelines initially seemed to grow organically—which is to say from the bottom up in accordance with organizational need—today they represent a "cascade" of authoritative sources linking guidance from the national level right down to the local emergency manager. At the same time, Business Continuity Management is gaining legitimacy and utility through a series of excellent and widely available frameworks.

Essentially, new thinking has created a new system depending mostly on cooperation rather than direction to address the new challenges of HS.

GOOD NEWS ABOUT IMPROVING OUR SYSTEM

Before the terrorist attacks of September 11, 2001, many people in the nascent field of homeland security thought some sort of terrorist event was bound to happen eventually, but few experts in either national security or public safety thought an attack was eminent.[1] This despite the fact that, as the 9/11 Commission concluded, "The system was blinking red" (Kean et al. 2004, x). Yet almost no one in the vast federal, state, or local bureaucracies was prepared for a major domestic attack by international enemies on that clear September morn in 2001.

Immediately after the attack, and especially following the anthrax attacks of October–December 2001, almost everyone expected a flurry of major terrorist attacks. Homeland security measures were put into place in what was, for the federal government, lightning speed. And then . . . nothing happened. At least, nothing seemed to happen.

In truth, there have been a number of terror attempts and many more "intents." Media reports record ninety-seven terrorist plots in the United States in the first sixteen years after 9/11 (Inserra, 2017). Several of these events resulted in significant casualties, including: 14 dead/30 wounded at Ft Hood, 2009; 3 killed/264 injured in the Boston Marathon Bombing, 2013; 16 dead/22 injured in San Bernardino, 2015; and 49 murdered/53 injured in the Pulse nightclub in Orlando, 2016. And of course, one American death from terrorism is too many.

---

[1] For the fascinating story of one lone individual who saw disaster coming and whose insistence on preparedness saved countless lives in the World Trade Center, see John O'Neill, "The Man Who Knew," *PBS Frontline*, https://www.youtube.com/watch?v=Tj6WbPG2GjU.

But it might have been much worse. None of the post-9/11 events comes close to the 168 deaths and 680 injuries in the Murrah office building bombing (Oklahoma City) in 1995, or the 2,977 victims killed on 9/11. There have been NO additional Weapons of Mass Destruction (WMD) attacks since five died and seventeen became sick in the 2001 anthrax attacks. And we have seen NO successful attacks on the government or national interests in the domestic arena.

It would appear that jurisdictions and authorities in the United States did a pretty good job of creating a system that minimized high probability–low consequences attacks and flat out prevented most low probability–high consequence events. The defense is not perfect. Our record is not clean. It is not a model of foresight, cooperation, or planning. No doubt aggressive action overseas has much to do with our success. And sometimes we were just lucky—as with an airline attacker who could not light his shoe bomb, another who set fire only to his own underwear, and a third who left a car bomb in Times Square, after locking the keys to his getaway vehicle inside. Lord, may all our enemies be like these.

But the point is that the homeland security program we cobbled together specifically because of a new type of international terrorist using a new type of weapon (WMD) against a new category of targets has largely worked.[2] Many attackers did try to hurt us and largely failed.

Yes, we could miss a clue and suffer a massive disaster with grievous losses before you can finish this sentence. But so far, so good. And the system that produced our success developed both "organically" (from the bottom up) and "systemically" (from the top down), with good people working hard to do their jobs and steadily improving guidance issuing from

---

[2] Terrorism is defined in PUBLIC LAW 107–296 107th Congress—November 25, 2002, 116 Stat. 2135, 6 USC 101 (15.) as: any activity that—
   (A) involves an act that—
       (i) is dangerous to human life or potentially destructive of critical infrastructure or key resources; and
       (ii) is a violation of the criminal laws of the United States or of any State or other subdivision of the United States; and
   (B) appears to be intended—
       (i) to intimidate or coerce a civilian population;
       (ii) to influence the policy of a government by intimidation or coercion; or
       (iii) to affect the conduct of a government by mass destruction, assassination, or kidnapping.
Most mass casualty attacks since 9/11 (VA Tech, 2007 [thirty-three dead]; Aurora, CO, 2012 [twelve dead]; Sandy Hook, 2012 [twenty-six dead]; Las Vegas, 2017 [fifty dead]; Sutherland Church, 2017 [twenty-six dead]; Stoneman Douglas High School, 2018 [seventeen dead]; etc.) do not meet this definition—most were public safety law enforcement issues.

DC. Working in fits and starts, and sometimes at cross purpose, various agents of public service and private industry adapted old solutions, modified existing programs, and created new ones in some quite effective ways.

Adaptation: FBI

An example of a longstanding organization that adapted to the new threat is the Federal Bureau of Investigation (FBI). Given its responsibilities, the FBI is actually spread quite thin. Today comprising thirty-five thousand agents (approximately the uniformed population of the NYPD), it was significantly smaller on 9/11.[3,4] While counterterrorism was one of its missions, that was not a top priority. The FBI's focus was on the arrest and conviction of criminals, not the prevention of their crimes (even if the crime was terrorism). In fact, the FBI and its parent, the Department of Justice, erected a famous "wall of separation" between those agents who developed intelligence and those who captured law breakers. Intel could not cross this wall if its source might ultimately threaten a prosecution. FBI resources devoted to "intelligence" were relatively meager. Joint Terrorism Task Forces (designed to share information with local law enforcement organization) were linked with local public safety officers, but with a minimal intelligence structure, there was relatively little intel to pass—especially on the topic of international threats to domestic national security targets. And while FBI policies were firmly controlled by the director and his staff in Washington, DC, the bureaucratic cultural of the organization strongly supported operational leadership by the Special Agents in Charge of the individual field offices. Headquarters told them what to do but not how to do it, and hence investigative priorities were to some extent determined locally.

It is important to understand that while the FBI may assist state and local officials, their focus is the enforcement of federal law. For example, the FBI might routinely be involved in a bank robbery since federal banking laws are violated. But the robbery of a convenience store next door would be addressed only by local police. This focus is restricted by Congress, the President, the DOJ, FBI leadership in DC, and the Special Agents in Charge of fifty-six field offices across the United States. Additionally, the focus is further narrowed by the fact that other federal officials take priority in enforcing some specific federal laws (DEA, ATFE, Sky Marshals)

---

3 "How Many People Work for the FBI?" https://www.fbi.gov/about/faqs/how-many-people-work-for-the-fbi (accessed December 18, 2018).

4 New York City Police Department, LinkedIn, https://www.linkedin.com/company/new-york-city-police-department. (accessed December 18, 2018).

and regulations (EPA, Department of the Interior, etc.). Within their purview, the FBI focuses on nine areas of criminal activity, divided into two categories.

These categories are then further subdivided into individual activities. So, for example, organized crime may include gangs, mafia, transnational trafficking of children, and so on. Of course, the prevalence of specific crimes may vary by geographic area and demographics—mafia activities might be greater in New York and Chicago; Transnational Criminal Organizations might pose a large problem in Houston. So local officials have always had some flexibility in the allocation of local priorities and resources. And specialized assistance (like fingerprint forensics or Hostage Rescue Teams) may be allocated from centralized resources in Washington, or Quantico, Virginia. Traditionally, the FBI operationalized their focus by investigation and prosecution. They responded to crimes and brought perpetrators to justice. Anticipating and preventing crimes was the subject of some efforts, as when the Civil Rights Division used informants and undercover agents inside groups suspected of planning and participating in hate crimes. But as previously mentioned, prior to 9/11, intelligence operations were generally separated from investigation and prosecution so criminal cases were not inadvertently contaminated by the vagaries of intel collection.

Textbox 12.1	Areas of FBI Law Enforcement Focus	
National Security	**Federal Criminal Activity**	
• Terrorism	• Violent Crime	
• Counter Intelligence	• White Collar Crime	
• Cyber	• Organized Crime	
• WMD[5]	• Civil Rights	
	• Public Corruption	

Although Robert Mueller served for many years in various jobs in the Department of Justice, he had been director of the FBI for only a week before international terrorists attacked US national security on domestic soil on 9/11. Sensing both a new national imperative and a new security

---

[5] Note that on the FBI's "Mission & Priorities" web site (https://www.fbi.gov/about/mission), all nine of these areas are listed under "What We Investigate." However, WMD is not listed as a priority. I interpret this to mean that the FBI remains in transition between the days of PPD-63, when the FBI had primary authority over WMD issues, and today, where others (to include the new the Department of Homeland Security [DHS] Countering WMD Office) share responsibility and jurisdiction.

mission, he rapidly adapted the mission priorities issued from FBI headquarters to place counterterrorism—and specifically the *prevention* of
terrorist attacks—as the top priority of every FBI office in the nation.
"The Wall" came tumbling down, and in coordination with FBI officials,
Congress modified provisions of existing and new laws (like the Patriot
Act) to broaden and clarify FBI powers on issues ranging from wiretap-
ping to querying internet service providers. FBI presence overseas was
increased dramatically, and teams actually deployed to combat zones to
teach and learn from military operations against terrorists. At home, a
Field Intelligence Group (now just Intel Office) was created for each FBI
field office to provide greater collection and prosecution power to local
agents and additional support to state and local officials.

This last action involved hiring, training, organizing, and employing
thousands of new personnel and using them in ways that required cultural changes to how field agents saw their FBI and themselves. And other
traditional organizations within the FBI adapted as well, like the well-
established InfraGard Public–Private Partnership, which quickly included
counterterrorism information in its nationwide effort to engage American
business in the fight against crime.

The transformation of the FBI from a crime-fighting organization to a
counterterrorism organization is not complete, nor should it be. The traditional criminal threats the FBI was created to address have not disappeared.
If anything, they have grown more challenging with the revolutions in
science, computers, and global transportation. But the innovations and
adaptations the FBI implemented helped to address the new international
threats in the domestic space and did much to create a new system for
domestic defense.[6]

Evolution: Department of Defense

As pointed out in the Author's Note at the beginning of this volume, the
name and concept of homeland security originated in a DOD document as
an effort to build a firewall between a postattack demand for resources and
the need to maintain those resources for overseas operations.[7] Thus, it is no
surprise that the department was quick to modify policy and organization

---

[6] It is worth noting that despite all this progress, tensions between intel collection and criminal prosecution remain an issue. Sometimes aggressive collection or early intervention
may prevent an attack but leave prosecutors without the charges required to keep a future
perpetrator off the street. The solution may be found in the drafting of creative new laws.
Domestic counterterrorism efforts have yet to see any new legal tools like the famous
RICO Act that has proven so effective against racketeering and organized crime.
[7] National Defense Panel, *Transforming Defense* (Washington, DC: Department of Defense,
1997), https://www.hsdl.org/?view&did=1834 (accessed December 18, 2018).

into a system allowing domestic agencies to request DOD support for emergencies, while controlling the use of those resources and minimizing the drain on national security assets.

Step one in the modification of DOD's approach to domestic involvement was a revision of language. The first *Quadrennial Defense Review Report* of the Bush 43 Administration was prepared for release on September 14, 2001. Given the events of 9/11, it was recalled, revised, and released on September 30. Adjustments were slight but important. The highest priority of the US military was specified as:

> the protection of the U.S. domestic population, its territory, and its critical defense related infrastructure against attacks emanating from outside U.S. borders . . . In addition, DoD components have the responsibility, as specified in U.S. law, to support U.S. civil authorities as directed in managing the consequences of natural and man-made disasters and CBRNE-related events on U.S. territory. Finally, the U.S. military will be prepared to respond in a decisive manner to acts of international terrorism committed on U.S. territory or the territory of an ally. (Rumsfeld 2001, 18–19)

To achieve these new roles, DOD would "institutionalize definitions of homeland security, *homeland defense* [emphasis added] and civil support, and address command relationships and responsibilities within the Defense Department" (Rumsfeld 2001, 92).

Thus an important early evolutionary step was the DOD establishment of "homeland defense" (a term they made up—not part of any previous studies or discussions) to define their mission and thereby focus (i.e., limit) their role in domestic operations. Today, DOD defines homeland defense as "the protection of United States sovereignty, territory, domestic population, and critical infrastructure against external threats and aggression or other threats as directed by the President. Also called HD" (DOD Dictionary 2018, 106).

Note the difference between this term and the broader definition of homeland security as: "A concerted national effort to prevent terrorist attacks within the United States; reduce America's vulnerability to terrorism, major disasters, and other emergencies; and minimize the damage and recover from attacks, major disasters, and other emergencies that occur. Also called HS" (DOD Dictionary 2018, 106).

Implementing the DOD organizational and mission changes began with the establishment of the US Northern Command (NORTHCOM) in October 2002, six months before the founding of the DHS. In a brilliant stroke of fiscal economy and political positioning, DOD located

NORTHCOM on Peterson Air Force Base in Colorado Springs, CO, next door to the North American Air Defense Command. In fact the same four-star commander was assigned to lead both—one general with two staffs.

NORAD is actually a "combined command," which is to say it provides air defense to both the United States and Canada. The subordinate units are made up of both US and Canadian personnel (and equipment) who report to their respective national organizations except for security planning and actual operations. Personnel from both nations make up the staff. And the second in command is a Canadian general.

In a clever reflection of NORAD's organization and operation, NORTHCOM is a "joint command" that plans for and supervises deployment of forces for all military services when used in a domestic setting. Depending on the situation, many of these forces may be National Guard or Reserve. Even when they remain under the control of their state governor, they coordinate with NORTHCOM, where the second in command is a Reserve (usually National Guard) general. The political and doctrinal message of this systemic design is clear. Just as NORAD provides a single point of command for all military air assets deployed for domestic national security, NORTHCOM provides a single point of command for all military assets deployed for domestic support of home-land security.

In theory of course, every soldier, truck, radio, and bandage owned by DOD could be diverted to homeland security. And those resources are con-siderable, including at a minimum:

Textbox 12.2	Areas of DOD Defense Support of Civil Authority
• Aviation	• Logistics
• CBRN	• Maintenance
• Command and Control	• Medical Support
• Communications	• Security
• Engineering	• Transportation

But the system, for what is now called Domestic Support of Civil Authorities (DSCA), ensures those resources are tapped sparingly and as a last resort. A detachment of military personnel built around a Defense Coordinating Officer (DCO) is collocated with each FEMA regional headquarters. In an emergency, they deploy with FEMA personnel; any request for military resources under the President's command must be funneled through them to the NORTHCOM staff. The staff requests those resources from a designated service headquarters (for example, Army resources are requested through US Army North in San Antonio). And simultaneously they request permission to use those resources through the Joint Staff and the Office of the Secretary of Defense.

As the commitment of resources grows, the deployment of headquarters elements to control them grows as well. But at each step, military staffs verify that the resources requested are not available through any civilian sources before DOD resources are dispatched. Those resources will in fact be the last deployed, and the first released, so that that the heaviest support burden falls on suitable and available civilian resources.

For example, if a city hard hit by a hurricane requests from FEMA "twenty trucks to move evacuees," the military detachment serving with FEMA will investigate whether the mission could be met by contracted civilian busses or some other means of transportation. Only as a last resort will the DCO validate the request and send it up the chain-of-command to be approved and provided from active duty or reserve resources when they are available. And at the first opportunity, those military assets will be withdrawn from service and returned to their primary mission.[8]

Of course, DOD was providing military forces in response to domestic crises (storms, fires, riots, etc.) long before NORTHCOM was established. Those forces were generally provided directly from units with other standing missions. They responded for one-time crises, received limited specialized training, and returned to their other duties when the crisis was over.[9]

But over time the resources dedicated specifically to homeland defense (and NORTHCOM's control) have evolved considerably. For example, a wide array of Active Duty, Guard, and Reserve troops, with specialized training and equipment, are now available for domestic deployment. Staffs

---

[8] This entire process will be described in greater detail in a subsequent volume.
[9] The first major deployment of US troops for support of civil authorities *besides civil disturbances and riot control* was to fight forest fires three decades ago. The troops and equipment were diverted directly from line units designated for short notice deployment in time of war, missing important cyclical training that left them less than fully prepared for their wartime duties for more than a year. Concern over such diversions convinced the authors of the previously mentioned National Defense Panel to recommend in 1997 that DOD consider how to plan for (and control) taskings for what would soon come to be called "homeland security."

have completed detailed plans to respond to every type of threat identified in the National Strategic Risk Assessment.[10]

And DOD itself has evolved with the establishment of an office housing the Assistant Secretary of Defense for Homeland Defense and Global Security, complete with a broad range of established policies and mechanisms for revising or establishing new policy on short notice to meet novel situations.[11]

The evolution of DOD's contribution to homeland security (or homeland defense if you prefer) has not been error or cost free. But it does reflect a steady, thoughtful, and systematic improvement in capability and doctrine. On 9/11 fighter jets launched to intercept the attacking aircraft flew in the wrong direction, based on outdated plans and perspectives. Thanks to years of hard work, our domestic defenses are not likely to make such a mistake again.

Creation: Department of Homeland Security

If the FBI demonstrates the *adaptation* of agencies with homeland security responsibilities, and DOD shows the *evolution* of such agencies, the DHS shows the systemic improvements possible when new organizations are *created* from scratch. Or almost. Because, of course, DHS was *not* created from scratch but rather cobbled together from more than twenty preexisting agencies with some sort of federal homeland security responsibility.

Actually the initial intent of the Bush 43 Administration was to leverage exiting capabilities for new effect with a minimum new "footprint." The overseas response to "terrorism with a global reach" was an "offensive defensive," featuring intervention, preemption, and regime change. But at home, the core philosophy featured a federal (not "national") solution, small budget, small government, and no civilian mobilization. The primary tool envisioned was NOT a large, new permanent bureaucracy but

---

[10] Joint Task Force–Civil Support (JTF–CS) was established in 1999 specifically to provide additional capabilities to prevent and respond to terrorist attacks as specified in Nunn-Lugar-Domenici legislation of 1998. According to JTF–CS FAQ, the organization was established "to develop the expertise and maintain the focus on the mission of providing command and control to domestic CBRN response missions." http://www.jtfcs.northcom.mil/About/FAQs/ (accessed December 18, 2018). Today it reports to NORTHCOM as command and control of military forces that would assist in managing the consequences of a domestic chemical, biological, radiological, nuclear, or high-yield explosive (CBRNE) event.

[11] This office itself continues to evolve. Originally focused largely on the Defense Security Cooperation Agency (DSCA), then expanded to include coordinating defense interaction with Canada, Mexico, and the Bahamas, it now oversees an array of issues that impact the domestic defense of the nation. Examples include Unmanned Aircraft Systems, DoD Support of the US Secret Service, National Preparedness, and Climate Change. These duties are most recently outlined in DOD DIRECTIVE 5111.13 dated March 23, 2018. https://fas.org/irp/doddir/dod/d5111_13.pdf (accessed December 18, 2018).

an Office of Homeland Security reporting directly to the president. It was to be supported by an associated Homeland Security Council, similar to the National Security Council, but limited to one hundred people, with most of them borrowed from industry and other government agencies. As directed by Executive Order 13228, the Homeland Security Advisor (former Pennsylvania Governor Tom Ridge was selected to be the first) would consolidate and pass guidance from the president to the Cabinet and call on the president as the enforcer for any laggards.

In the midst of the anthrax attacks, constant terrorism warnings, and the run up to wars in Iraq and Afghanistan, that approach simply did not work. For one thing, as the creation of an executive order and not legislation, the organizations had no budget line for permanent funding. Meanwhile, in Congress, Senator Lieberman and Congressman Gephardt led a vocal campaign to create a new cabinet department. In the winter of 2002, the president set a small team to work designing both a National Strategy for Homeland Security and a department to implement it. In the spring of 2002, both were announced, followed by a spirited debate over personnel (and in particular labor union) policy for the new department. After the November election, the lame-duck Congress approved bipartisan legislation, and in March 2003, DHS was born.

The department's history since then has been, to borrow a term from economics, one of "creative destruction."

Some organizations, like FEMA, have seen their role contract and then expand considerably. Initially buried several layers deep in the now defunct Office of Emergency Preparedness and Response, the agency now enjoys standalone status and reports directly to the Secretary. It has primary responsibility for DHS operations under PPD-8, which established the National Preparedness Goal and System and plays a major role in incorporating Risk Management into HS operations nationwide, both inside and outside the federal government.[12] As changing demographics have driven increases in the magnitude of disasters, FEMA's role has steadily expanded, both "left of boom" (in Mitigation, Prevention, and Protection before events) and "right of boom" (in Response and Recovery after disastrous events). This is reflected in the creation of documents and policies that impact the whole of the HLS community, like the series of national frameworks that make national preparedness possible. And FEMA's online education program, available for free through the Emergency Management Institute, together with the Center for Homeland Security and Defense at

---

[12] FEMA has primary proponency for CPG-201, the THIRA (Threat and Hazard Risk Identification and Assessment Guide), by which every community in the nation should be conducting Integrated Risk Management.

the Naval Postgraduate School, have become leading sources of curriculum for HLS training and education programs nationwide.

Other DHS organizations, like the TSA and the Cybersecurity and Infrastructure Security Agency (CISA, formerly the National Protection and Programs Directorate, or NPPD), have been created entirely new.

With nearly sixty thousand employees (about one-third of the DHS total), TSA replaced a patchwork of private contractors operating independently under the supervision of each airport.[13] Created by law three months after 9/11, TSA initially reported to the Department of Transportation and was transferred to DHS after its activation in March 2003. While best known for providing checks of passengers and luggage at airports, TSA also inspects cargo and security systems, operates canine detection teams (bomb-sniffing dogs), trains pilots in law enforcement duties as Federal Flight Deck Officers, oversees the Federal Air Marshall Program, and conducts Visible Intermodal Prevention and Response (VIPR) operations for nonaviation transportation platforms (busses, rail, etc.).

Many TSA policies and operations have generated controversy since their creation. Some pat-down procedures have actually resulted in sexual assault investigations. One entire class of body scanners was replaced after images were deemed too intrusive. And unhappy passengers regularly blame TSA for their inclusion on the "No-Fly List," even though that list and the longer Terrorist Watch List are actually products of the interagency Terrorist Screening Center, housed in the National Security Branch of the FBI.

More importantly, however, the 9/11 attackers began their fateful trips with connecting flights from small airports, hoping to defeat the various security checks presented by private contractors trained to a variety of standards. It worked. A similar effort would be less likely to work against the system of defenses in place today. In the modern world of low probability–high consequence risk management, that constitutes a success.

The CISA (until October 2018, the NPPD) presents a similar story of creation, change, and frustrating but steady system development. Born from PDD-63 and the President's Commission on critical infrastructure, both established in 1998, the term "critical infrastructure" initially referred to energy, banking and finance, transportation, vital human services, and telecommunications, with a special emphasis on cyber platforms

---

[13] Airports are still allowed to use contractors if they are approved by the TSA. A handful of the 450 airports in the United States make use of this legal provision.

and linkages.[14],[15] At the direction of PDD-63, the FBI formed the National Infrastructure Protection Center. Shortly thereafter, the Y2K problem increased federal focus on cyber issues, with efforts coordinated primarily out of FEMA and the Department of Justice. As a result, the FBI really had the national lead on cyber issues before 9/11 and ceded control only grudgingly to DHS after 2003. The FBI InfraGard program remains a legacy of the FBI interest in critical infrastructure, and a valuable public–private program for the distribution of security info to business, as well as the collection of leads for law enforcement.

The redirection of lead responsibility for CI (again previously called CIKR for Critical Infrastructure and Key Resources) to DHS shifted emphasis from law enforcement to "identification and prioritization of critical infrastructure" in order to "to protect them from terrorist attacks."[16] Under the Bush 43–era HSPD-7, seven areas of critical infrastructure were identified, and "Sector Specific Agencies" from the federal government were charged with assisting private industry in those sectors. The number of CI sectors grew over time, even as responsibility shifted within DHS from a Directorate of Information Analysis and Infrastructure Protection in 2003, to Preparedness in 2007, to National Protection and Programs in 2008, to CISA where it remains today. Meanwhile the list of critical infrastructure sectors grew to sixteen, the primary tool for federal guidance became the *National Infrastructure Protection Plan (NIPP)*, and the focus shifted (under PPD-21) to "resilience," defined as:

> the ability to prepare for and adapt to changing conditions and withstand and recover rapidly from disruptions. Resilience includes the ability to withstand and recover from deliberate attacks, accidents, or naturally occurring threats or incidents.[17]

---

[14] The White House, PDD-63 Critical Infrastructure (Washington, DC: The White House, May 22, 1998), https://fas.org/irp/offdocs/pdd/pdd-63.htm (accessed December 18, 2018).

[15] Robert Marsh, *Critical Foundations: Protecting America's Infrastructures* (Washington DC: President's Commission on Critical Infrastructure Protection, October 1997), https://fas.org/sgp/library/pccip.pdf (accessed December 18, 2018).

[16] Homeland Security Presidential Directive 7: *Critical Infrastructure Identification, Prioritization, and Protection* (Washington, DC: The White House, December 17, 2003), https://www.dhs.gov/homeland-security-presidential-directive-7 (accessed December 18, 2018).

[17] PPD-21, *Critical Infrastructure Security and Resilience* (Washington, DC: The White House, February 12, 2013), https://obamawhitehouse.archives.gov/the-press-office/2013/02/12/presidential-policy-directive-critical-infrastructure-security-and-resil (accessed December 18, 2018). The document states specifically, "It is the policy of the United States to strengthen the security and resilience of its critical infrastructure against both physical and cyber threats."

Fully aligned with PPD-21, the Obama era NIPP (2013) and its supplemental documents represent a continuing reinvention of the federal approach with increased emphasis on: integration of cyber and physical security efforts; closer alignment to national preparedness efforts [read "FEMA"]; and increased focus on partnerships with private and nonprofit sectors.[18] Especially noteworthy is the citation of the *Comprehensive Preparedness Guide 201: Threat and Hazard Identification and Risk Assessment Guide* (promulgated primarily by FEMA and now in its third edition) as the NIPP approved approach to Risk Management for critical infrastructure.[19] This is an important step as these two organizations (FEMA and NPPD/now CSIA) have not always taken a common view of Risk Management.

If these organizational changes seem dizzying, well hang on. DHS in particular is far from done with creation, adaptation, and evolution. "Continuing reinvention" is clearly a central theme for DHS. For example, under recent changes three organizations that reported directly to the Secretary in 2008 (Health Affairs, National Cyber Security Center, and Counter Narcotics Enforcement) are missing entirely from the current DHS organizational chart.[20]

But that said, as with the FBI and DOD, DHS efforts have produced a systematic approach to homeland security, which was missing on 9/11.[21]

BEYOND ADAPTING, EVOLVING, AND CREATING: A HYBRID APPROACH TO SYSTEMIC IMPROVEMENT

Adaptation, evolution, and creation are good approaches to developing improved solutions within single categories of actors. But the

---

[18] NIPP 2013 Partnering for Critical Infrastructure Security and Resilience (Washington, DC: Department of Homeland Security, 2013), pp. 16–17, https://www.dhs.gov/sites/default/files/publications/national-infrastructure-protection-plan-2013–508.pdf (accessed December 18, 2018).

[19] *Comprehensive Preparedness Guide 201: Threat and Hazard Identification and Risk Assessment Guide 3d Ed* (Washington, DC: Department of Homeland Security, May 2018), https://www.fema.gov/media-library-data/1527613746699-fa31d9ade55988da1293192f1b18f4e3/CPG201Final20180525_508c.pdf.

[20] Health Affairs was incorporated into the Countering WMD Office, the National Cyber Security Center was incorporated into the NPPD (now the CISA), and Counter Narcotics Enforcement is apparently now spread across US Customs and Border Protection, the US Coast Guard, and US Immigration and Customs Enforcement. See *DHS Organizational Chart* dated December 04, 2018. Available at: https://www.dhs.gov/sites/default/files/publications/18_1204_DHS_Organizational_Chart.pdf and Department of Homeland Security Counternarcotics Doctrine dated July 20, 2015. Available at: https://www.dhs.gov/publication/department-homeland-security-counternarcotics-doctrine. (both accessed December 18, 2018).

[21] While government organization is always dynamic, changes in DHS are especially common. Check the DHS website often for document and organization updates.

most fundamental problem we face in improving the homeland security "system" is not improving single agencies like the FBI, DOD, or even the new DHS. The problem goes by a lot of names: cross-breeding; cross-polarization; interagency cooperation; interdisciplinary collaboration; or the homeland security favorite, "Unity of Effort." To brand the issue we might use "hybridization," which has traditionally meant the blending or cross breeding of two or more plant or animal species in order to combine desirable characteristics. However, you can hybridize other agents like cultures, music, art, or even chemical elements.[22] This process is ongoing within homeland security, although no one uses the term (yet).

The problem, of course (as anyone who has tried to raise hybrid roses knows), is that as desirable characteristics are blended in a new agent, undesirable characteristics may be imported as well. Hybrid beef cattle may grow more rapidly to a larger size but be plagued by a skeletal structure too small for their now much larger weight. The interagency processes created by PPD-56 Managing Complex Contingencies is a case in point. The coordinating process prompted by the series of committees and linkages directed by the 1997 presidential memoranda has had a positive influence on the interagency process during subsequent crises. Whether the routine, day-to-day, long-term effectiveness has improved across the entire enterprise or simply made the whole system vulnerable to the flaws of individual organizational cultures remains an open question. A good way to apply this question to homeland security is to look at the systemic hybridization of intelligence.

As the introduction to this chapter suggested, the idea that 9/11 was an intelligence failure of a system that was "blinking red" but unable to "connect the dots" has become a national meme. Actually this idea is not born out by the report of the 9/11 Commission, which suggests the failure was not of intel collection and analysis but imagination among leadership, management, and bureaucracy. Analysts identified the dots and issued warnings—well-meaning bureaucrats erected the wall between intelligence and enforcement that proved fatal.

After 9/11 the FBI, DOD, and DHS (along with other agencies) rushed to adapt, evolve, and create. But the Intelligence Community (IC) as a whole made no such immediate changes.

The term "community" implies a common relationship to the professional knowledge required but not necessarily a formal relationship between agents. Pilots of military, commercial, private and ultralight aircraft are all members of the aviation community. Their experiences and perspectives—and agendas—may be quite different. The term "Intelligence Community"

---

[22] TexMex food is my favorite example of a successful cultural hybrid.

refers to the collection of federal agencies with the statuary responsibility to collect raw information, analyze it, and release it for action through appropriate channels. The term came into general use sometime after the creation of the Central Intelligence Agency (CIA) through the National Defense Act of 1947, which named the head of the CIA the "Director of Central Intelligence." In practice, however, organizations with an intelligence function operated more or less independently, with some actually displaying periodic hostility toward others.[23] There was simply no mechanism to integrate efforts across the intelligence enterprise.

What changed this situation significantly was not 9/11 but the clear failure of intelligence research, analysis, and evaluation (and many would argue, senior leadership) leading up to the Iraq War in 2003. Intel developed by members of the IC and briefed to the president, the UN, and the world suggested Saddam was developing nuclear, chemical, and biological WMD (to include, for example, mobile labs to avoid detection) and was willing to share those resources with terrorist organizations bent on attacking the United States in the homeland. When the analysis turned out to be faulty (no WMD was discovered, no such connections identified) and the primary sources were revealed as self-serving charlatans, the Administration created commissions and study groups to investigate, and Congress stepped in with hearings and legislation.[24,25] A formally structured IC with a new Director of National Intelligence (DNI) as the overall director / coordinator and multiple newly delineated responsibilities was one outcome of the resulting *Intelligence Reform and Terrorism Prevention Act of 2004* (signed December 17, 2004).

---

[23] Antagonisms between the FBI and CIA were legendary, as were periodic differences between DEA and ATF, etc.

[24] The first report released was the Senate *Report of the Select Committee on Intelligence on the U.S. Intelligence Community's Prewar Intelligence Assessments on Iraq.* Phase I was released on July 9, 2004. It focused on problems in intel gathering and analysis leading to false conclusions about Iraq WMD. Phase II, released in May 2007 focused on resulting policy decisions. Note that in its public history, the ODNI begins its own story with a congressional study in 1955 and suggests that creation of the agency (in December 2004) was a direct outcome of the 9/11 Commission Report released July 22, 2004. Perhaps so. But the momentum provided by the highly critical Senate report should not be underestimated.

[25] A major point of discussion, then and now, was CIA National Intelligence Estimate *NIE 2002-16HG Continuing Programs for Weapons of Mass Destruction.* It was distributed in highly classified form in October 2002. An unclassified version was released by the CIA in 2004 (see https://nsarchive2.gwu.edu/NSAEBB/NSAEBB129/nie_first%20release.pdf). The full version was released in 2014 and is available at https://www.scribd.com/doc/259216899/Iraq-October-2002-NIE-on-WMDs-unedacted-version#download&from_embed. An interesting explanation of the problems with this intel effort is located at https://news.vice.com/article/the-cia-just-declassified-the-document-that-supposedly-justified-the-iraq-invasion. It argues that *as the NIE worked its way through the drafting and approval process, important caveats were dropped so the final version seemed both more certain and more dire than the basic intelligence warranted. The United States then went to war based on a faulty intelligence report rather than a faulty intelligence assessment.*

Table 12.1 The United States Intelligence Community, Post-Iraq War

Independent Agencies			
Office of the Director of National Intelligence	Central Intelligence Agency		
Department of Defense Elements			
Defense Intelligence Agency (DIA)	National Security Agency (NSA)	National Geospatial-Intelligence Agency (NGA)	National Reconnaissance Office (NRO)
Army Intelligence	Navy Intelligence	Air Force Intelligence	Marine Corps Intelligence
Elements of Other Departments and Agencies			
Department of Energy: Office of Intelligence and Counter-Intelligence	Department of Homeland Security: Office of Intelligence and Analysis (OIA)	US Coast Guard Intelligence	Department of Justice: Federal Bureau of Investigation (FBI)
Department of State: Bureau of Intelligence and Research	Drug Enforcement Agency: Office of National Security Intelligence	Department of the Treasury: Office of Intelligence and Analysis	

Note: This is a table listing the seventeen agencies, NOT a wiring diagram denoting a chain of command.

Source: Office of the Director of National Intelligence, Members of the IC, https://www.dni.gov/index.php/what-we-do/members-of-the-ic (accessed December 18, 2018). The DNI has the authority to coordinate external intelligence efforts, but not direct internal activities like hiring or firing. For example, National Intelligence Estimates must now be formally coordinated across all agencies and either endorsed or disputed.

So the events of 9/11, the Global War on Terrorism in general, and the search for WMD in Iraq in particular had a significant impact on the organization and practice of intelligence at the national security level. What does that have to do with homeland security and the public safety personnel who practice it? After all, except for the DNI and the Office of Intelligence and Analysis (OIA) of DHS, all of the other agencies existed before 9/11. So except for the requirement to coordinate through the DNI and his huge new staff, what's different?

Other members of the IC reviewed the document and disagreed but had no requirement to state those reservations. This account is from a heavily opinionated news source and not a peer-reviewed academic journal. But to date no credible sources have emerged to argue with the presentation or interpretation. A more academically oriented version of the same story (written before the full release of the NIE) is available at Richard K. Betts, "Two Faces of Intelligence Failure: September 11 and Iraq's Missing WMD," *Political Science Quarterly*, vol. 122, no. 4 (Winter, 2007/2008), pp. 585–606.

First, **today we see a new focus on international terrorist threats likely to impact the domestic arena.** For example, the Coast Guard had long had the responsibility for risk management and security for ports, but the new situation saw the creation of entirely new systems for the identification and tracking of ships and cargo, not to mention maritime passengers and crew. The Department of the Treasury found itself on the pointy end of the global hunt for terrorists, their resources, and those who provide their financial support. The Drug Enforcement Agency expanded its focus on trans-national crime to include possible collusion with terrorism organizations and the use of cartel networks to smuggle terrorists in the country. The Department of Energy applied its international expertise domestically through the creation of the Domestic Nuclear Detection Office (DNDO)— "a jointly staffed office within the DHS Countering WMD Office . . . the primary entity in the U.S. government for implementing domestic nuclear detection efforts for a managed and coordinated response to radiological and nuclear threats, as well as integration of federal nuclear forensics programs" (DNDO web site). Without exception, every element of the IC eventually found itself in an expanded fight against an elusive international enemy that became a top priority because of the potential for attack on US soil.

Second, **this new focus led directly to the creation of domestic intel organizations, the proliferation of systems for information distribution, and new thinking about domestic intelligence as a career, both at all levels of government and in private industry.**

Today there are several claims on the origin of the "fusion center," but the truth is that the idea of "fusing" all available information to provide a better understanding of potential threats is such a good idea (and so obvious) that it emerged in many places at roughly the same time. New York City was an early adopter of the concept as was Los Angeles County. As already mentioned, the FBI developed an intelligence center at each of its field offices. Every state developed a center and some border states developed mini-fusion centers for specific geographic sectors. Given the broad DHS definition as a "collaborative effort of two or more agencies that provide resources, expertise and information to the center" with the goal of coun-tering criminal or terrorist activities, a huge number of new and preexisting efforts now qualify as fusion centers (DHS Fusion Center 2018).

Think for a moment about any nationwide retail company with a central office that collects reports of criminal activity, analyzes them for patterns, and coordinates prevention and prosecution efforts with store managers and local law enforcement. Technically that's a fusion center. The organizations they contact to identify threats and trends outside their own databases (aided by the Internet revolution) are fusion centers, too. What makes this a hybrid effort is that while many commercial organizations have long thought about prevention (as in "loss prevention" activities), the concept is relatively new to policing.[26] And while the nexus between crime and terrorism has long been obvious to law enforcement organizations, the idea that commerce and the elements of critical infrastructure (transportation, etc.) have a role in stopping terrorism is relatively new to industry. So the new organizations and efforts represent neither a creation of something entirely new nor an adaptation or evolution of something old but rather the blending of new and old to create something different and useful in a unique way.

Although the OIA was established in the department with the idea of fusing intelligence in mind, DHS fell a bit behind the state and local rush to establish centers in the 2004–2005 timeframe. As a result, many organizations were established without central guidance or standards. But in fairness, DHS took a methodical, structured approach to the subject, which has paid off in a cascade of guidance and assistance in a field that did not exist a decade ago. Rather than try to summarize their work, I commend to you their extensive website on the subject.[27]

Along with hybridization of the domestic intelligence effort has come the realization that intelligence offers many career opportunities outside the traditional overseas-focused IC. And that has led to a significant increase in the number of university programs producing certificates or full degrees in intelligence. Unfortunately they are hampered by the same lack of theory as the field of homeland security itself (see chapter 15 of this volume). But because the field is so focused on practice rather than policy, that does not seem to make much difference to teachers, students, or prospective employers. Between the intel cycle, tactics/technique/procedures, past history, future technology, opponents, and integration with potential customers (like business or law enforcement organization) domestic intelligence education programs have found plenty to teach and a sure path to making a genuine contribution to the fight against the New Normal in homeland security.

---

[26] Law enforcement officers will argue that deterrence as a form of prevention has always been a duty of law enforcement which is correct. But I am talking about the hiring of intel analysts and the formation of intel sections to collect and analyze data and exchange information with other jurisdictions, which *is* a new and growing field.

[27] See the website of the DHS Office of Intelligence and Analysis (https://www.dhs.gov/office-intelligence-and-analysis), the link to its State and Major Urban Area Fusion Centers page (https://www.dhs.gov/state-and-major-urban-area-fusion-centers) and especially the resources collected for fusion centers at (https://www.dhs.gov/resources-fusion-centers) .

Figure 12.1 The Intelligence Cycle

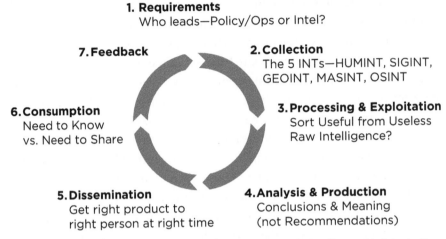

1. Requirements
Who leads—Policy/Ops or Intel?

7. Feedback

2. Collection
The 5 INTs—HUMINT, SIGINT,
GEOINT, MASINT, OSINT

6. Consumption
Need to Know
vs. Need to Share

3. Processing & Exploitation
Sort Useful from Useless
Raw Intelligence?

5. Dissemination
Get right product to
right person at right time

4. Analysis & Production
Conclusions & Meaning
(not Recommendations)

Drawn from William Lahneman, "Chapter 5: Homeland Security Intelligence," in *Introduction to Homeland Security* (ed. Keith Logan and James Ramsey), Boulder, CO: Westview Press, 2012, 103–06. Some other publications use a slightly different description of the cycle.

A third point of progress in the hybrid development of domestic intelligence is the production and distribution of intelligence in new ways across old boundaries. Having already used as an example the extensive FBI information exchange through its JTTF and InfraGard systems, let me cite instead the DHS Homeland Security Information Network (HSIN).[28] Although not available to the general public, this source provides a steady stream of intelligence, data, and reference links to approved users, who include most public safety officials working HS issues. And this is only one of many such sources available to public safety practitioners of homeland security today.

In fact, one problem in the hybridization of domestic intelligence is the explosion of material available. Before 9/11, one of the problems facing the IC was the lack of central management over the products of a dozen or so major organizations. There was no way to focus efforts or evaluate products, reduce duplication, identify underlaps, set priorities, or adjudicate disagreements. Today with at least 150 federal, state, and local fusion centers and scores of private organizations issuing intelligence products of one sort or another, the problem of quality control has multiplied ten-, twenty-, or maybe thirtyfold.

And of course, law enforcement fusion centers have naturally applied the new capabilities to their traditional criminal responsibilities as well, so intelligence on high-probability dangers like dope dealing and car theft rings vie with harder to interpret reports about radicalized personalities and

---

[28] For access to HSIN, see https://www.dhs.gov/homeland-security-information-network-hsin.

opportunistic "lone wolves." DHS training guidelines help, but still local operators could be paralyzed if they responded to every "what if" from on high, and they in turn could jam the system if they reported every suspicion from the street. So the problem is not really a technical or training or even a funding problem. It is a strategy, policy, and operational problem: what exactly do we want to achieve; what will cause the outcome we want to achieve; how do we get the organization to achieve that outcome? And as we will see in the next three chapters, these answers really turn on systemic challenges with jurisdictions, perspectives, and theories of homeland security.

The good news is that in addition to all the systemic progress made in HS, in general, and domestic intelligence, in particular, we actually know how to address this problem. The bad news is that it will require a systemic change in how we think about homeland security.

Again jumping ahead, this time to Volume 2 of this series, we will see that major parts of DHS and many state and local practitioners (especially emergency managers) address this problem of evaluation and prioritization using Risk Management (RM). National security specialists talk about RM but do not apply it as regularly or with the same fidelity as, say, those local officials preparing their required Threat and Hazard Identification and Risk Analysis (THIRA). Although DHS claims in its Quadrennial Review that "Homeland Security is Risk Management," we are not training, educating, or preparing IC to think about their job as a driver of Risk Management. In fact, law enforcement organization and many other public safety officials barely consider the DHS-sanctioned Risk Management approach at all.

We are simply not training, educating, or preparing the IC to think about their job as a driver of Risk Management. Without some such method of prioritizing intelligence reports on threats, we are putting the burden on operators to figure out what intel can do for them and then submit a proposal in the language of intel specialists rather than familiarizing intel with operations and demanding they think, write, and speak in terms that operators can understand. A quick solution might be to incorporate Risk Management into the Intelligence Cycle. (Perhaps as part of Step 4: Analysis and Production: Conclusions and Meaning.) But this would take a concerted effort in the homeland security community writ large.

This observation is not offered as an example of intel failure. HS can point to lots of successes at identifying and forestalling threats. Rather, the hybrid nature of HS intel offers an opportunity for improvement. Here is a low-hanging fruit that should have been picked long ago, except that systemic failures highlighted in the next three chapters (tensions between jurisdictions, narrow traditional practitioner perspectives, lack of educational theories of practitioner integration) all mitigate against such improvement.

SYSTEMATIC BUT NOT A SINGLE SYSTEM

All of these efforts have benefited from new thinking that includes a new structure for preparedness nationally, a new emphasis on capabilities required to meet these needs, and (with the exception of intel) a new approach to risk management. What was once a federal effort focused primarily on emergency management and civil defense, has been reconceptualized in much broader terms. For example, organizations, jurisdictions, and responsibilities in the cyber security realm are evolving so quickly that it is hard to keep up. A robust family of concepts and documents has been developed to promote protection of critical infrastructure and preparedness for organizations and individuals alike. While the guidelines initially seemed to grow organically—which is to say from the bottom up with limited central connectivity—today they represent a "cascade" of authoritative sources linking guidance from the national strategic level right down to the local emergency manager.[29]

Perhaps the most recent example of systemic improvement is the DHS innovations in Business Continuity Management. Once the purview of private specialists (the National Fire Protection Association, the American Society for Industrial Security, the International Organization for Standardization, DRI International, etc.), DHS has recently developed its own extensive framework under its Ready.com program.[30]

All of these efforts (to include state, local, and private contributions) are explained and critiqued in greater detail in future volumes in this series. All of them represent systemic progress in national security in a domestic arena.

However, it is hard to tell at this point whether our success in preventing catastrophic attacks has been a matter of right action or good luck. Threats remain, and in some ways, risk increases as technology bounds ahead. Enemies both foreign and domestic continue to lurk in the shadows, and the danger remains of a single spectacular failure that would negate all our hard-won success. If we encounter such a problem, it will probably result from one of three systemic challenges that produce seams in our domestic defense. We will address these challenges in the next three chapters.

---

[29] See as an example, *The National Preparedness System*, a comprehensive program of frameworks, guidance, and even exercises (with lessons learned). https://www.fema.gov/national-preparedness-system (accessed December 18, 2018).

[30] See *Business Continuity Planning Suite*, https://www.ready.gov/business-continuity-planning-suite (accessed December 18, 2018).

REFERENCES

Business Continuity Planning Suite. n.d. Washington, DC: The Department of Homeland Security. Accessed December 18, 2018. https://www.ready.gov/business-continuity-planning-suite.

DHS Counternarcotics Doctrine. July 20, 2015. Washington, DC: The Department of Homeland Security. Accessed December 18, 2018. https://www.dhs.gov/publication/department-homeland-security-counternarcotics-doctrine.

DHS National Network of Fusion Centers Fact Sheet. December 17, 2018. Washington, DC: The Department of Homeland Security. Accessed December 18, 2018. https://www.dhs.gov/national-network-fusion-centers-fact-sheetm.

DHS Organizational Chart. December 04, 2018. Washington, DC: The Department of Homeland Security. Accessed December 18, 2018—Note: this chart changes frequently. https://www.dhs.gov/sites/default/files/publications/18_1204_DHS_Organizational_Chart.pdf.

DOD Dictionary of Military and Associated Terms. November 2018. "Homeland Defense." Washington, DC: Department of Defense. Accessed December 18, 2018. http://www.jcs.mil/Portals/36/Documents/Doctrine/pubs/dictionary.pdf.

———. November 2018. "Homeland Security." Washington, DC: Department of Defense. Accessed December 18, 2018. https://www.dhs.gov/xlibrary/assets/nat_strat_homelandsecurity_2007.pdf.

DOD Directive 5111.13, Assistant Secretary of Defense for Homeland Defense And Global Security(ASD (HD & GS)). March 23, 2018. Washington DC: Office of the Chief Management Officer of the Department of Defense. Accessed December 18, 2018. https://fas.org/irp/doddir/dod/d5111_13.pdf.

Domestic Nuclear Detection Office (DNDO). Washington, DC: The Department of Homeland Security. Accessed December 18, 2018. https://www.dhs.gov/domestic-nuclear-detection-office.

Federal Bureau of Investigation. n.d. "How Many People Work for the FBI?" Accessed December 18, 2018. https://www.fbi.gov/about/faqs/how-many-people-work-for-the-fbi.

Inserra, David. October 18, 2017. "Foiled Terror Plot Raises Number of Plots, Attacks to 98 Since 9/11." *The Daily Signal*. Accessed December 18, 2018. https://www.dailysignal.com/2017/10/18/foiled-terror-plot-raises-number-of-plots-attacks-to-98-since-911/.

Kean, Thomas, and Lee Hamilton et al. 2004. *National Commission on Terrorist Attacks upon the UnitedStates. 9/11 Commission Report*. New York: W.W. Norton.

Lahneman, William. 2012. "Chapter 5: Homeland Security Intelligence." In *Introduction to Homeland Security*, edited by Keith Logan and James Ramsey, 103–06. Boulder, CO: Westview Press.

National Defense Panel. 1997. *Transforming Defense*. Washington, DC: Department of Defense. Accessed December 18, 2018. https://www.hsdl.org/?view&did=1834.

National Preparedness System. n.d. Accessed December 18, 2018. https://www.fema.gov/national-preparedness-system.

New York City Police Department. LinkedIn. Accessed December 18, 2018. https://www.linkedin.com/company/new-york-city-police-department.

NIPP 2013 Partnering for Critical Infrastructure Security and Resilience. 2013. Washington, DC: Department of Homeland Security. Accessed December 18, 2018. https://www.dhs.gov/sites/default/files/publications/national-infrastructure-protection-plan-2013–508.pdf.

NORTHCOM. n.d. "Joint Task Force Civil Support FAQs." Accessed December 18, 2018. http://www.jtfcs.northcom.mil/About/FAQs/.

O'Neill, John. "The Man Who Knew." *PBS Frontline*. Accessed December 18, 2018. https://www.youtube.com/watch?v=j6WbPG2GjU.

PPD-21. 2013. *Critical Infrastructure Security and Resilience*, Washington, DC: The White House. Accessed December 18, 2018. https://obamawhitehouse. archives.gov/the-press-office/2013/02/12/presidential-policy-directive-critical-infra-structure-security-and-resil.

Public Law 107–296 107th Congress—NOV. 25, 2002, 116 STAT. 2135. 6 USC 101, (15). "Terrorism Definition." Accessed December 18, 2018. https://www.google.com/sea rch?q=PUBLIC+LAW+107%E2%80%93296+107th+Congress+%E2%80%94+N OV.+25%2C+2002+116+STAT.+2135&ie=utf-8&oe=utf-8&client=firefox-b-1-ab.

Rumsfeld, Donald. 2001. *Quadrennial Defense Review Report*. Washington, DC: Department of Defense. Accessed December 18, 2018. http://archive.defense. gov/pubs/qdr2001.pdf.

13

Systemic Challenge #1: Tensions

★ ★ ★

BOTTOM LINE UP FRONT

So the good news is that the United States has done a solid job of creating a systematic solution to the new domestic challenges to national security (NS). The not-so-good news is that while a few new organizations have been created to respond to these new threats, most assets now used for homeland security (HS) were already fully committed to public safety, and most are not federal resources to begin with.

Consequently, the very concept of homeland security is plagued from its beginning by tensions baked into its DNA. In simplest terms, nobody is in charge.

- *Jurisdictions: Unlike with national security where the president and his Executive branch have almost sole jurisdiction over threats and responses to those threats, the Constitution (and especially the Tenth Amendment) divides jurisdiction for homeland security challenges between the federal government and thousands of state, local, and even private organizations. Essentially, no single person or organization—not even the President—is in charge.*
- *Authorities: National security resources are numerous and spread around the globe, so NS authorities over those people and assets trace a huge geographic footprint. But the lines of authority are generally well defined by law and regulation. In contrast, homeland security issues impact the entire domestic community, so authorities may overlap or remain unclear along the seams between jurisdictions.*
- *Responsibilities: With national security the lines of responsibility are generally clear from the lowest private to the National Command Authority.*

But the complexity of homeland security issues, and the overlapping of new and traditional authorities raise some entirely new questions about who is responsible for what both before and after HS events occur.

- *Bureaucracies: When traditional organizations are pointed in new directions, well-established organizational cultures may resist the change.*
- *Funding: Because demands for domestic security always exceed available resources, prioritization remains a challenge.*

The systemic challenge of inherent tensions to homeland security means there will be no unity of command. Unity of effort is the best we can expect. But given the scale and scope of the challenge even that will prove difficult. Participants will have to sacrifice some degree of power or control for larger purposes. But why would they agree to that? Unity of perspective is probably the best answer—a common view of what is at risk and what can be done might drive a new community culture of cooperation as it has with NS. But creating a common HS perspective is itself a challenge.

The most important single thing to understand about Homeland Security in the United States is that **the entire concept is built upon an irreconcilable set of tensions that <u>cannot be solved</u> because of the imperfect intersection of national security concerns with public safety resources.** This systemic challenge can be managed but never resolved.

These inevitable tensions arise from multiple sources. For example, the United States of America was born as a response to the domestic abuse of centralized power. Consequently, the Constitution, which establishes the structure of the national government, is designed to prevent the concentration of domestic power and decision-making. The three branches of the federal government—Executive, Legislative, and Judiciary—are designed to check and balance each other. As an example, the Administration proposes annual federal budgets, but the Congress decides what is actually spent, and the Judiciary is sometimes called on to determine if those expenditures are legal under the Constitution.

Furthermore, the day-to-day implementation of the Constitution remains caught between conflicting political ideas that reach back to the Founding Fathers. Historians call this a clash between Jeffersonian and Hamiltonian visions. Thomas Jefferson argued that power should remain as close to the people as possible, so he pushed for constrained federal power with most authority reserved to the state and local levels. Alexander Hamilton advanced the idea of power flowing predominantly to a national political elite, with states directed accordingly. Legal scholars call this constitutional tension between centralized and decentralized decision-making "an invitation to struggle." Because the struggle is purposely designed into the DNA of our government, it can never be "solved." It can only be "managed" as the people and their leaders adjust laws and policies in accordance with changing challenges.

The Tenth Amendment to the Constitution—approved at the same time as the main body of the Constitution and having equal weight under the law—attempted to square this circle by specifying that those powers not enumerated to the federal government in the Constitution were reserved to the states. But 220 years of federal lawyers have proven creative in arguing for alternative interpretations, and tensions over the division of powers between levels of government remain strong today.[1]

What is especially disorienting about homeland security is that if the same international threats were mounted against national interests in overseas locations, the provisions of the Constitution would allow unified planning and control by the Executive branch. Some examples of tensions follow.

Multiple Jurisdictions

One way this argument over powers plays to our domestic disadvantage is through the tensions between jurisdictions. Definitions of "jurisdiction" become technical very quickly. But for our purposes a focus on "the extent of power to make decisions" is close enough. The key word is "extent," meaning boundaries, whether geographic or legal or administrative—the divisions of power.

In national security, divisions of power are generally formal and clear. US ambassadors have jurisdiction over US government activities within their assigned nations. US military or intelligence activities require coordination with and generally the permission of the local ambassador, who is the president's primary local representative. Military jurisdictions are also

---

[1] Actually we are probably using the whole concept of higher and lower wrong when we distinguish between federal, state, and local levels of authority and jurisdiction. The founders who drafted the Declaration of Independence (especially Jefferson) and the Constitution were very clear that primary political authority in the United States resides with the people where they live, and thus at the local level. Authorities enumerated for the federal level were all intended to support the people by advancing their interest, not to rule and control them. So step one in understanding security perspectives is to recognize that local homeland security officials see themselves as the apex of government, not the bottom. And business tends to see all government in a utilitarian manner, largely agreeing with President Calvin Coolidge that "the chief business of the American people is business."

generally clear. From a the Department of Defense (DOD) perspective, the world is divided between "combatant commands," and staff charged with military operations in one area of the world (say the Pacific Ocean), would never dare to intrude in another command's business (say in Europe or the Mideast). Even in the most complex of all international operations—combat operations with allies—jurisdictional divisions are routinely bridged by formal networks allowing, for example, different units from different commands and different services from different nations to fly and fight through the same battlespace.[2] These mechanisms of cooperation are not perfect. Conflicts between intelligence agencies and other components of the administration are legendary. But the bridges across jurisdictions are constantly reinforced by education, practiced by training, and implemented by common national security culture.

Nothing like this routinely occurs between elements of public safety working homeland security missions. Imagine a volunteer fire department from a rural county in one state called on to support police in a large city in another state, under direction of a Department of Energy team responding to a radiological event. That would be very difficult with extensive planning. It is not going to happen in an emergency. And not just because the skills and training are incompatible. There simply are no mechanisms to connect those jurisdictions.

That said, bridging across domestic jurisdictions is much better today than it was even a decade ago. The difference in coordination between federal, state, local, and private organizations after Hurricane Katrina, and cooperation between the same agencies after Hurricane Harvey, is striking. But the efforts put into education, training, planning, and operations for the threat of recurring hurricanes are unique. Efforts toward cooperation in the face of some other major threats cannot boast the same progress.

Multiple Authorities

Besides the imperfect alignment of boundaries between decision-makers in homeland security, domestic power itself is distributed among thousands of federal, state, local, and private authorities, all pulling in different directions.

With national security issues, authorities may be convoluted, but there is an underlying structure. All formal matters with other international

---

[2] An excellent example of how boundaries between operators and decision-makers are routinely bridged in national security issues is the operation in Mogadishu, Somalia, in 1993 where American infantry joined Pakistani tanks and Malaysian armored personnel carriers to rescue US Army Rangers and Navy Seals while covered from the air by Special Operations helicopters. The units and personnel did not know each other, and some did not even speak English, but jurisdictions were bridged in an emergency under combat conditions because of common training and culture. It was not clean or easy . . . but it worked.

states, whether treaties or declarations of war, are ultimately coordinated through the Department of State. All military issues, whether involving a lance corporal or an aircraft carrier, are ultimately directed by the Secretary of Defense. All intelligence matters are ultimately coordinated by the Director of National Intelligence.[3] Again, execution is not always perfect, but with national security somebody does ultimately have the authority to "connect the dots" all the way back to the president.

With homeland security, not so much. In fact, not at all. There is no single, consolidated domestic authority over homeland security. The president can issue orders to federal authorities who report to him (US Marshalls, for example), and he can call to federal service some state resources (the National Guard). But the president has no authority at all over state and local law enforcement or firefighters, governors, or mayors. He cannot issue orders to private hospitals or medical personnel. He cannot close schools or order grocery stores to remain open.

Even worse (from the perspective of central domestic coordination), the authorities granted these many different jurisdictions are not uniform across the nation. For example, some state constitutions mirror the federal approach, with those powers not enumerated to the state reserved to counties, cities, parishes, townships, and so on. But some states (Texas, for example) invert this relationship, with the state holding all the cards and the lower-level governments acting as suppliants in issues ranging from school funding to tax rates to police authority. Additionally, five US territories and the District of Columbia have unique arrangements with the federal government.[4] Also Native American tribes actually function as separate "nations" in some regards, including the management of their domestic security.

This patchwork quilt of jurisdictions and authorities creates a similar patchwork of government organizations. For example, at the federal level, most emergency management functions are delegated to FEMA, which is subordinate to the Department of Homeland Security (DHS). Yet the Department of Justice has authority over the crime scene of a terrorist attack, even though it has no emergency management authority. In some states, the emergency manager reports to the state highway patrol. In some cities, emergency managers report directly to the mayor but with no authority over police and fire "first responders." Other governments entirely separate

---

[3] Well . . . in theory. Bureaucratic culture still gets in the way of this new relationship once in a while.

[4] There are technically fourteen US territories, but they are sometimes counted in different ways. Only five are permanently occupied (America Samoa, Guam, the Northern Mariana Islands, Puerto Rico, and the US Virgin Islands).

security responsibilities (vested perhaps in the state commander of the National Guard) from emergency management planning and coordination. The resulting smorgasbord of organizations makes centralized planning and execution virtually impossible. Unity of Command must give way to Unity of Effort—and that requires constantly managing multiple tensions.[5]

Multiple Responsibilities

So what exactly do these overlapping jurisdictions and authorities in homeland security do? As we established in chapter 3, national security is about physical protection against foreign attack or encroachment upon the nation, its interests, and its elements of national power. As we will discuss in greater detail in chapter 14, public safety is about protecting people, property, and what might be called the "civil environment"—the whole range of physical and intellectual resources that comprise the nation state and allow it to function and prosper in a safe and lawful environment. Homeland security uses some national and mostly domestic resources to secure the space where national security and public safety overlap. That would include everything from individuals and businesses, to critical infrastructure, to the mechanisms and even the legitimacy of the state.

This creates tensions between overlapping and underlapping responsibilities. For example, I once visited a border town in Texas that had about three miles of frontage on the Rio Grande River and was several miles deep, for a total area of about twenty square miles. In that space resided more than two dozen law enforcement agencies all with individual jurisdictions, authorities, and responsibilities. They included city police, county sheriffs, district constables, state police, Texas Rangers, ICE, CBP, US Marshalls, TSA (they had an airport), DEA, FBI, ATFE, Military Police (there was a military facility), and university police. Also present were National Guard and State Guard personnel working for the governor to support law enforcement, as well as special personnel from K-9 and bomb squad units. When counterfeit currency crossed the border, the Secret Service joined the show. From outside the city boundaries, DHS worked to prevent cyber attacks on critical infrastructure, and DOD did the same for the military facility. Meanwhile a variety of private security forces guarded banks and select businesses. When necessary, law enforcement from outside jurisdictions crossed in to help local police. And of course, much of this structure was paralleled by various legal agencies that advised the different

---

[5] As will be explained in detail in a later volume, Unity of Command means one person can issue to orders to everyone involved in an operation. Unity of Effort means different organizations direct their own activities, while senior leaders meet to coordinate operations without a single individual in charge.

law enforcement organizations (LEOs) and prosecuted any criminals that stumbled into this web of relationships.

So who exactly coordinates the efforts of these dozens of LEOs? Answer: Everybody. Which means nobody.

And the lack of coordinating structure is even greater in other organizations where responsibilities parallel, cross, or disappear. Who was in charge of the response to the Ebola outbreak in Dallas in 2014? The mayor. The county judge. The governor. The local department of public health. DHS. FEMA. HHS. CDC. The board of the privately owned hospital. The national accrediting agency for hospitals.

These are not questions. These are the answers. And the problem gets worse the deeper you look into the private ownership of most of our critical infrastructure.

Again, these overlaps and underlaps in the assignment of responsibility cannot be "solved." They are an artifact of our system of government. They can only be managed.

Multiple Bureaucracies

Bureaucracies have been with us forever. The Pharos had ranks of scribes, accountants, and record keepers. Even Alexander needed data collection and policy managers to promote efficiency and effectiveness. But the Industrial Revolution made bureaucracy a primary enabler of the economy and thus of modern life. Even more than for government, bureaucracy enabled business and capitalism to collect and analyze the information necessary to improve their processes and products, and then create and enforce productive policies in multiple factories, multiple cities, and finally multiple countries. The industrial-scale bureaucracies in government and industry that we created to win the Cold War eventually came to dominate the planet.

But the Information Revolution is changing all that. Almost overnight, middle management has become an obstacle to the rapid flow of data up to decision-makers and policies back down to operators. Sensing their vulnerability, bureaucracies in many organizations respond by tightening their grip on information (and resources) and enforcing their prerogatives, slowing and complicating decisions rather than accelerating them. The driving (or rather constraining) factor in modern business and government is not capability but bureaucratic culture. Stanford lecturer Steve Blank identified this tension in a number of citations taken from the 2018 National Defense Strategy (Mattis 2018; Blank 2018):[6]

---

[6] In his online essay in War on the Rocks, Steve Blank draws these examples from the *2018 National Defense Strategy*. https://warontherocks.com/2018/02/national-defense-strategy-compelling-call-defense-innovation/ (accessed December 18, 2018).

- "Maintaining the Department's technological advantage will require changes to industry **culture**, investment sources, and protection across the National Security Innovation Base" (p. 3).
- "Defense objectives include: . . . Continuously delivering performance with affordability and speed as we **change Departmental mindset, culture, and management systems**" (p. 4).
  - "Cultivating a lethal, agile force requires more than just new technologies and posture changes; . . . it depends on the ability [to] . . . **change business practices**" (p. 7).
  - "**The current bureaucratic approach,** centered on exacting thoroughness and minimizing risk above all else, **is proving to be increasingly unresponsive. We must transition to a culture of performance**" (p. 10).
  - "Deliver performance at the speed of relevance . . . **Current processes are not responsive to need** . . . We must **not accept cumbersome approval chains** . . . Delivering performance means we will **shed outdated management practices and structures**" (p. 10).
  - "**Culture change is hardest in the middle of a large organization.** It will be interesting to see how each agency in the Department of Defense adapts the strategy **or whether the bureaucratic middle kills it or waits it out**" (p. 10).

These national security examples are striking but not unique. In a later volume we will examine at length the frustrations of Bob Gates, former Director of the CIA, Secretary of Defense, and president of a major university, with the bureaucracies and bureaucratic cultures that repeatedly impeded his efforts at innovation, even during time of war. And we will explore the solutions offered by business legend John Kotter concerning how to promote change in business and government bureaucracies. Unfortunately, these challenges in large but unified organizations are simple compared to the difficulty of promoting change in thousands of independent public safety organizations as the field of homeland security matures.

Multiple Lines of Funding

For complexity and power to generate emotional response, few tensions can match the intensity of battles over funding. With national security, it is clear that we all contribute to funding a military that goes abroad to secure the nation collectively. But for homeland security, things are not so simple.

When President Bush 43 first announced his plans for a National Strategy for Homeland Security, he foresaw an expense of about $100 billion, divided between federal, state, and private industry. This at a time when federal national security expenditures were regularly topping $500 billion. But businesses never came close to investing "their share" in their own security. And state and local governments actually turned to their federal representatives to supply much of their funding from grants. The amount of those grants has waxed and waned with differing perspectives on the threat, and the way the money was delivered has varied as well, with Congress sometimes placating governors by routing funding through states, and sometimes satisfying pressure from big city mayors with direct funding for local projects.

Further tensions are introduced when homeland security funds come from different sources (say FEMA and the Department of Justice) with different priorities (storm mitigation vs. terrorism prevention or protection). Sometimes federal funds come with restrictions that prevent locals from spending the money on what they need most (as in basic IT architecture). And it is not unknown for locals to use federal grants to pay bills they previously covered themselves, reducing local taxes rather than increasing local capabilities.

At another level it is worth asking whether citizens of one city or state should really be footing the bill for securing bridges and airports and conducting basic law enforcement functions for another city or state in the first place. With defense funding, citizens everywhere contribute to the purchase of ships or planes or soldiers that protect us all equally. But with HS funding, nationwide taxes frequently pay for special local projects. Essentially, every locality has the same desire: local control and outside funding. The resulting tensions can imperil the homeland security mission.

Many Other Tensions

This short list of tensions just scratches the surface of the systemic challenges posed to homeland security. For example, the tensions between public safety and national security priorities remain unresolved. There are simply not enough resources to secure every power plant and every school bus. How do we prioritize? And ownership of assets poses a tension all its own. How much taxpayer money should go to securing the 85 percent of infrastructure that belongs to private industry?

And by the way, what are we securing potential targets against? There is a profound tension between assigning limited DHS resources to high probability–low consequence events (like domestic crime) and low probability–high consequence events (like an attack with a bio agent or a nuclear weapon). Even deciding how to prioritize our actions involves significant tension: how do we strike the right balance between Mitigation, Prevention, Protection, Response, Recovery, and Resilience? What types of events threaten us most—terrorist attacks, natural disasters, or man-made hazards?

And finally, a major question: What exactly is it we are securing, anyway? America (our economic and political system together with the sinews of national power) or Americans (meaning individual citizens at home, work, and play)? Even more to the point, do we want complete security for everyone everywhere at the cost of our constitutional liberties? Or do we want to maintain all our liberties at the cost of some periodic casualties?

THESE TENSIONS LEAD TO A SECOND SYSTEMIC CHALLENGE

Taken together, these many tensions lead to a further tension produced by the work of homeland security itself: differing perspectives (read "agendas, cultures, and priorities") between HS practitioners.

Most of the people who work in national security think of themselves as full-time national security professionals. Even the newest private in the army understands that he has sworn to "protect and defend the Constitution of the United States against all enemies foreign and domestic." But most people who work in the homeland security enterprise do so by default— they have full-time jobs in public safety, or even private enterprise, which just happen to apply to securing the homeland. Securing the nation as a whole is not the reason they signed up.

The perfect solution to these tensions would be self-management—that is, practitioners recognizing the need to adjust to the perceptions of others in the service of a greater whole. But as we will see in the next chapter, that turns out to be a systemic challenge of its own.

REFERENCES

Blank, Steve. February 12, 2018. "The National Defense Strategy: A Compelling Call for Defense Innovation." War on the Rocks. Accessed December 18, 2018. https://warontherocks.com/2018/02/national-defense-strategy-compelling-call-defense-innovation/.
Gates, Robert M. 2016. *A Passion for Leadership*. New York: Alfred Knopf.
Kotter, John. 2012. *Leading Change*. Harvard Business School.
Mattis, James. 2018. *National Defense Strategy*. Washington, DC: Department of Defense.

14

Systemic Challenge #2: Perspectives

★ ★ ★

BOTTOM LINE UP FRONT

Thus far in this volume of essays we have looked at the reasons national security developed into the system we know today and the reasons home-land security is developing differently. But it is not just the subject matter that is different or the tensions between of the participants. The perspectives of the practitioners are different as well.

Since the attack on Pearl Harbor and the entry of the United States into a global struggle against enemies who sought to undermine our interests overseas, the national security community has perceived that threats to the power and existence of the nation originate primarily overseas and play out there. Even the threat of nuclear attack is addressed primarily by the threat of retaliation overseas.

Consequently, <u>national security practitioners</u> may vary greatly in their bureaucratic culture (Army, Navy, CIA, Department of State, etc.), but as institutions, they share a number of common perspectives. They think about threats and interests globally. They see their jobs as fitting into a matrix of policies and organizations, addressing similar goals, and making similar contributions to the national interest. There is some distance between them and the impact of their decisions, and for most, physical danger is the exception, not the rule. They focus on the security of the nation, not the lives and property of individual citizens. One of the unifying elements of the national security perspective is a requirement for theory-based graduate education that appreciates the interagency perspective for advancement to the highest ranks in most national security organizations.

In contrast, <u>public safety practitioners</u> perceive that their duties involve preservation of private property and individual well-being against domestic threats to public order and safety. They do not exist to ensure the survival *of the nation, its institutions, its sources of power, or its legitimacy. They see threats and risks as local, personal, and pervasive. Attacks, hazards, and disasters are not periodic events like wars, but daily occurrences. Their efforts draw more on training and lessons learned than education and theory. And those lessons involve a variety of different missions and objectives: safety from the threat of fire or a natural disaster is quite different from safety from criminal intent. Consequently, perspectives of public safety practitioners are much different from those of national security participants, and indeed from each other.*

And <u>security practitioners in private industry</u> have yet another perspective, focused as they are on minimizing cost and maximizing profit.

These differing perspectives make unified thinking about HS difficult— perhaps even impossible.

Given the differing origins, focus and priorities of national security and public safety in the United States and the imperfect way these two concepts intersect in the field of homeland security, we might expect different perspectives and even cultures between participants in these various fields. And that is in fact the case.

PERSPECTIVE OF THE NATIONAL SECURITY COMMUNITY

Let's begin with the perspective of professionals in the national security community. That would include everyone who protects and advances American interests and power outside the US borders.

Figure 14.1 Differing Homeland Security Perspectives

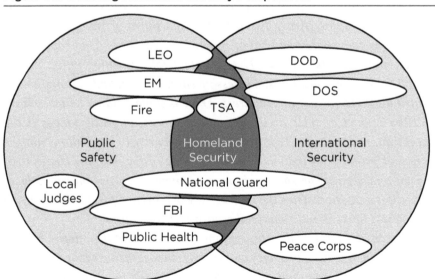

From a motor pool gate guard in Afghanistan, to the press officer at the US Embassy in Japan, to a watch officer in a missile silo, to a treasury analyst tracking money from transnational criminals, to the director of the National Security Council, every NS employee is focused on supporting the national security policies of the United States. Violence, destruction, and danger are part of the calculus of national security, and for some participants (pilots, spies, USAID officers operating alone in distant corners of the earth), even peacetime duties can be risky. Casualties are part of the price of doing business. But this business operates on a global scale, and avoiding violence to the nation is a top priority. In fact, most national security employees never face real risk at all.

To accomplish national security priorities, each national security practitioner occupies a precise location in a huge matrix and executes well-defined missions within a gigantic, mostly twentieth-century industrial structure. Information flows up. Strategy, policy, plans, and operational guidance flow down. The workforce is well-educated and expected to use that education within well-defined boundaries. Unauthorized initiative can be dangerous to the entire enterprise.

While it is the instinct of all bureaucracies to collect power and guard information, and agency parochialism has long been a major barrier to effective national security operations, formal and informal mechanisms to promote cooperation across internal jurisdictions are valued. Organizational rivalry remains a major concern, especially when budgets are at stake. But the legacy of the Cold War and the operational realities of nearly two decades of global war against vicious and dedicated terrorist enemies have created a focus on mission accomplishment that overcomes many of those barriers and well serves the nation's international interests.

The Starship Enterprise might serve as a modern metaphor for the national security enterprise. The hugely expensive and astonishingly complex human and technological marvel rockets through a hostile environment, with shields up and sensors deployed, seeking to make friends, encourage trade, deter or destroy enemies, and benefit the Federation that created it. The massive structure is highly compartmentalized, each workspace occupied by crew performing vital if sometimes mundane functions. Some set policies for communicating with aliens, some navigate, maintaining the momentum and direction, or operate the weapons. Some provide resources and repairs; some prepare meals or take out the trash. But ultimately, every crew member has a function that contributes to the mission. There is a reason that Plato called a nation performing its international functions "the ship of state."

This is not to suggest that the national security community consists only of technically oriented Starship Troopers. As with any ship underway, some crewmembers are awake and others asleep. Some are working hard, and some are hardly working. Some are steering the ship away from rocks, and some are provoking rocky relationships with other members of the crew. Some are planning for engagements with the enemy; some are planning for early retirement. But the metaphor of a large organization with expensive and extensive structure, navigating daily between the calm channels of peace and the dangerous shoals of war, with a focus and mission to which everyone more or less contributes, is a good one.

What then is the perspective of the national security community? The focus on national security missions means most participants are well versed in national security threats. They understand that *at the national level* those threats may be accepted, addressed, or mitigated, but not transferred.[1] They collaborate instinctively (if imperfectly). They operate mostly within their jurisdictional boundaries and may train for a narrow mission. But they understand through education that their tasks contribute to a larger effort with a greater purpose than individual safety. They live, think, and breathe at the national level.

PERSPECTIVE OF THE PUBLIC SAFETY COMMUNITY

Most HS practitioners live in an entirely different reality.

As discussed in previous essays, "domestic security" and "internal security" are terms sometimes used in other countries to describe organs of government that protect the state against internal threats. Other nations sometimes combine this role with guarding against both crime and terrorism at the national level. France, for example, has both a national civilian police force to combat crime (the Police Nationale) and a national military police force to promote security (the Gendarmerie Nationale). Local police forces are a relatively new development for them.

Given its concern from birth about the consolidation of power at the highest levels, the United States never created a national police force. Although there are several dozen federal law enforcement agencies (FBI, DEA, ATF, etc.), each focuses on a relatively narrow range of federal crimes. Many of these agencies contribute to **national security** despite their domestic location and focus. For example, one of the FBI's two major divisions is national security, and they work issues like counterterrorism and counterespionage every day. Similarly, the Department of Homeland Security (DHS)

---

[1] You can't simply transfer national security risk to some other party. See the discussion of Risk in Volume 2 of this series.

is charged with coordinating at the federal level preparedness for major attacks, hazards, and disasters that would impact the nation as a whole.

But in the United States, there is no single, overarching federal enterprise focused on **public safety.** That term is generally used to describe state and local organizations that provide services like police, fire and rescue, emergency medical services, emergency communications and management, and enforcement of certain laws and regulations like the Department of Motor Vehicles. While these roles may overlap with national security and some federal law enforcement duties, they actually have a quite different focus, and consequently, a quite different perspective.

If anything, the individual agents of public safety have more varied (and sometimes competitive) cultures than those of national security. They have a long tradition of local control. Ben Franklin started the first public fire company in Philadelphia in 1736, and volunteer fire departments remain a mainstay of many smaller American communities today. Policing was generally ad hoc until Boston established a formal police department in 1836. Throughout the nineteenth century policing efforts were not standardized and were sometimes augmented by the efforts of posses or militias. State law enforcement organizations (LEOs), state emergency management assets, and state wildfire organizations (in the states that have them) belong entirely to the governors. They cannot be activated or controlled by any federal officer.

A quick look at how several public safety professions see the world will show that their differing perspectives create a systemic problem for homeland security.

Public Safety: Law Enforcement

Today, regardless of the size of the department, most state and local law enforcement officers work in very small units—often by themselves and rarely in patrols larger than two. Manpower is usually quite limited. Calling for assistance means some other patrol area goes unprotected. Special organizations like SWAT teams are usually comprised of officers with standard duties, called together only for special training or missions. Because of resource constraints, duties are highly compartmentalized. Officers working burglary, auto theft, counter narcotics, violent crime, or street patrols may cross paths infrequently. While efforts at cooperation like the FBI-sponsored Joint Terrorism Task Forces may exist, interagency operations remain the exception and not the rule. Jurisdictional constraints are tightly enforced: state police may patrol state highways through a town, but not residential streets a block away. And the sheer number of nonfederal LEOs is remarkable, numbering in the scores of thousands. A single county or parish may contain multiple city police departments, constables, sheriff's deputies, and one or more university police force. It may also contain federal law enforcement representatives from the FBI, DEA, ATFE, TSA, US Marshalls Service, Postal Service, ICE, BCP, the National Guard, the state guard, the military services, and several entirely separate state, local, or federal intelligence fusion centers, all operating inside the same geographic boundaries. They may collaborate, if necessary, but work alone as a matter of routine.

Additionally, many officers interact personally with the victims of crime. Public safety provides protection to individuals as opposed to security (international or domestic) that may benefit citizens but does so as a byproduct of protecting society. Protecting pedestrians from assault on Wall Street is a matter of public safety. Protecting "Wall Street" from attack (meaning the markets and firms that provide the foundation of the American economy) is a matter of national security—with assistance from public safety and private business security personnel.

As a result, law enforcement officials working public safety missions tend to focus on well-defined legal and jurisdictional parameters rather than grander and more general concepts of "national interest." Their perspective is rooted in the name of their profession: law enforcement. They enforce the law by pursuing law breakers. "Intelligence-led policing" that would deter or prevent crime is a relatively new concept. LEOs worry about the practical effects of crimes against individuals and seek solutions from experience and lessons learned. For this reason they focus on training for "how?" rather than education on "why?"

Public Safety: Fire

If anything, fire departments are even more insular and independent than LEOs, so their perspectives are even more varied. Of course there are many large organizations charged with coordinating fire prevention and response across large swaths of state and federal lands. The United States Fire Service manages fire protection for 193 million acres of public lands. The California Department of Forestry and Fire Protection (CDF) has similar responsibilities for the State of California (Lundberg 2009, 301) But among the fire jurisdictions that protect most citizens of the United States, there is no hierarchy of fire departments, as there is between constables, local police, state police, and federal investigators. Some crimes are divided by law into federal, state, local, or even tribal jurisdiction, allowing, for example, the FBI to take over a criminal investigation from local law enforcement if it concerns a terrorist event. Excepting wildfires, there is no such thing as a federal, state, or local fire. There is no case where a "higher" fire department might arrive and claim a jurisdiction from a "lower" fire department already on the scene.

A case in point was the fire response to the attack on the Pentagon on 9/11. The Pentagon was in the jurisdiction of the Arlington Virginia Fire Department. Four other departments responded to assist. Together they established a Unity of Effort whereby Arlington provided leadership and the other departments cooperated. But there was no Unity of Command whereby the Arlington department could give an order that other departments were legally bound to obey.

Fire jurisdictions frequently strike agreements with neighboring jurisdictions to borrow resources in moments of crisis. If one city were to commit most of its resources to a multi-alarm fire it could, as a general rule, rapidly activate existing agreements to borrow crews and equipment from other departments. An Emergency Management Assistance Compact (EMAC) is an interstate mutual aid agreement that enables states to share resources during times of disaster.[2] Cities and local communities frequently strike similar agreements. But fire equipment and people are usually employed as teams or mission packages with the structure previously agreed upon in writing. Individual crewmembers or pieces of equipment are rarely lent across jurisdictional lines on an ad hoc basis.

Also, fire departments are by their natures geographically tethered and thus geographically oriented. The vast majority of the time they respond in their own jurisdiction, fight a fire saving local lives and property, and return to the station house, all in a single shift. As a rule, they have no logistical support system outside their home jurisdiction. Such support can be coordinated through the National Incident Management System (see the later volume on Emergency Management). But despite this possibility, the perspective of fire departments and fire personnel tends to be local, focused on practical solutions to local fires, hazards, and disasters.

Public Safety: Emergency Management (EM)

EM comprises a relatively small group of people who help coordinate participants from other areas of public safety in preparing for or dealing with an emergency. It is actually more a managerial function than an operational function. Its goals are to reduce the loss of life, minimize damage to property and to the environment, and protect the jurisdiction from all threats and hazards. Between emergencies, they and their small staffs are engaged in a continuous cycle of planning, organizing, equipping, training,

---

[2] See FEMA's comprehensive explanation at "Emergency Management Assistance Compact (EMAC)." https://www.fema.gov/pdf/emergency/nrf/EMACoverviewForNRF.pdf (accessed December 18, 2018).

exercising, and evaluating/improving. During disasters they manage operations centers and support the Incident Commander in the execution of plans and operations using the National Incident Management System (NIMS) and the Incident Command System (ICS) (again, see the future volume on EM).

Because so many of their duties revolve around integrating the plans and operations of other public safety participants and exercising and evaluating that cooperation, emergency managers tend to have a broader perspective on homeland security than some of their more locally focused compatriots. This broader perspective is further promoted by the existence of FEMA. EM is the only complement of public safety to have a single, unified federal point of contact to assist them in training, educating, and exercising their participants for homeland security responsibilities. That single federal agency then supports them in operations during a crisis. Although there has been some tension since 2003 as FEMA adjusted to its position within the DHS hierarchy, it now seems committed to a fully cooperative perspective on homeland security and provides training and educational resources to help spread that perspective nationally.

Thus the perspective of EM on homeland security seems to be more favorable toward higher-level understanding and integration than some other more narrowly focused public safety organizations.

PERSPECTIVE OF THE BUSINESS COMMUNITY
(SAFETY AND SECURITY)

We began this volume of essays with the observation that we cannot get answers right unless we get the questions right. And we cannot get the questions right unless we get the language right. Few issues demonstrate this conundrum more clearly than safety and security in business.

Merriam-Webster gets us off on the wrong foot by leaving something important out of the definition of business as: "commercial or mercantile activity engaged in as a means of livelihood." (Merriam-Webster, "Business"). This leaves out the essential concept of profit: the characteristic which most distinguishes business from government. Both may provide a livelihood and a service to the public at large. But government finances those services by taxes. The public has little choice in paying for the services or even using them, regardless of cost or quality. When government outlays exceed income, they simply raise taxes, and the public has no choice but to pay. Business, however, even a not-for-profit business, exists only because the public determines its product to be worth the cost. If the products from one business rise in cost or decline in quality because of mismanagement or a failure of internal safety or security, the public takes their business elsewhere. Thus safety and security are areas of mission focus for government. They are issues of life-and-death for business.

That said, the government has no real choice but to provide safety and security even if their measures turnout to be faulty or incomplete. Business, however, can and frequently does fool itself and its investors concerning its exposure to risk and its level of preparedness for safety and security.

Business Safety

Safety is a relatively new concept to business as a whole. In the past it was frequently driven by the risk of lawsuits should employees or customers be injured by something a company did or failed to do. To maintain its profitability, business must actively balance <u>risk reduction</u> (perhaps from employee training or new construction), <u>mitigation</u> (sometimes by planning and the distribution of assets), <u>transfer</u> (primarily by insurance), or <u>acceptance</u> (essentially a bet that significant uncovered losses will not arise). Over the last several decades, many companies have come to understand that poor safety practices risk not just lawsuits but the loss of value that employees contribute to the firm.[3] The rise of social media has caused companies to consider the cost that safety events may inflict on their brand. All of these issues usually fall under the purview of the company safety officer or occupational safety department, giving them a unique perspective on the subject.

Business Security

Business security is a new area of business activity prompted by the increasing scale and frequency of major crimes and physical attacks against business accounts and facilities.[4]

Obviously physical security is a long-standing concept for business. It mostly refers to passive measures designed to guard against theft and petty crime or even product tampering. In some special cases, as when tensions between unions and management degenerate into serious confrontation, special security officers have been employed. But major or sustained attacks against malls and restaurants or the paralysis of hospitals by ransomware are relatively new developments—so new that the term "business security" does not even have an agreed-upon definition.

---

[3] Relatively new practices include insurance to compensate the company for the loss of specific experts, and wellness programs to reduce the cost of health insurance.

[4] Further confusing the issue of language is the fact that crimes and physical attacks dealt with in-house as a matter of business *security* are addressed externally by law enforcement and other public *safety* officials in the government.

Companies that provide specialized perimeter monitoring and personnel tracking within facilities advertise as business security providers. So do companies that specialize in the protection of executives and their families against kidnapping, extortion, and other threats. Some information technology specialists have argued that the protection of information systems is so critical to company survival that these activities should now be called "business security." Emergency managers and other *public safety* officials may provide government response and recovery efforts for hazards and disasters, but within major corporations this is called "business continuity" and increasingly falls in the purview of *business security personnel.* The same is true of insider threats. Corporate security personnel are charged with loss prevention and the even larger dangers of data theft, sabotage, employee misconduct, and industrial espionage. When they find a problem they refer it to government public safety personnel for action. Or even (as in the hack of Sony industries by North Korea) to national security personnel.

The central point for our immediate purposes is that all this causes business *security* personnel to have a somewhat different perspective from both public safety and national security personnel. Indeed, they do not even think like business *safety* personnel, except for their understanding that the lifeblood of business is profit—a perspective quite different from public safety practitioners.

CONCLUSION

After two decades of effort, people in national security, public safety, and business have found ways to work together in the still undefined space we call homeland security. But fundamental differences in perspective concerning missions, jurisdictions, bureaucracy, and culture, not to mention resources, remain. These differences constitute a major systemic challenge to homeland security.

What we need is a way for participants to maintain their expertise and professional identity while gaining a broader understanding of other contributors to homeland security who harbor different perspectives based on their duties. We might even need a new term—something that suggests a common goal bridging national security and public safety without the overtones of an authoritarian state, which "homeland security" seems to suggest.

My candidate for this term is "Civil Security."[5] I like it because it suggests a focus on protecting and maintaining civil government, civil

---

5   While I developed this term independently after conversations at many homeland security conferences, I have discovered that author Amanda Dory suggested it in a report for the

rights, civil liberties, and the civil compact between the people and the government forged by our Constitution and our history. While homeland security seems like something stuck onto our republican form of government, civil security feels like the culmination of the entire American experiment—a higher purpose served by national security and public safety rather than some vaguely threatening way to entangle them.[6]

But unfortunately, for better or worse, "homeland security" is the term we are stuck with for now. And whether we call the domestic fusion of national security and public safety, civil security, homeland security, or some other term, *a major systemic challenge continues to be establishing a common perspective in the minds of those who perform homeland security duties.*

REFERENCES

Federal Emergency Management Agency. "Emergency Management Assistance Compact (EMAC)." Accessed December 18, 2018. https://www.fema.gov/pdf/emergency/nrf/EMACoverviewForNRF.pdf.

Lundberg, Kristen. 2009. "The 2003 San Diego Firestorm." In *Managing Crises: Responses to Large Scale Emergencies*, edited by Arnold Howitt and Herman Leonard, 307. Washington, DC: CQ Press.

Merriam-Webster. "Business." Accessed December 18, 2018. https://www.merriam-webster.com/dictionary/business.

Center for Strategic and International Studies back in 2003. See https://www.csis.org/analysis/civil-security (accessed December 18, 2018).

[6] Some have suggested the alternative term "human security," and several academic programs that include this concept at their core have been established in the United States. I have no objection to this effort. But it doesn't quite address my concern about differing perspectives between national security and public safety. In fact if anything, it creates a new perspective with a new emphasis on social and global issues. I am looking for a term that will fuse existing safety and security concepts, not shift the focus from the nation-state.

15

Systemic Challenge #3: Theory (or Lack Thereof)

★ ★ ★

BOTTOM LINE UP FRONT

National security (NS) involves a coordinated effort to use nationally controlled resources to prevent violence between states and manage it if it does take place. This effort begins with intellectual constructs that explain the nature of the problem and theories (concepts of cause and effect) that can be tested with deductive research and analysis. Most importantly, NS is built upon the <u>integration</u> of constituent academic disciplines (political science, security studies, economics, etc.) and types of power (diplomatic, informational, intelligence, military, economic, domestic, etc.)

Homeland security offers no such central construct or integrated theoretical effort. Most of its constituent parts (from public safety) are practical professions whose application is based largely on inductive best practices and lessons learned. HS operators are mostly practitioners (police, fire, emergency responders, medical personnel, etc.) who work with minimum resources and see the victims of public safety failure "up close and personal" on a daily basis. They have little time for theoretical concepts, war games, and thought experimentswhen most of the answers they need can be gleaned from practical experience. While some homeland security–related disciplines are built on academic theory and inquiry (criminal justice, fire science, disease pathology, etc.), there are few sustained academic efforts to integrate those theories or address public safety as an interdisciplinary study. This is because there is little demand for HS theory. Most HS issues (traditional threats, vulnerabilities, and consequences) can be managed without reconceptualizing fundamental authorities, jurisdictions, and cultural norms. For day-to-day public safety challenges, lessons learned work just fine.

Additionally, NS theory development was additive. New military theories were developed for the new (nuclear) military context, with all their implications for budgets, personnel, organizations, operations, and so on, and then theories for the security and employment of other elements of national power were added. And because of the immediacy of their Cold War threat, those new requirements came with new resources. NS theory was built by adding responsibilities and resources.

In contrast, HS concepts are subtractive. Public safety originations, structures, policies, and careers are already in place. New duties impose new burdens—they rarely come with new resources. The integration of new responsibilities requires someone to surrender existing authority, funding, etc. This creates an inherent resistance from practitioners, especially when most homeland security events since 9/11 have been variations of problems public safety was already handling. The resulting climate throughout the HS enterprise is not conducive to the development of theories.

And yet, what if a Weapons of Mass Destruction (WMD) attack killing or injuring thousands actually took place? Is the "parallel play" between HS practitioners to which we have become accustomed adequate to meet the needs generated by such a system-changing event? Or do we need some sort of a forcing function to take our thinking beyond the solutions we know, to the challenges we may face?

The next (and final) chapter in this volume will see what Maximum of Maximums (MOMs events) can tell us about how to think about homeland security.

ACADEMIC THEORY AS A FOUNDATION OF NATIONAL SECURITY

French Prime Minister Clemenceau is credited with having said, "War is too important a matter to be left to the military." Many suppose this to mean that it should be left to politicians. But in the United States, the fundamental ideas that move national security generally emerge from academia. Scholars provide definitions, concept development, theory formulation, and data interpretation that shapes, bounds, and directs national security discussions. They educate the mid-level bureaucracy where the first drafts of strategies, policies, operational plans, bureaucratic organization, and resource budgets are written. And they analyze and evaluate the strategies and policies proposed by senior government leaders. Politicians and their staffs may popularize or delegitimize security ideas before the public. But those ideas usually arise from the halls of academia—especially if they involve the elements of national power—diplomacy, information, intelligence, military, and economics.

The trail that leads to current US diplomatic theory begins about the middle of the nineteenth century. Prior to the American Civil War, political issues were regarded in most major American universities as an extension of religion and ethics mixed with classical political philosophy. The few early courses and programs based on secular political inquiry were joined by many more in the late nineteenth century as science continued its shift from inductive to deductive (theory based) inquiry, and scientific discoveries accelerated the Industrial Revolution. A combination of government money (the Morrell Act of 1862) and private support (from new industrialists) joined with a new American model for universities that combined teaching and research. The result was a new emphasis on theory and applied research in many fields.

One of these academic fields was political science, energized by Colombia University's development of the first such academic department in 1880 and the founding of the American Political Science Association (APSA) in 1903. The fifth president of the APSA was Woodrow Wilson, who held the office from 1909–10, departing just four years before his election to president of the United States. Political scientists of the time thought of themselves as practical people developing practical solutions to real-world problems. But there is no question that some of the solutions they offered looked more like political theories than historical lessons learned. Many scholars regard the two big ideas that emerged from Wilson's Presidency— the 14 Points and the League of Nations—as political theories put into action.[1]

One academic response to the shocking carnage of World War I was the rise of a new subdiscipline within political science. International Relations (IR—first established circa 1919) consciously disregarded political concerns between people and within nations and focused on the interaction between states. IR labored for recognition in academia for twenty years before gaining general acceptance with the publication of *The Twenty Year Crisis* by Edmund Carr (1939). Carr's work codified a number of IR concepts to include realism and liberalism (addressed previously in chapter 7). After World War II, Carr became a strong voice for grounding diplomatic action

---

[1] For an excellent short summary of the development of political science in America, see "'Schools of Political Science' and the Formation of a Discipline" by Erkki Berndtson (2009)—a paper prepared for presentation at the XXIst World Congress of the International Political Science Association, July 12–16, 2009, Santiago de Chile, Chile. http://paperroom.ipsa.org/papers/paper_3767.pdf (accessed December 18, 2018).

on a theory-based view of statesmanship rather than the previous approach that tried to base behavior on an inductive review of the past.

With the emergence of the Cold War and thousands of nuclear weapons deployed on each side, it became clear that the world had entered a new age where relying on centuries-old lessons learned for political and military guidance was no longer advisable. With this new context in mind, IR theory sought ways to test and verify ideas about the new world of nuclear gamesmanship. And so academic theory emerged as the guiding force in diplomatic and military relations between nations—at least from a Western perspective.

"Military science" took a similar turn toward the theoretical at about the same time. For millennia concepts of military employment were driven largely by weapons technology and the ability to grow enough food to field a professional army. Bronze, iron, steel, sword, shield, javelin, spear, pike, musket, bayonet, rifle, machine gun, catapult, smooth bore cannon, rifled artillery—not to mention the steel plough, the railroad, and mass production—each of these technical advances was followed by new ways of generating and employing force. But about the middle of the twentieth century, the relationship between new technology and new ideas changed. Advances in science and engineering allowed military theorists to think about what they wanted to do to the enemy *in the future* and then develop the technology that accomplished it. Or to look at what a potential enemy might develop *in the future* and counter it.[2]

For example, although the limitations of early technology prevented aircraft from exerting a decisive role in World War I, forward-thinking military officers recognized that aviation would change the context in which war was waged forever. Visionaries saw that new concepts of employment (that is, theories) would be required, even if they differed over which concept to embrace.

German military theorists in the 1930s saw the aircraft as a way to support and advance ground combat. They built bombers with one or two engines and limited payload and range for use close to the front lines. This worked to their advantage on the European battlefield early in World War II. But later in the war they lacked the range to project decisive power against either English cities or the troops and logistical support massed in England for the invasion of France.

However, American and British air theorists of the 1930s anticipated using the airplane to leap over the front lines and strike industry, logistics,

---

[2] Today the Department of Defense (DOD) calls this approach a "Capabilities-Based Strategy."

and the populace in the enemy's rear. They pressed for long-range four engine bombers to support those theories. As a result, they were able to destroy their opponents' manufacturing, transportation, and population centers, thereby shortening war. New theories (like airpower) demanded new science and engineering, which drove successful practice.

When nuclear weapons appeared on the scene, practitioners immediately sought new ways to use them, first for attack and then for deterrence. Many senior military officers (including General Eisenhower) initially saw the atomic bomb as just a larger version of conventional munitions. But academic theorists like Brodie, Kahn, and Kissinger pressed for new concepts such as second-strike deterrence, penetrating bombers, ballistic missiles, submarine launched missiles, multiple independent reentry vehicles, and finally ballistic missile defense. These capabilities and many others grew out of theories about how opponents would act and react in this entirely new context. Because of the political implications of these ideas, the theories were primarily created, "tested," and advanced by political scientists and IR specialists.

These approaches to friend and foe were then converted into policy and practice by the various national security communities—DOD, Department of State (DOS), intelligence organizations, and so on—as strategies, treaties, doctrines, plans, operations, bureaucratic structures, capabilities, and budgets. Should we ally ourselves more closely with Pakistan or India? Defend forward in Europe or distribute forces to the Far East? Use tactical nuclear weapons early as a warning to an enemy or as a last resort after a breakthrough? Plan for a long-term presence in Afghanistan to build a stable government or announce an early withdrawal to pressure locals to act? Challenge Chinese military activities in the Pacific or tell our ships to give them a wide berth? Distribute space and cyber capabilities across the federal government or concentrate them in cyber and space Commands? Spend limited resources on more special operations forces or long-range bombers or State Department diplomacy? And what concepts and skills do we need to teach our upcoming public servants through training and education? The answers to all these questions and many more depend on how we think about NS.

In the years leading to the Cold War, academic theory also became a driving force in developing national economic power. By 1950, the great clash seemed to be between capitalism (generally recognized as emerging with Adam Smith, and in particular with his book *The Wealth of Nations*, published in 1776) and Marxism (a theory of the role of labor and class first fully presented in the *Communist Manifesto* in 1848). But actually, the more fundamental clash of theories was between the "Austrian School" (grounded in the Enlightenment and the concept of private ownership and decision-making) and socialism (a conceptual wedding of Marxism and Romanticism). The desperate search for economic solutions prompted by the Great Depression led to an American embrace of liberal Keynesian economics (emphasizing government intervention), followed by a push back by F. A. Hayek and other conservatives (emphasizing the "creative destruction" of free markets).

For nine decades this clash of economic theories has driven a clash of national economic strategies and policies. Can we make the United States richer and the liberal world order more stable at the same time? Should we implement the Trans-Pacific Partnership or not? Expand NAFTA or end it? Risk a trade war to protect American jobs? Raise military spending or cut taxes . . . or both? The answers we adopt spring from how we think about the intersection of economics and national security.[3]

So as the United States settled into what Churchill called "the long twilight struggle" against communism, academics adjusted to the new context by developing new concepts for leveraging all the powers of the state. Borrowing a term from the National Security Act of 1947, which put new military and intelligence structural approaches in place, academics called the new subdiscipline of political science *Security Studies*. After the jarring experience of Vietnam (and in the new postwar political context), many other theoretical subdisciplines emerged, including Peace Studies.

Table 15.1 presents a list of just some of the many academic theories that led to the strategies, policies, organizations, and technologies employed to advance and defend national security.

The point here is NOT to make the reader an expert in any of these ideas. The point is to understand that today the "operators" who populate the Department of State, Intelligence Community, the DOD, and various national economic programs derive guidance on the Ends they seek and the Ways and Means they employ largely from theories developed in academia and then expressed through the political process. This is possible because national security efforts are all focused on one goal: advancing national security interests within the context of international relations. Academia can design, test, and teach theories for achieving that goal.

---

[3] For an informative and hilarious short explanation of the battle of theories between Keynes and Hayek, see "Fear the Boom and Bust," https://www.google.com/search?q=keynes+vs.+hayek+rap+battle&cad=h , and "Fight of the Century," https://www.youtube.com/watch?v=GTQnarzmTOc.

Table 15.1 Examples of National Security Theoretical Constructs

Diplomacy (IR)	Intel Cycle[a]	Economics
• Realism	1. Requirements	• Mercantilism
• Liberalism (Values)	2. Collection	• Colonialism
• Balance of Power	3. Processing/ Exploitation	• Austrian Free Market
• Collective Security	4. Analysis and Production	• Keynesian
• International Regimes	5. Dissemination	• Government Market
• Hegemonic Stability	6. Consumption	• Marxist / Socialist
• Democratic Peace	7. Feedback	• Third Way
• Power Preponderance		

Military	Military (cont.)	Nuclear Conflict
• Attrition	• Precision War	• Massive Retaliation
• Annihilation	• Sequential War	• Deterrence; MAD
• Disruption/Paralysis	• Cumulative War	• First Strike–Second Strike
• Exhaustion	• Deterrence	• Counter value vs. Counter Force
• Symmetric vs. Asymmetric Attack	• Punishment	• Game Theory; Triad
• Sinews of War	• Denial	• Civil Defense, COG, COOP
• Nodal War	• Preemption	• Offense-Defense
• War of the Rings	• Combat Multipliers	• Massive Retaliation

[a] Note that some practical disciplines like intelligence substitute "frameworks" for theory. This is a promising way forward for homeland security academics.

HOMELAND SECURITY ACADEMIC THEORY: MISSING IN ACTION

In contrast, homeland security cannot lean on academic theory for either practical guidance or intellectual direction despite the entirely new context in which it operates. There is no single set of concepts of cause and effect to link HS Ways, Means, and Ends. Inherent tensions, narrow practitioner perspectives, and a lack of a common intellectual vision all mitigate against the development of theories as the basis for an integration of HS efforts.

When homeland security was first developed, in discussions before 9/11, and then after the creation of the new department, many people (including academics) thought there would be multiple parallels between homeland security and national security. This has turned out not to be the case.

First, while the elements of *International power* are clear (DIME), and the international interests they secure and advance are relatively well defined, the elements of *domestic power* are not so well delineated.[4]

- Is there a domestic equivalent of Diplomacy? Would that be federal, state, and local *politics* and the government agencies that implement policies after elections? Is the American political system a form of domestic power that must be protected? Against whom? And who is charged with that duty? The lingering questions about Russian interference in the 2016 presidential election, and the uncertainty about what to do in response, demonstrate how far we are from a theory of cause and effect that we could teach as part of HS curriculum.
- Does someone have a HS duty to protect domestic Information from hostile actors? Well, what information? Info belonging to whom? Isn't protecting bank records a bank responsibility? Isn't protection of local property records a local government responsibility? When does protection of industry information so endanger our military or economic power that it becomes a government homeland security issue?
- What is the HS version of military power? Law enforcement? Domestic intelligence? Should we be trying to protect them or enable them? Or maybe control them as new technology pushes old constitutional boundaries. But didn't our system already address this before HS was born? And by the way, when does an empowered police force become a police state? How do we avoid that outcome?
- Concerning economics, we actually have many theories for creating, protecting, and advancing domestic economic advantage. But they are manifested as domestic political arguments not security theories, played out in elections and legislative decisions, not public safety activities.
- And there may be other elements of domestic power. How about political legitimacy? Or the will and capability of the government, the military, or the people? Clausewitz sees maintaining a balance between these elements as a primary task of leaders (Clausewitz 1976, 89). Shouldn't they be secured from domestic attack? How?

I could go on. As explained in chapter 13, the jurisdictions and responsibilities for homeland security are fragmented, and ownership is divided

---

[4] See chapter 3. And please note my preference for a more expansive acronym (DIIME-D) which distinguishes between Information and Intelligence and adds Domestic Power as an element of national power. See chapter 9.

between federal, state, local, and private interests. By design of our Constitution, there is no central authority controlling every aspect of domestic security. The president cannot issue orders to local authorities; Congress cannot make laws concerning many local concerns; the federal courts are constrained from ruling on purely local issues. The Secretary of Defense must deal with only four military services, and he can issue orders to all of them.[5] The Secretary of Homeland Security must consider dozens of non-DHS federal law enforcement agencies and thousands of officers who carry badges and guns under nonfederal authority. Yet the Department of Homeland Security (DHS) can issue orders to almost none of these officers. The same is true concerning emergency managers, fire and medical personnel, operators and managers of critical infrastructure, and most of the other people and agencies that comprise homeland security. What sort of cause-and-effect relationship (theory) may be studied when so many independent variables are in play?

Second, almost everyone who works on national security issues does so full-time. By contrast, outside of DHS, most people who work on homeland security issues do so part-time and not as their primary responsibility. The result is a work force not inclined toward concepts that constrain their independence.

For example, first responders (police, fire, and emergency medical services, etc.) in any large city will be at the core of the response to a terrorist attack. But this is an additional duty for most of them, as they are hired, trained, and equipped for day-to-day police, fire, and medical duties. These daily duties are based on best practices and lessons learned rather than theories like those that drive national security operatives. In academia, those who teach HS-related individual professions at the university level (fire science, criminal justice, etc.) do not, as a rule, focus on how the professions integrate with others. There is no homeland security equivalent of Security Studies, which looks at how the various elements of national power are integrated to support an international objective.

Lastly, most of the professionals who contribute to homeland security as a part of their daily duties are really focused on public safety, not national security. The difference is not just semantic. Where the security of the nation as a whole is at stake, a certain level of loss of resources, infrastructure, and even lives is accepted as "the cost of doing business." But the whole point of public safety is to prevent precisely that kind of loss. A general who loses a battalion or an admiral who loses a ship in securing a national objective may still have accomplished his mission. A police chief

---

[5] Five Services in time of war as the Coast Guard transitions to duties in DOD. Six Services if you count the yet to be created Space Force.

who loses thirty students in an attack on a school but saves the rest of the people involved is not likely to regard his operation as a success. What theory can put the round peg of safety in the square hole of security?

The bottom line here is that national security plays out as an integrated effort to use nationally controlled resources in an effort to prevent or manage violence against the state externally. This effort begins with theories (concepts of cause and effect) that can be tested with research and analysis.

Homeland security offers no such centrally focused theoretical effort.

WHY NOT?

Actually, that is not quite correct. If there is one unifying idea—one core principle—at the heart of all homeland security efforts it is this: "Unity of Effort, not Unity of Command." The phrase comes from the Integrated Command System (ICS), a component of the National Incident Management System (NIMS).[6] Born before DHS or even HS, from efforts by the National Fire Service to coordinate unrelated units who show up to fight forest fires, it is a form of management by objective.

That is, an Incident Commander, who has no legal authority over units or individuals or equipment, may nonetheless coordinate their efforts successfully by getting all to agree on common objectives. If all the participants use a common map and lexicon, and a common organizational structure (so they know who is in charge of planning, food, fuel, medical assistance, etc.), and a central communications system for scheduling meetings, releasing information, and so on, then they can conduct complex operations with a minimum of confusion.[7] They can achieve unity of effort despite the fact that no single individual is technically "in command."[8]

---

[6] See the term "Unified Command" in *National Incident Management System*, 3rd ed. (Washington, DC: FEMA, October 2017), p. 22, https://www.fema.gov/media-library-data/1508151197225-ced8c60378c3936adb92c1a3ee6f6564/FINAL_NIMS_2017.pdf (accessed December 18, 2018).

[7] ICS, NIMS, and the National Preparedness System will be discussed in greater detail in a subsequent volume.

[8] Of course, with many safety and security issues it is quite clear who is in charge. A bar fight is almost always a matter for local courts. Prosecution for the murder of a state judge will usually fall to the state attorney general. An air attack on the United States is a matter for the NORAD commander; a ballistic missile attack, for the NORTHCOM commander (who conveniently is the same person). Addressing an improvised nuclear device itself is the business of the Department of Energy. Tracking the network that delivered it domestically is a task led by the FBI. Stopping drugs at the border is a Border and Customs Protection (BCP) task. Confiscating drug shipments inside the border is generally an ICE (or DEA) matter. Coordinating national health warnings is for the CDC. National terrorist threat warnings are issued by DHS. National storm warnings by NOAA's Storm Prediction Center. No one shares these duties through "unity of effort." But while individual issues

While the phrase was created for emergency management operations, the central idea (we will all share information and trust to each other's professionalism to get the job done) is a pretty good summary of how DHS does much of its business inside the department. FEMA crafts frameworks, provides guidance, and controls funding in many areas but enforces few regulations. The Cybersecurity and Infrastructure Security Agency distributes information, publishes guidance, matches corporations with Special Interest Groups, and oversees protection of some special interest sites but has little directive authority. The same is true for DHS interaction with fusion centers and risk managers. Outside of DHS, the rules differ by department, states, and localities, but the same approach generally applies: the concept of central command authority common among national security organizations is missing among most HS organizations *by design*.

The result across the entire homeland security enterprise is exactly what you might expect: everyone is enthusiastic about maintaining their own authority and increasing their resources, but no one wants to surrender anything in order to integrate with others. Child psychologists have a term for the situation where young children play close to others but do not make the sacrifice of toys, autonomy, and decision-making required to integrate their activities. It is called "parallel play." It is not my intent here to denigrate anyone, and especially not the heroic responders who spend their lives (sometimes literally) in the service of others. But parallel play is not an unfair description of ICS.

The results of all these independent operations are mixed. For example, in Texas where emergency management is well funded and preparedness a high priority, Texas Task Force 1 demonstrated in Hurricane Harvey that its global reputation is well deserved. In Puerto Rico, where funding and expertise are in shorter supply, local efforts in Hurricane Maria quickly proved insufficient.

The bottom line is that all this autonomy and independence makes creating unified theories nearly impossible. There are just too many actors, too many variables, too many novel conditions, and too many unique outcomes as a result. Homeland security does not have anything like the array of theories that mark the national security community or the clear line to strategies, policies, operations, and resource decisions that those theories produce.

---

and situations may be assigned to specific chains of command, complex situations like national preparedness (prevention, protection, mitigation, response, and recovery) for major earthquakes, storms, WMD, etc., generally involve multiple agencies who must collaborate without surrendering their autonomy. Unity of Effort is the current solution.

THIS LACK OF THEORY IS NOT FOR LACK OF TRYING

Graduate education is about understanding and changing the world by analyzing, evaluating, synthesizing, and creating theories. Educators who teach at this level know that something is missing in HS. Without theory, inquiry is unfocused—it can be used reliably only to understand the past, not to influence the future. Without theory, researchers do not know what data to collect, how to focus on what matters, how to identify cause and effect, or how to establish a standard for peer review. Without theory, there is no basis for recommendations that go beyond the case at hand. We are constrained to lessons learned from individual case studies from the past instead of frameworks that provide insights into different cases in the future. Without theory, HS education is reduced to addressing training issues from a different perspective, which is where many educational programs reside today.

But this lack of theory is not for lack of trying among dedicated academics.

- Nearly two years before 9/11, Colonel Randall Larsen (USAF), Director of the Department of Military Strategy at the National War College, organized the first academic conference on homeland security. Attendees included William Sessions (former head of the FBI), Newt Gingrich (Speaker of the House of Representatives), and numerous other strategists and government leaders. As Dean of the National War College, I sponsored the meeting. We spent the entire day trying to define HS. We did not identify a single theory of national security that applied to the new topic.
- Shortly thereafter, Analytic Services, Inc. (a public service research company) hired Colonel Larsen to head a small think tank focused on HS. In the months after 9/11, Larsen made several thousand media, academic, and public presentations in which he noted the early focus on operations over strategy. No theories of HS were ever identified.[9]
- In the days just before and soon after 9/11, a number of DC think tanks, including CSIS, CATO, Brookings, and Heritage published articles and hosted events focused on homeland security. Topics addressed were consistently policy related. None ever offered an academic theory to advance the discipline.

---

[9] Full disclosure: Larsen hired me as his deputy three weeks before 9/11. I had the same experience he did, conducting thousands of presentations and interviews with business, government, media, and academia. No one ever suggested a theory of HS . . . or asked for it.

- Soon after DHS was created (spring 2003), it established a Director of Education. His focus quickly turned to satisfying requirements generated within DHS. This approach spawned the many "Centers of Excellence" that involve more than a hundred universities addressing DHS needs today. But developing general theories of homeland security is not among their duties. Nor is that the business of the DHS Education Officer (who focuses on training and higher education for the DHS workforce) or of the Homeland Security Academic Advisory Council (a group of university leaders sponsored by the DHS Office of Academic Engagement who provide high-level input but do not propose curriculum development).
- US Northern Command (NORTHCOM) in Colorado Springs was created six months before DHS. Its first commander, General Ed Eberhard (USAF) was a product of the extensive military education system and commanded the North American Air Defense Command on 9/11. He was determined not to be caught by surprise again, and NORTHCOM soon emerged as the early national leader in HS education. Under the guidance of his Education Officer, Dr. Stan Supinski, NORTHCOM hosted multiple academic meetings and one of the largest HS public conferences in the nation for several years in a row. The meetings were key to the formation of early HS curriculum, and many attendees went on to successful academic careers with leading universities. I attended all of these meetings. Although the lack of a HS theory was identified, no one ever offered a useful answer to the problem.
- With the support of Leon Panetta (former Clinton chief of staff, former director of the Office of Management and Budget, and former Budget Committee chairman, US House of Representatives), the Center for Homeland Defense and Security was established at the Naval Postgraduate School in Monterrey, California, in 2003. Although located at a military facility, the program was developed as a partnership with the National Preparedness Directorate of FEMA. Over time it came to offer the world's best online library on HS topics, a wide variety of training programs (including for faculty), a master's degree in homeland security that today is the gold standard for such programs in the United States, and a university partnership program that includes more than 350 schools. One of their most important offerings is an annual academic conference which has become the leading such event in the nation. But despite many panels and discussions over the years, no central HS theory or set of theories has emerged from their efforts.[10]

---

[10] The staff and leadership of the Center of Homeland Defense and Security (CHDS) should be commended for the positive influence they have had in the teaching of HS nationwide. Stan Supinski set the proper tone as the first outreach coordinator to the CHDS University

- At roughly the same time, the FEMA Higher Education Program (a part of the Emergency Management Institute at Emmitsburg, Maryland) matured into a serious academic endeavor. Born out of Civil Defense efforts, energized during James Lee Witt's tenure as Clinton's FEMA administrator, and sustained through many lean years by the efforts of Dr. Wayne Blanchard, the program has traditionally offered four major benefits to emergency management participants:
  - an excellent set of free college level online courses for individuals;
  - connectivity to high-quality FEMA training courses (so that training and education curriculum may be integrated);
  - an excellent newsletter providing a review of EM educational issues nationwide;
  - an annual conference helping hundreds of faculty and EM officials to update curriculum with the latest information.

Most recently the program has added regional conferences to increase its unifying influence on university programs. But the program continues to focus on lessons learned and lessons to be learned, not theories.

- In the years between 9/11 and Hurricane Katina, the EMI program and EM as a whole struggled to define its relationship with homeland security. Dr. Claire Rubin helped to resolve what might be called a momentary crisis of confidence among EM educators by publishing an excellent history of disasters that showed the continuity of EM development over the last century.[11] And Dr. Dave McEntire (no relation to this author) solidified the intellectual foundation of EM as the sparkplug of a working group that published the *Principles of Emergency Management*, now widely used to help define the subject.[12] That said, there are still some who believe HS should be a subset of EM rather than the other way around. And despite all these efforts, no coherent HS theory has emerged.

---

and Agency Partnership Initiative (UAPI). His extraordinary effort and results have been matched by the current coordinator, Steve Recca, https://www.chds.us/c/academic-programs/uapi (accessed December 18, 2018). A turning point of sorts was reached at the October 2018 conference at SUNY Albany, when an entire plenary session was devoted to the issue of Homeland Security Theory (and the lack thereof).

[11] Claire B. Rubin, *Emergency Management: The American Experience 1900–2010,*2nd ed. (Boca Raton, FL: CRC Press, 2012).

[12] Wayne Blanchard et al., *Principles of Emergency Management*, Emergency Management Institute (Emmitsburg, MD: FEMA Higher Education Program, September 11, 2007), https://www.fema.gov/media-library-data/20130726-1822-25045-7625/principles_of_emergency_management.pdf (accessed December 18, 2018).

- Many of the nation's military educational institutions (staff colleges, war colleges, etc.) have worked hard to fit HS curriculum (focused on the military role of Defense Support of Civil Authorities) into a curriculum built on strategic NS theories. The most sustained effort (and in many ways the most influential) has been by Bert Tussing of the Army War College, whose insightful presence at dozens of conferences over the last fifteen years has inspired countless faculty to redouble their efforts to integrate the elements of HS studies.[13] Alas no one has yet integrated these efforts with theory.
- In addition to these institutional efforts, several private organizations have attempted to establish a national academic footing for HS. One of the most notable was the Homeland Security/Defense Educational Consortium, directed by Lydia Staiano and Vince Henry of Long Island University. More recently members of the International Society for Preparedness, Resilience and Security (INSPRS—with James Ramsey, University of New Hampshire, as ramrod) put two years of effort into creating a core curriculum for undergraduate programs in HS, based on knowledge domains and skill sets identified by HS subject-matter experts.[14] But neither of these efforts produced anything that looked like the theory base that defines national security studies.[15]

In print, where academia leaves its mark, several efforts to address the lack of HS theory stand out.

- Chris Bellavita's early work at CHDS laid the groundwork for theory by trying to define homeland security (nearly ten years after Randy Larsen's initial effort—see above). In the process he demonstrated the difficulty of a creating a theory that combines a focus on terrorism, all hazards, catastrophes, jurisdictions, meta hazards, and national security (Bellavita 2008).
- His subsequent article comparing the search for HS theory with Albert Camus's famous existential work "Waiting for Godot" captures

---

[13] This is not to denigrate the efforts of other military institutions. The Naval War College and the Command and General Staff College at Ft. Leavenworth, KS, in particular, routinely provide valuable contributions to academic conferences.

[14] Paul Stockton et al., *Development of Competency Based Education Standards for Homeland Security Academic Programs: Report for Undergraduate Degree Programs,* INSPRS, January 2017. It is impossible to name everyone who has worked on this and similar projects, but the efforts of John Comiskey, Monmouth University; Mike Collier, Eastern Kentucky; Nadav Morag, San Houston State; Irmak Renda-Tanali, University of Maryland; and Paul Thompson, Penn State Harrisburg deserve special note.

[15] To this list I would add my own efforts first at ANSER and then with the Integrative Center for Homeland Security Texas A&M. These are listed in some detail in the introduction to this volume. I do not yet count a theory of HS among my accomplishments. But see chapter 16.

the frustration many serious scholars felt (and still feel) about their discipline's inability to create a paradigm to describe the HS effort as a whole (Bellavita 2012).

- Given the importance of this topic, the population of academic articles addressing it is surprisingly thin. Like Larsen and Bellavita, James Ramsay, and Linda Kiltz tried to frame the subject by suggesting that we view HS through several different "lenses" at once. That is, think of HS as a problem in criminal justice, international relations, and organizational design all at the same time (Kiltz and Ramsay 2012). It is a useful explanation of the complexity of our problem, but it needs several examples in order to show how such a complex problem could be addressed by a simple theoretical approach.

- Richard White, Tina Bynum, and Stan Supiski took a big step forward in describing the holistic nature of our problem in their seven-hundred-page text that redefines homeland security as "safeguarding the US from domestic catastrophic destruction" (White 2016). The idea is to focus efforts on the effect (catastrophic destruction), regardless of the cause (attack, hazard, or natural disaster) (White 2016, 139). It is a clever way to sidestep the problem of addressing so many threats and highlights the limitations of the "All Hazards" approach from EM. Clearly all catastrophes are not the same—preparing for one will not prepare for all. But this excellent opus stops just short of telling us what to do about the problem, which is pretty much the definition of a theory.[16]

- And finally, a number of fine conventional texts are now available for educational purposes, most describing in detail the history, organization, and challenge of homeland security today. One of my favorites is *Managing Crises* by editors Arnold Howitt and Herman Leonard (2009). Although a little dated, the long list of case studies drives home the point that the challenge of PS/EM/HS events is not their scale but their novelty. That is, with training and resources we can respond to easily recognized big events based on lessons learned. Problems arise when we face new types of disasters that defy our efforts at "unity of effort" based on previous experiences. For these events, we need theories and concepts, not doctrine and dogma.

---

[16] Richard and I have spent many profitable hours discussing this idea over coffee. His excellent treatment of "catastrophic destruction" is not far from the suggestion at the core of this work that we focus our academic inquiry on MOMs, which quickly demonstrate the flaw in the "all hazards" approach. It doesn't address all hazards. I take the argument a bit further in suggesting that there may be too many variables in HS to ever craft a "theory of everything." My solution (Spoiler Alert) is to identify the core problem—bureaucracy—and use existing theories to create solutions unique to the homeland security context. See chapter 16.

Unfortunately, my twenty-one years of experience in this field of study teaches me that despite the best efforts of a number of first-class institutions and academics, no theory of HS has emerged.

SO WHAT? WHAT DIFFERENCE DOES ALL THIS MAKE?

Our problem is that working without theories leaves HS education exactly where NS education was at the dawn of the nuclear age: trying to apply lessons learned from the past in an entirely new context. The next volume in this series focuses on this new context as the New Normal.

This is fine if you assume that "All Hazards" training really does prepare you for all the hazards you are likely to face.

- But the fact that we have not faced a global pandemic since the Great Influenza of 1918–19 does not mean that we won't face an even worse biological challenge in the future. In fact, new technology makes biological disasters increasingly likely.[17]
- Earthquake experts tell us that modern growth and population density turn inevitable earthquakes along existing fault lines into inevitable disasters.[18]
- In mid-2018, the Federation of American Scientists moved the hands of their famous "Doomsday Clock" (predicting the likelihood of a nuclear conflict) to the most dangerous position since the height of the Cold War.[19]

---

[17] On December 13, 2017, in testimony before the US Senate Committee on Agriculture, Nutrition and Forestry, former Senator Joseph Lieberman explained the concern of a year-long study by the Blue Ribbon Panel on Biodefense that animals and agriculture can become major targets of biological terrorism. https://www.agriculture.senate.gov/imo/media/doc/Testimony_Lieberman.pdf (accessed December 18, 2018).

[18] To explain the implications of a major earthquake for our modern society, the US Geological Survey created a scenario showing the impact of a 7.0 event along the Hayward fault line. This single fifty-two-mile fault line, one of many just in California, could leave 18,000 injured, 22,000 trapped, and 150,000 households displaced. Such an event has occurred at this location roughly every hundred years for the last two millennia. The next is fifty years overdue. https://www.usgs.gov/media/videos/haywired-scenario-movie (accessed December 18, 2018).

[19] While there is a political aspect to the judgments of the Bulletin of the Atomic Scientists, they do represent a respected voice in the debate over nuclear weapons since its founding in 1945 by "University of Chicago scientists who helped develop the first atomic weapons in the Manhattan Project." In 2018 the organization moved the clock to "2 minutes before midnight . . . the closest the Clock has ever been to Doomsday, and as close as it was in 1953, at the height of the Cold War." Their argument is that "nuclear weapons are poised to become more rather than less usable because of nations' investments in their nuclear arsenals. This is a concern that the *Bulletin* has been highlighting for some time, but momentum toward this new reality is increasing." https://thebulletin.org/2018-doomsday-clock-statement/ (accessed December 18, 2018).

- A congressionally sponsored research commission has argued that "the critical national infrastructure in the United States faces a present and continuing *existential* [emphasis added] threat from . . . manmade electromagnetic pulse (EMP) attack, as well as from natural EMP from a solar superstorm."[20] In his *New York Times* bestseller *Lights Out*, respected newsman Ted Kopple (2015) warns against the same sort of nation-paralyzing impact on the electrical grid, but based on a cyber attack.

The list goes on. Practically every major threat identified in the National Strategic Threat Assessment has a civilization-ending version involving modern technology in the hands of modern fanatics or something nearly as bad produced by the statistical inevitabilities of a merciless Mother Nature.[21]

Given the changes in our nation's population density, geographic distribution, and vulnerabilities, these new catastrophes would make our previous disasters look like a minor league warm-up game. Are our leaders and our responders, our citizens and our families, really ready for this? The answer is no, first and foremost, because we have not come to grips

---

[20] *TheCommission to Assess the Threat to the United States from Electromagnetic Pulse (EMP) Attack* was established by Congress in FY 2001, in order to investigate and report on the potential for and implications for the United States of an EMP event (natural or man-made). It has released a number of reports to include executive reports in 2004, 2008, and 2018. The last was apparently one of ten prepared before the commission was dissolved. Seven are reportedly awaiting declassification by DOD. The reports by sober and recognized experts in the field are apocalyptic in substance and tone, arguing that large parts of the United States can be reduced to "life without electricity" for years and perhaps decades. They argue for immediate, dramatic Congressional action. https://michaelmabee.info/wp-content/uploads/2018/05/2017-Life-Without-Electricity-FINAL-April2018.pdf (December 18, 2018). Not everyone agrees. In particular, The Electric Power Research Institute (which promotes "A (more) Electrified Future") argues the threat of EMP is significantly overblown and expensive new protections are not required. https://www.epri.com/#/?lang=en (accessed December 18, 2018).

[21] Writing nightmare scenarios is not difficult. I used to ask my students to imagine and describe one. I stopped. It was too easy. But what is striking is the number of such Jeremiads written over the last two decades by sober-minded politically astute professionals from across the political spectrum. Clinton National Security Adviser Anthony Lake (*6 Nightmares* [2000]), Pulitzer Prize winner Judith Miller (*Germs* [Miller, Engelberg, and Broad 2001]), CDC Champion of Prevention award winner Richard Preston (*The Demon on the Freezer* [2003]), Kennedy School sage Graham Allison (*Nuclear Terrorism* [2004]), internationally acclaimed newsman Ted Kopple (*Lights Out* [2015]), Chairman of the House Homeland Security Committee Michael McCaul (*Failures of Imagination* [2016]), former chair of the Senate Homeland Security Committee Senator Joe Lieberman and first Secretary of Homeland Security Tom Ridge (co-chairs, *Blue Ribbon Study Panel on Biodefense*, 2018), and many more national thought leaders have penned clear, fact-based warnings that something really wicked is coming this way. The nation has sighed, and returned to *Dancing with the Stars*.

intellectually with the domestic threats we face and the actions required to meet them.

Thus, the third systemic challenge we face is that we lack theories for domestic security in the New Normal of looming catastrophic disasters.

Theories teach the habit of inquiry—questioning cause and effect—so that even if the theory is wrong, it prepares you to think your way through new and novel situations in the future. This is what makes graduate-level thinking different from training and graduate-level approaches useful even in an entirely new context. Without theories, homeland security thinking can't take full advantage of the educational leverage that has marked the progress of the Western world since the Enlightenment.

WHAT CAN WE DO ABOUT THIS? ASK OUR MOMS

So . . . what is to be done?

In one respect the intellectual challenge of HS is the inverse of what NS faced in the 1950s. **With NS the problem was additive.** We developed new theories of military (nuclear) force and added new theories (and funding) for the additional elements of national power (diplomatic, economic, etc.) over time. Fitting the powers together was somewhat intuitive as our holistic concept of national security grew. And we had a forcing function that gave the work momentum and immediacy—the threat of the Cold War turning Hot at any moment.

With HS our problem is subtractive. Public safety jurisdictions and practitioners already exist with tasks, powers, authorities, and resources divided between them. To integrate these elements of domestic power, even in theory, somebody—in fact, just about everybody—has to give something up. To overcome the resistance from inherent tensions and hostility from parochial practitioners, *we need a reason to compromise and think anew as national security had to do in the face of threats to our national survival.*

Interestingly, we have such a forcing function: the MOMs, including WMD attacks. We just have not used it.

In chapter 12, we saw that since 9/11 we have been able to adapt procedures (the FBI), evolve capabilities (DOD/ NORTHCOM), and create organizations (DHS) resulting in a new systemic response to domestic safety. And that system now seems to work well with traditional challenges (storms, routine criminal issues, etc.). But homeland security was created because of nontraditional threats (WMD) so great that the security of the nation as a whole was endangered. These threats have not disappeared, but they have not been fully addressed either, largely because the cost (not just in money but in surrendered authority and autonomy) of addressing the systemic challenges identified in chapters 13, 14, and 15 is higher than most charged with HS are willing to pay.

In chapter 16, we will investigate whether the start point for homeland security—the threat of WMD (MOMs)—might provide the motivation we need.

REFERENCES

Allison, Graham. 2004. *Nuclear Terrorism*. New York: Henry Holt.

Bellavita, Christopher. June 2008. "Changing Homeland Security: What is Homeland Security?" *Homeland Security Affairs* 4 (1). Accessed December 18, 2018. https://www.hsaj.org/articles/118.

Bellavita, Christopher. August 2012. "Waiting For Homeland Security Theory." *Homeland Security Affairs* 8 (15). Accessed December 18, 2018. https://www.hsaj.org/articles/231.

Berndtson, Erkki. 2009. "'Schools of Political Science' and the Formation of a Discipline." Department of Political Science, P.O. Box 54 (Unioninkatu 37) 00014 University of Helsinki, Finland. Accessed December 18, 2018. http://paperroom.ipsa.org/papers/paper_3767.pdf.

Blanchard, Wayne, et al. 2007. *Principles of Emergency Management*. Emmitsburg, MD: Emergency Management Institute, FEMA Higher Education Program. Accessed December 18, 2018. https://www.fema.gov/media-library-data/20130726-1822-25045-7625/principles_of_emergency_management.pdf.

Bronson, Rachael, et al. January 25, 2018. "It Is Now Two Minutes to Midnight." Chicago, IL: Bulletin of the Atomic Scientists. Accessed December 18, 2018. https://thebulletin.org/2018-doomsday-clock-statement/.

Clausewitz, Carl von. 1976. "Book One, Chapter One What is War?" In *On War*. Translated by Machael Howard and Petr Paret. Princeton, NJ: Princeton University Press.

FEMA. October 2017. *National Incident Management System*. 3d ed. Washington, DC: FEMA. Accessed December 18, 2018. https://www.fema.gov/media-library-data/1508151197225-ced8c60378c3936adb92c1a3ee6f6564/FINAL_NIMS_2017.pdf.

Howitt, Arnold, and Herman Leonard, eds. 2009. *Managing Crises: Responses to Large-Scale Emergencies*. 1st Edition. Washington, DC: CQ Press.

Kiltz, Linda, and James D. Ramsay. August 2012. "Perceptual Framing of Homeland Security." *Homeland Security Affairs* 8 (16). Accessed December 18, 2018. https://www.hsaj.org/articles/230.

Kopple, Ted. 2015. *Lights Out (A Cyberattack. A Nation Unprepared. Surviving the Aftermath)*. New York: Crown.

Lake, Anthony. 2000. *6 Nightmares*. New York: Little, Brown.

Lieberman, Senator Joseph. December 13, 2017. "Safeguarding American Agriculture in a Globalized World." Hearing of the Senate Committee on Agriculture, Nutrition, and Forestry: Washington, DC: US Senate. Accessed December 18, 2018. https://www.agriculture.senate.gov/imo/media/doc/Testimony_Lieberman.pdf.

Mabee, Michael. Mike's Blog. Accessed July 10, 2018. https://michaelmabee.info/category/mikes-blog/ [Mabee is an author who maintains the most comprehensive list available at a single location of reports by the now defunded *Commission to Assess the Threat to the United States from Electromagnetic Pulse (EMP) Attack*.]

McCaul, Michael. 2016. *Failures of Imagination*. New York: Crown Forum.

Miller, Judith, Stephen Engelberg, and William Broad. 2011. *Germs: Biological Weapons and America's Secret War*. New York: Simon & Schuster.

Preston, Richard. 2002. *The Demon in the Freezer*. New York: Random House.

White, Richard, Tina Bynum, and Stan Supiski. 2016. *Homeland Security: Safeguarding the US from Domestic Catastrophic Destruction*. Colorado Springs, CO: CW Productions.

Rubin, Claire B. 2012. *Emergency Management: The American Experience 1900–2010*. 2nd ed. Boca Raton, FL: CRC Press.

Stockton, Paul, et al. January 2017. *Development of Competency Based Education Standards for HomelandSecurity Academic Programs: Report for Undergraduate Degree Programs by the Education Standards Committee*. INSPRS.

16

How to Think about Homeland Security: Go Ask Your MOMs

★ ★ ★

THE MOTHER OF ALL BOTTOM LINES UP FRONT

In the first fifteen chapters of this volume we learned that homeland security poses a unique problem for our nation because it exists at the imperfect intersection of two major functions of government—national security and public safety. Accomplishing these tasks is tough enough when the threats and challenges are isolated into traditional fields with their own perspectives, histories, cultures, theories, beliefs and training, and education regimes. When they overlap in a new way—when international threats are manifested in the domestic space—then adhering to successful practices that worked in the past may actually impede the new ideas, perspectives, and solutions required for the future.

Today, our national security thinkers and practitioners remain focused primarily on international threats in the international space. Most public safety officials charged with homeland security responsibilities already have other full time duties and see Homeland Security (HS) as an extension of the lessons they have learned while focused entirely on traditional domestic challenges. And the few leaders and practitioners charged with homeland security as a primary duty—with securing national power and interests at home—lack the authority, and frequently the vision, to require a new synthesis of domestic actors and actions focused on national level security threats in the domestic space.

The good news is that many of our federal, state, local, and industry organizations have done a good job of adapting, evolving, and creating new ways to cooperate—especially for the traditional high probability–low consequence events where professional experience from the past may be applied.

The bad news is that we have not made the same progress against the national-level threats HS was intended to address. Progress is especially hindered by three systemic challenges: jurisdictions and authorities; practitioner perspectives; and inadequate theories.

The problem is not that these challenges are impossible to meet. We are meeting them regularly for traditional threats (minor criminal attacks and major hazards/natural disasters). And we are getting better and better at cooperating in complex contingencies.

But for high-end, nontraditional challenges, especially the extreme consequences of Weapons of Mass Destruction (WMD), voluntary cooperation (Unity of Effort vice Unity of Command) may not be enough. Meeting the extreme challenges of the most extreme situations (Maximum of Maximums [MOMs]) will require existing practices and practitioners to surrender existing power, authority, and resources so their efforts can be integrated. We are still not thinking clearly about that problem.

Examining even a single Security MOM (for example, a nuclear event in the United States) demonstrates why current thinking about HS remains inadequate. The challenge is just too enormous, too complex, for well-established bureaucracies to make the major adjustments required in the moment of crisis.

Researching, analyzing, evaluating, and synthesizing new theories to address this New Normal, and creating in the process new professional perspectives, is the job of the academic community. Its tool of choice is inquiry—using the right language to ask the right questions, in a way that will promote clear thinking and elicit useful analysis, evaluation, and solutions. But despite hard work and the best of intentions, most HS inquiry remains focused on best solutions to the manageable challenges of the past instead of new solutions for the nation changing mega-disasters that threaten our future.

The distressing fact is that after nearly twenty years of hard work at every level (federal, state, local, and industry), our HS efforts today prepare us least for the threats most likely to damage our national security. We need a new mental construct—a new way of thinking—to explain the special danger of extreme homeland security challenges and the necessity of combining national security and public safety contributions in the domestic space.

One way to break through to a new paradigm so we can create new ways to think about HS is to <u>shift our focus for intellectual inquiry from the worst that is likely to happen to the worst that could reasonably happen</u>: from high probability–low consequence events to low-probability-but-decidedly-possible-high-consequence events (MOMs). The highest *consequences would be from major events that threaten the power and existence of the nation. I call such events Security MOMs.*[a]

University-level analysis and evaluation of these extreme threats and systemic challenges, combined with the application of well-established theories about changing bureaucracies, might begin to address the gap in HS thinking. The work of Bob Gates in leadership, John Kotter in business, Donald Kettl in governance, Graham Allison in crisis, and Edward Deming in Quality Systems Management would be a good place to start.

WOULDA-COULDA-SHOULDA: WHAT WE MIGHT HAVE DONE

Homeland security (HS) was born of the realization that the security of the nation could now be threatened in the domestic arena by international attacks from nonstate actors. After 9/11, "National Security Threat" was the key to our alarm. We were not worried about being hurt at home. We were worried about being *destroyed* at home by a new sort of enemy using a new sort of attack—terrorists wielding WMD.

For most of our history, domestic dangers—crime, wildfires, hazardous material spills, major storms, and so on—played out as localized events and were rightly addressed as matters of public safety. Even when events caused significant casualties (at least eight thousand dead in the Galveston Hurricane of 1900) or struck a large region (twenty-seven thousand square miles in the Great Mississippi Flood of 1927), the security of the nation as a whole was not imperiled. Localities might struggle, local officials call for assistance, and federal officials supply resources, but a coordinated nationwide solution was not imposed. The one exception was Civil Defense, which was actually more about the survival of the nation with its ability to fight back intact than the survival of individual citizens.

Only recently have domestic risks (threats, vulnerabilities, and consequences) risen to a level that demands a true national-level response. Federal, state, and local public safety organizations have responded well in evolving, adapting, and creating traditional capabilities to meet ever larger traditional challenges. But our ability to prepare for, respond to, and recover from catastrophic events that challenge the national security has

---

[a] Risk Management (prioritizing resources against risks) is the way thoughtful leadership addresses the fact that the nation faces more threats and vulnerabilities than its resources can address. This essay is NOT a call to change that rational approach to National Preparedness. But it IS a call for the academic community to take a different approach to homeland security education. Instead of regarding their programs as a broader and deeper extension of existing public safety training and ideas, educators should be asking how the security of the nation is threatened by the potential of new Security MOMs and what new synthesis of strategies, policies, operations, bureaucracies, etc. could best address those concerns.

not yet been proven, or really even tested. In particular, our preparedness for terrorist attacks on the sinews of national power—the events homeland security was founded to address—seems to have plateaued.[1] And our shortcomings appear to be not just minor flaws but systemic.

In other disciplines (economics, politics, defense), systemic flaws are investigated, theories tested, and policies developed by intellectual inquiry; concepts of cause and effect born in academic institutions are used to organize and interpret practical lessons learned, which are then converted into policy and taught in training venues. But in HS . . . not so much.

Unfortunately, our early decisions about homeland security education were made under pressure. We expected another attack soon after 9/11, so our intellectual approach to the new threat was built backwards. We should have looked closely at what was new and started from scratch. We should have thought differently about homeland security.

But we were in a hurry. So we began with public safety training already in place (like CBRNE response to natural and man-made hazards), and educational programs already established (like courses on traditional state-sponsored terrorism). We built on these existing programs and tried to extend them into the new ill-defined space called homeland security.

Not surprisingly, the result has been imperfect. Today, surveillance and security capabilities designed to protect national assets are bleeding over into routine law enforcement activities. Special preparedness required for national-level catastrophes is taking second place to improving routine response, recovery, and resilience, under the theory that training for "all hazards" is the same as preparing for "the worst hazards." A focus on high-probability/local-consequence events is winning out over low-probability/national-consequence threats.[2] And one of our primary tools for analyzing and creating preparedness capabilities (CPG 201: Threat and Hazard Identification

---

[1] As we will discover in a later volume, terrorism has many different definitions, depending on how the person or organization using the term wants to leverage it against a perpetrator. The FBI may wish to leverage the law against individual lawbreakers; the Department of State may wish to leverage sanctions against a nation or group; academics may wish to leverage data sets to advance a theory; nonprofits may wish to leverage statistics to promote domestic abuse laws; etc. This widespread habit of shopping the definition of terrorism in order to maximize leverage makes developing counterterrorism strategies, policies, and operations difficult. For the purposes of homeland security, I focus on the concept of terrorism as a form of insurgency—as criminal war, waged against the nation for political purposes. When armed with WMD, the result is a form of terrorism that poses a Threat at the National Security Level (a danger to the "TNSL Strength of the Nation"). This concept will be further examined in Volume 2.

[2] As just one of many examples, Senator Lieberman cited before Congress (December 13, 2017) the discovery of his own Blue Ribbon Study Panel on Biodefense that although threats to agriculture constitute a serious threat to the nation itself, "Agrodefense appears to be an orphan, with long-view funding and policy priority finding a home in neither the Department of Homeland Security (DHS) nor USDA." www.agriculture.senate.gov/imo/media/doc/Testimony_Lieberman.pdf.

Risk Analysis Guide) emphasizes a local rather than a regional or national perspective. It is as though the Department of Defense (DOD) focused their efforts on doctrine, training, and equipping of the entire force for counter-insurgency and stability operations, trusting that the resulting capabilities would be adequate for major war against China or Russia in a pinch.

This is not to suggest that DOD ignore the small wars that are now a daily reality in favor of focusing exclusively on unlikely but catastrophic major wars. Nor should homeland security practitioners abandon their focus on the routine dangers that face the citizens they serve every day. But we need to strike a balance.

One way to strike that balance would be for practitioners to continue their focus on lessons learned, while homeland security educators explore the potential national level incidents, called in the vernacular MOMs, that most endanger the nation.[3,4] The resulting findings, conclusions, and recommendations (constantly revised by new scholarship) could then balance traditional lessons learned with ideas for new policies, operations, organizations, and resources to address the New Normal in national-level threats.

To be clear, this is not a criticism of public safety practitioners or of DHS. Every major event since the retooling of DHS after Hurricane Katrina in 2005 has seen:

- Improved anticipation of risk based on the adoption of Risk Management concepts and guidance created by DHS, and Coordinated Planning Guidance 201;

---

[3] This FEMA terminology may have originated with the National Hurricane Center, which calculates MOM storm surges as "a worst case snapshot for a particular storm category under 'perfect' storm conditions." See National Hurricane Center. "Storm Surge Maximum of Maximums." http://www.nhc.noaa.gov/surge/momOverview.php (accessed December 18, 2018). Today the term is extended to imply the worst-case situation for all threats. David Graham describes the concept and implications clearly in "The Mothers of All Disasters," *The Atlantic*, September 2, 2015, https://www.theatlantic.com/national/archive/2015/09/the-disaster-next-time/403063/ (accessed December 18, 2018). A good starting point for understanding the scale of maximum disasters is the FEMA list of fifteen National Planning Scenarios. See https://emilms.fema.gov/IS800B/lesson5/NRF0105060t.htm (accessed December 18, 2018). A list of executive summaries of these scenarios is maintained by Global Security at https://www.globalsecurity.org/security/library/report/2004/hsc-planning-scenarios-jul04_exec-sum.pdf (accessed December 18, 2018).

[4] While the term MOM is common in HS and Emergency Management discussion, routine use does not quite capture the point I am trying to make. A nuclear accident like Three Mile Island would clearly be a MOM impacting the nation as a whole. But it would not threaten the security, legitimacy, or existence of the nation. However, one or more covert nuclear attacks leaving tens of thousands dead, huge areas contaminated, the national economy disrupted, and the population doubting the national leadership might undermine the nation itself. These "Security MOMs" should be our top priority for inquiry and education. And yes, I am playing a bit with words for effect. Part of gaining acceptance for a new idea is marketing it in a memorable way.

- Improved preparedness in accordance with The Bush 43 Administration's HSPD-8 (Homeland Security Policy Directive) and the Obama Administration's subsequent PPD-8 (President Policy Directive), which standardizes the five "mission areas" of mitigation, prevention, protection, response, and recovery, as well as new national frameworks and interagency coordination documents;
- In particular, improved planning that focuses on thirty-two core capabilities identified by PPD-8 and incorporated into FEMA educational documents;
- Nationwide acceptance and use of the National Integrated Management System (NIMS), and especially its subordinate operational concept, the Integrated Command System (ICS);
- Improved protection of critical infrastructure (per HSPD-7, its replacement, PPD-21, and the National Infrastructure Protection Plan), as well as information exchange between the Federal Sector Specific Agencies, private CI owners, and State, Local, Tribal and Territorial (SLTT) partners;
- National assistance and robust local action in establishing more than 150 intelligence fusion centers, many focused narrowly on specific industries and sectors;[5]
- Improved integration and coordination between various levels and agencies of government, especially in largely law enforcement–related events like the Boston Bombing, "The Pulse" Florida nightclub attack, and the San Bernardino shooting;
- New guidance, capability, and success in promoting resilience, especially after major national disasters, in order to reduce the cost and shorten the timeline for recovery; and
- Dramatically improved communications with the public, again especially with use of emerging social media like texting, Twitter, Facebook, WhatsApp, and the like.[6]

In short, new preparation for and execution of mission areas and core capabilities for traditional threats, hazards, and national disasters

---

[5] I list this as an accomplishment. I also consider it a concern. Where did we get the thousands of trained intelligence analysts and managers who are suddenly populating these centers? Many are training themselves, On The Job. Who is providing oversight? Frequently, nobody outside the parent organization. What constraints are placed on their capabilities? Frequently none, as technology races ahead of the law-making process. So we have tens of thousands of people with limited training in domestic intelligence work, often directed by managers lacking domestic intel backgrounds themselves, using technology (drones, cell tower spoofing, etc.) designed for targeting enemies overseas. What could possibly go wrong?

[6] All of this is with the single exception of Hurricane Maria in Puerto Rico, where special historical, cultural, political, financial, and social circumstances combined to create a preparedness failure so complete that it required the assignment of the US Army Corps of Engineers as the primary federal agency in charge of rebuilding the island's entire electrical grid.

is extensive, elaborate, and practiced. An extensive collection of lessons learned has been established. A broad range of training is available for a wide variety of risks and disasters and for an increasing number of what the Obama Administration called "adversarial actions"—criminal attacks, school shooters, "sacrificial zealots" (a term explained in chapter 1), and even the dangers of the opioid/fentanyl epidemic.[7]

These advances are not limited to FEMA or even DHS alone. The FBI, Secret Service, DEA, ATFE, HHS, and many public–private Special Interest Groups (SIGs) are fully and constantly engaged in improving all aspects of preparedness, with a new emphasis on Recovery and Resilience (areas of effort traditionally left mostly to state and local officials). And while less standardized in their approach (and frequently underresourced), many efforts at state and local level have shown similar dramatic improvements. Many in private industry have become full partners in these efforts, and Business Continuity Management is now routinely accepted as an essential element of business planning and operations.

In short, those who count meeting traditional threats on a traditional scale with improved capabilities as a success have reason to be proud of their efforts. We are thinking in an effective way about traditional HS issues.

BUT WHAT ABOUT NONTRADITIONAL THREATS? WHY WE NEED TO DO SOMETHING DIFFERENT. NOW.

As the Bush 43 Administration drew to a close, those working HS tried to accomplish several major administrative tasks.[8]

First, they sought to fill permanent deputy positions under political appointees in order to provide continuity during changes of administrations. In this, they were largely successful. While some suspected that Bush 43 appointees would use this opportunity to "burrow in," the transition between Administrations (at least in homeland security) proved effective. Both "sides" deserve credit.

Second, they sought to implement key lessons learned as identified in the various Hurricane Katrina postmortems. Given that the Republicans and Democrats in Congress issued different reports, this proved challenging. But one gratifying success was the way a late Bush-era interest in preparedness and risk management was expanded and implemented through

---

[7] See, for example, DEA *Roll Call Video Advises Law Enforcement to Exercise Extreme Caution*, June 10, 2016, https://www.dea.gov/press-releases/2016/06/10/dea-warning-police-and-public-fentanyl-exposure-killsm (accessed December 18. 2018).

[8] You are not going to find this in any text, and DHS does not have an official historian. But I knew some of the key players in DHS at the time. I watched this unfold.

Obama's PPD-8, which superseded Bush's HSPD-8 with a broader and more mature approach.

Lastly, Bush's HS team attempted to create a new focus on Response and Recovery (and hence mitigation, prevention, and protection as well) from a clandestine nuclear attack on the United States—a situation we might call a "Nuclear Security MOM." This effort carried over into the first years of the Obama Administration. Important efforts included the following.

- High-profile reports (RAND, *Effects of Attack*, 2006 [Mead and Molander 2006]) (Physicians for Social Responsibility, *Nuclear Terrorism*, 2006 [Helfand et al. 2006]).
- Federal strategies and playbooks (HHS, National Health Security Strategy for the United States, 2009 [Sebelius 2009]) (Medical Planning and Response Manual for a Nuclear Detonation Incident: a Practical Guide, 2011 [Laffan 2011]);
- Productive, high-profile conferences (*Center Bio Security*, *Advancing Resilience*, 2011);
- A highly regarded volume of focused scholarly research (*Medical Response Nuclear Detonation*, 2011 [Murrain-Hill, Coleman, and Hick 2011]);
- A federally sponsored ten paper series on nuclear event health and medical education from the CDC (CDC, *Scarce Resources for a Nuclear Detonation*, 2011);
- And useful emergency management and medical planning documents (Lawrence Livermore, *Planning Factors*, 2011 [Buddemeier et al. 2011]; ASPR, *Medical Planning Nuclear Detonation*, 2013 [Coleman et al. 2013]).[9]

After this flurry of activity, the focus on nuclear terrorism was gradually diluted during the late Obama era by emphasis on more traditional hazards and disasters (hurricanes, etc.) Since then, experts in MOM preparedness (both nuclear and biological) have continued their work but with a lower profile. As a result, publications from major new studies and conferences about nuclear MOMs have slowed. For example, one of the most referenced documents in this field today remains the interagency *Planning Guidance*

---

[9] The Johns Hopkins Center for Health Security (formerly UPMC) has been a national leader in the field of biosecurity and, by extension, other WMD threats. Results from their studies, workshops, etc. are available at http://www.centerforhealthsecurity.org/our-work/search%20publications?search=nuclear (accessed December 18, 2018).

for Response to a Nuclear Detonation, 2nd edition (Executive Office of the President et al. 2010).[10],[11]

A review of material produced during this high point of federal focus on nuclear MOMs reveals that such an event is quite different in scale and substance from more traditional disasters, and despite practitioners' claims to the contrary, an All-Hazards Approach will not meet the challenges of such a homeland security event.[12] Let's look at some of that material.

RAND, Considering the Effects of a Catastrophic Terrorist Attack, 2006

This RAND report used a number of games and gaming techniques to think through the implications of an event similar to scenario number one on the DHS list of fifteen national planning scenarios: a ten kiloton nuclear bomb concealed in the shipping container and smuggled into the Port of Long Beach near Los Angeles.[13] Anticipated outcomes included:

- Sixty thousand people might die instantly from the blast itself or quickly thereafter from radiation poisoning.
- One-hundred-fifty thousand more might be exposed to hazardous levels of radioactive water and sediment from the port, requiring emergency medical treatment.
- The blast and subsequent fires might completely destroy the entire infrastructure and all ships in the Port of Long Beach and the adjoining Port of Los Angeles.
- Six million people might try to evacuate the Los Angeles region.

---

[10] This chapter is focused on the aftermath of a nuclear event. While major academic efforts slowed somewhat during the Obama Administration, efforts on prevention continued apace. Some of the best work is to be found at NTI (Nuclear Threat Initiative) http://www.nti.org/about/nuclear-terrorism/, The Belfer Center at the Kennedy School https://www.belfercenter.org/nuclear-issues, and the Union of Concerned Scientists https://allthingsnuclear.org/category/nuclear-terrorism-2#.WwW1rYoh3IU.

[11] This is not to suggest that interest in a nuclear MOM has disappeared. Publication of related material continues, including Michael McCaul's (2016) *Failures of Imagination* mentioned in chapter 15. And NORTHCOM recently conducted a major exercise related to the subject. But when President Obama declared that terrorism did not pose "an existential threat" to the United States, focus on terrorist attacks with WMD waned.

[12] Kelly McKinney's (2018) book, *Moment of Truth: The Nature of Catastrophes and How to Prepare for Them*, drives this point home in distressing detail.

[13] The fifteen National Planning Scenarios were created by DHS to establish the range of response capabilities required for preparedness planning under the Bush 43 HSPD-8 (ultimately replaced by the Obama PPD-8). All of them constitute major emergency events (MOMs). Only a few (a nuclear attack, a national pandemic, etc.) present a threat to the nation's power and security (a Security MOM).

- Two to three million people might need relocation because fallout will contaminate a five-hundred-square-kilometer area.
- Gasoline supplies might run critically short across the entire region because of the loss of Long Beach refineries—responsible for producing one-third of the gasoline west of the Rockies (Mead and Molander 2006, xvi).

As with other studies, this one highlighted the need for massive emergency response. But the report was unique in that it extended its focus until several months after the event and demonstrated how long-term challenges would greatly exceed the recovery problems of more traditional hazards and natural disasters. For example:

- The early cost was estimated to exceed $1 trillion in 2006 dollars—perhaps twenty times the cost of Katrina.
- A policy conflict would likely develop between the imperative of closing all ports to prevent future attacks and rapidly reopening ports so the global shipping supply chain and the global economy could continue to operate.
- Restoring orderly economic relationships would be a major challenge as loans and mortgages went into default, insurance companies went bankrupt, and financial markets were unable to meet contract obligations for futures and derivatives. (Mead and Molander 2006, vii)
- The entire civil court system would be stressed to the breaking point.

In short, this nuclear MOM would play out very differently from large-scale natural disasters where effects are primarily local or regional, and recovery is mostly a matter of rebuilding damaged infrastructure. The combination of massive destruction, nationwide impact displacement of millions of people, economic cascade between various industries, and the uncertainty of subsequent attacks, would present decision-makers with problems that could not be addressed by organizations, perspectives, and lessons learned from the past (Mead and Molander 2006, 8).

Physicians for Social Responsibility, *The US and Nuclear Terrorism*, 2006

Like other medical stakeholders, the Physicians for Social Responsibility concluded that traditional government organizations were unprepared to: meet the medical needs of the many people who would be injured; plan for the decisions that would be required; coordinate and deploy essential resources; or even communicate real-time information and guidance to citizens and government officials (Helfand et al. 2006, 5). Experiences in Texas and Florida during the 2017 hurricane season suggests that progress has been made in communicating with citizens and between officials in traditional emergencies. But the lack of recent focus on novel MOMs (specifically WMD attacks) does not instill confidence.

HHS, National Health Security Strategy for the United States, 2009

This document is included as part of the broad effort to prepare for MOMs for two reasons.

First it is a great example of a new initiative by a traditionally nonsecurity-related federal department making a conscious effort to contribute to domestic security by minimizing "the risks associated with a wide-range of potential large scale incidents" (Sebelius 2009, 2). The reference is clearly to the major threats that most concern DHS (including nuclear attack), as the language is closely coordinated with that department's documents concerning preparedness, threats, and risk management.

Second, the Health Security Strategy provides an excellent insight into just how hard that is likely to be by establishing ten essential strategic objectives:

1. Foster informed individuals and communities.
2. Develop the required workforce.
3. Ensure situational awareness.
4. Foster integrated, scalable health care delivery systems.
5. Ensure timely and effective communications.
6. Promote an effective countermeasure enterprise
7. Ensure prevention or mitigation to emerging threats to health.
8. Incorporate postincident recovery into planning and response.
9. Work with cross-border and global partners to enhance global health security.
10. Ensure that all systems that support national health security are based upon the best available science, evaluation, and quality improvement methods.

The effort required to achieve all this in preparedness for an event like that described in the Rand report (above) is truly sobering. We are NOT prepared for such an eventuality today.

UPMC, Advancing US Resilience to a Nuclear Catastrophe, 2011

This high-profile conference asked two dozen experts to suggest new "policies and proposals to strengthen the capacity of major U.S. cities, and the nation as a whole, to withstand a nuclear catastrophe . . . with particular emphasis on response to a terrorist detonation of a nuclear weapon and early lessons emerging from the [then] recent Fukushima Daiichi nuclear disaster" (Center Bio Security, introduction). The results in some areas were surprisingly positive, including good news about advances in plume modeling for radiation dispersal and the ability of individuals to survive fallout radiation by sheltering in place. Progress was noted in planning, medical knowledge, and medical treatment for radiation issues, as was the creation of networks of experts (like the European Group for Blood and Marrow Transplant [EBMT] and the Nuclear Accident Committee [NAC] who responded effectively to the Fukushima incident). And the results of research into disaster communications were particularly encouraging, as Dr. Dennis Mileti noted that:

> people of all stripes will respond to calls to prepare for disaster if 3 conditions exist:
> 1. They can observe others—friends, family, coworkers—taking the encouraged action.
> 2. Preparedness messages are clearly focused on action, not risk. People want to know what to do, how to do it and how taking such action will cut their losses. People are not interested in messages that focus on risk and science.
> 3. Messages must be consistent, and they must be delivered repetitively by a variety of trusted sources, across multiple channels. [Center Bio Security, p. 3]

The sponsoring Center for Biosecurity also announced an initiative to produce "radiation (rad) resilient cities" by providing information on fallout preparedness to high risk cities, as well as an idea for a public–private partnership capable of screening up to one million people for radiation in a matter of days after an event (Center for Biosecurity 2011; Adalja et al. 2011).

But several major issues echoed our previous conclusions about systemic problems, including a lack of unified authority and guidance, differences in focus and perspective between practitioners, and the need for coherent concepts (theories) to drive preparedness, planning, and public communications.

- For example, Admiral Thad Allen, the Federal Incident Commander for the BP oil spill and Hurricanes Katrina and Rita, emphasized the need for understanding the complex legal framework for US disaster response as well as the role of technical experts and political leaders in both decision-making and execution. In fact, as long as state and local governments are functioning, there is no legal authority for the federal government to preempt their authority. Coordinating around this reality is much more difficult in major WMD events than in the smaller disasters upon which most disaster training is predicated (Center Bio Security, p. 5).

- Similarly, David McKernan, an emergency manager in Fairfax County, VA, reinforced the challenge to local practitioners of dealing with national security events (like a Nuclear MOM) and the need for research to identify specific needs for such events, to include unique resources and techniques for utilizing them (Center Bio Security, p. 3).

In sum, most professionals do not know how to think about the special challenges of a Nuclear MOM.

Murrain-Hill, Medical Response to a Nuclear Detonation, 2011

This comprehensive medical article makes the point that "the US Department of Health and Human Services (HHS) has substantial experience planning for and supporting the medical and public health needs for large civilian gatherings and mass casualty incidents in the United States and globally." And they have the legitimacy to apply that experience to nuclear events. The authors draw on their expertise to design a "playbook" (including templates) for use in short and mid-term nuclear response. Their considerations include: using damage zones to organize response activities; the number and spectrum of injuries; radiation contamination; safety of response workers; triage; venues for medical response; and even a list of measures for pre-incident preparedness.

But practitioners and elected official must be able to apply this expertise across a broad region of the nation on a moment's notice. And there's the rub. There is no evidence that anyone beyond a small number of emergency management specialists and a few specially prepared DOD units routinely think in these terms.

Lawrence Livermore, Planning Factors in the Aftermath of Nuclear Terrorism, 2011

Written with a broader emergency management audience in mind, this publication offers more than one hundred pages of detailed explanations of what responders and government leaders should expect, with attention to topics ranging from prompt effects (blast, blindness, electromagnetic pulse, and fires) and fallout concerns (close-in, long range, and agriculture) to shelter and evacuation. Its recommendations are extensive (emergency management priorities; responder priorities; public health and medical priorities; long-term recovery issues; and preparedness).

But it does not answer the central issues raised by Admiral Allen earlier: Who exactly has the authority and responsibility to make all this happen? And how many are trained and prepared, constantly thinking about how to respond on short notice to such an event impacting millions across a broad swath of the nation?

HHS, Medical Planning and Response Manual for a Nuclear
Detonation Incident: A Practical Guide, 2011

This excellent document provides a quick, broad overview of complex
topics, with an ability to drill down deep into details as necessary. The thir-
teen manuscripts were designed to be no more than seven to fifteen journal
pages in length, with illustrations, tables, and bulleted points so the reader
can quickly get a full sense of the topic, accompanied by clear guidance on
where to find more detailed information. The resulting 125-page manual
provides much of the information that would be needed to understand and
help manage a major nuclear or radiological disaster. Topics include:

- Health Risks from Exposure to Radiation: The Basics
- Response, Resources, and Resilience: Preparedness and Planning for a
  Nuclear Detonation
- Acute Radiation Syndrome: Medical Guidance and National Response
- Nuclear Fallout Protection in a Nutshell
- What to Do, What Not to Do, and Why
- Preparing the Home for Sheltering in Place Following a Nuclear
  Detonation
- Involving the Community: Operationalizing a Playbook, Engaging
  Regional Emergency Coordinators, and Considering Ethical Issues
- Communicating about a Nuclear Detonation
- The Federal Response Structure and Plans: NRF, NIMS, ESFs, and
  Directives
- Population Monitoring after a Nuclear Detonation
- Radiation/Nuclear Medical Countermeasure Research and Product
  Development Efforts for Public Health Emergencies
- Strategic Framework for Providing Radiation Sickness Medical
  Countermeasures and Supplies in a Scarce Resources Setting: Local,
  Regional and Federal Resources
- The Increasing Role of Technology in Educating Responders and
  Planners about Mass Casualty Radiation Emergencies
- International Agencies, Networks, and Radiation Safety Guidance

But despite providing information to help think through this national
security challenge, the authors identify a problem with leader and practitioner culture:

> Public health and medical leaders typically make decisions once data
> have been collected and analyzed. In a crisis, the available data will
> be insufficient to make fully informed decisions, and it is critical that
> leaders learn the important skill of making decisions with incomplete
> information. (Laffan 2011, 3)

In other words, those in charge really have think through this problem before the moment of crisis. Some victims will have to be abandoned. Some communities who thought they had prepared adequately will find their resources diverted. Leaders will have to make life and death decisions on incomplete data as a radioactive cloud climbs skyward and fleeing citizens fill the streets. Some of those decisions will be wrong. Traditional thinking in such a novel situation will leave our system of response, recovery, and even governance paralyzed.

Executive Office of the President et al., *Planning Guidance for Response to a Nuclear Detonation, 2nd ed.* June 2010 (2nd ed. updated 2012)[14]

In an attempt to provide one stop guidance to response planners and their leadership across the nation, this document addresses: nuclear detonation effects; a zoned approach to recovery; shelters and evacuation; early medical care; population monitoring; and public preparedness. The inescapable conclusion is that state and local rescue efforts will be on their own and left to make their own judgements for the first three days or more after a national nuclear security event. Many victims will be unreachable, and leaders will have to balance the risk to rescuers against the chance of reaching those who are injured but survivable. The information required to make such decisions will be limited and perhaps unreliable. And the physical and moral challenges will extend well past the response phase and into recovery, where every traditional effort by law enforcement, repair crews, medical personnel, and even commercial owners, operators, and workers will be vastly complicated.

Finally the challenge presented to private industry of working after a nuclear event is sobering. What employees will report to work in face of concerns over contamination or contagion? How many will leave their families at such a dangerous time to purify water, sell groceries, clean hospitals, or even provide administrative support to law enforcement? Just the challenge of maintaining multistate logistical chains will be daunting in the face of a region impacted by fallout. This situation is not like sending truck drivers to wait just outside the "wind line" of a major hurricane. Who will send cargo and drivers into harm's way when their return unscathed is in question? Who will go?

---

[14] The sources in this section have been placed in chronological order, except for this one which was released in 2010 and updated in 2012. Given its origin, it remains the single most authoritative source for the federal vision of planning for and responding to a Nuclear MOM. It addresses gaps noted in the earlier *DHS Planning Guidance for Protection and Recovery Following Radiological Dispersal Device (RDD) and Improvised Nuclear Device (IND) Incidents (2008)*.

Not mentioned in this extensive treatment are the legal and political ramifications of the situation. When are responders obligated to respond? When can they say no? What about workers in critical infrastructure? Who pays for what? Is there any point at which Unity of Effort must be replaced by Unity of Command for the sake of the nation? Citizens can be drafted to defend our national security overseas. Should similar provisions be made for compelling service in the domestic security arena?

To their credit, DOD and the military services (especially the National Guard) have established military units trained to collect some of the data needed to make these nontraditional decisions. And some of the troops do have specialized equipment to allow them to work amid the dangers of "high radiation levels, wide spread fires, deep rubble, structural instability, and other hazards" (Executive Office of the President et al. 2012, 56). But the number of such troops available at any given time is limited and unlikely to be adequate for multiple simultaneous attacks (as I think we should expect).

Also in fairness, it must be noted that a number of individuals and organizations have created training regimes to address the most obvious and immediate concerns for a nuclear or radiological event. For example, FEMA addresses these concerns with a number of excellent courses available online for free at the Emergency Management Institute.[15] And NORTHCOM recently used a similar event as the focus of an annual exercise program. The Nuclear Security MOM is not being ignored. It is just a very hard task, and trainers have little in the way of lessons learned to draw upon. This is why educators who concentrate on inquiry, analysis, and evaluation need to be involved.

MAMA MIA! MULTIPLE MOMS!

The question from our look at a single Security MOM is whether the progress we have made in HS efforts since the concept was created in 1996 is adequate to address such a situation. Examining this example suggests the answer is "No." Are there other examples?

Yes. Because unfortunately, not all MOMs are created equal.

The type of MOM matters. The footprint of extensive damage to New Orleans from Katrina flooding was probably larger than the Severe Damage Zone anticipated by a ten kiloton nuclear weapon. But the New Orleans scenario created hardly a blip in the national economy. A nuclear attack (perhaps followed by a second or third) would doubtlessly impact national power for years.

---

[15] https://training.fema.gov/is/crslist.aspx (accessed July 20, 2018).

The location of a MOM matters. A chemical MOM on the order of Bhopal but in a Gulf Coast setting would have a major impact on the nation, but it would probably not imperil our national power or our ability to use it overseas. A radiological event like Chernobyl but located in rural South Texas would probably have a similar limited impact. However, the same events unfolding near the heart of a major financial or government center (like New York, Dallas, or DC) would most certainly be a Security MOM, impacting the security of the nation as a whole.

The target of a MOM matters. The explosion that created the Texas City Disaster (sinking ships at dock, knocking airplanes from the sky, killing nearly six hundred and injuring eight thousand) was surely a MOM. But it did not impact the nation's security. A similar event targeted at naval facilities at San Diego or Norfolk would probably qualify as a Security MOM.

The identity of the MOM targeteer matters. The Great Influenza of 1917–18 killed more American soldiers than World War I, but the American public saw it as just another battle in man's endless war with Mother Nature. If the same level of biological attack were launched by a sovereign state, we would no doubt see it as a cause for war.

The impact of a MOM matters. The New Madrid fault runs roughly under the Mississippi River from the Midwest to New Orleans. A major slip along the fault in rural Missouri would obviously be a MOM. But a change in location and degree, severing rail and road connections across the Mississippi from the Gulf of Mexico northward, could split the nation with national security implications.

The novelty of a MOM matters. If the Galveston Hurricane of 1900 were to be repeated (despite the seventeen-foot seawall that has since been created), we would know how to think about the disaster, and thus we could respond properly, recover eventually, and show resilience as a city, state, nation, and as a people. But if a cyberattack were to compromise property records in a state or destroy health records from a major healthcare provider, or actually delegitimize an election—with the promise to repeat the event again—the sheer novelty of the crisis and the fear of repetition might weaken the nation in unforeseen ways.

The number of potential Security MOMs is large but finite. All of these eventualities could be considered, explored with experts, and "tested" through academic inquiry if we chose to think about homeland security the way the founders of national security thought about their new world in the 1950s and 1960s. They left the management of tanks and troops, of aircraft and aircraft carriers, to the professional practitioners in the field and focused on the core issues that drive national security theory and practice. How might we do that with homeland security?

A COMMON FEATURE OF ALL SECURITY MOMS

By now you should recognize that the three systemic challenges we noted in chapters 13, 14, and 15 (authorities, organizations/perspectives, and concepts) all apply to the worst cases we might face. But is there something even more fundamental underlying these problems?

One characteristic all of the potential Security MOMs share in common is likely leader indecision (in some cases, perhaps paralysis) because of the novel nature of the disaster. I have no doubt that in the face of a nuclear detonation, or a terrible pandemic, or complete interruption of communications from cyberattack, public safety personnel would respond bravely and to the best of their ability. But could leaders reason their way to entirely new solutions, or would they be constrained by well-established protocols now inadequate to the type and scale of disaster?

To address this question in my classes, I use the book *A Passion for Leadership* by Bob Gates (2016). In it he notes that he led four very large organizations in his life: the CIA, Texas A&M University, the DOD, and the Boy Scouts of America. In all of them, good, well-meaning people struggled with change. The problem, he concludes, is not individual workers and administrators but the very nature of bureaucracy. "No one set out to make bureaucracies the enemy of ordinary people," he argues (Gates 2016, 5). But that is frequently the way they ended up, making today look like yesterday and tomorrow look like today, in slavish devotion to old cultures and perspectives, despite new situations with new demands. His example of the difficulty he had as Secretary of Defense in pushing through the immediate fielding of mine resistant vehicles against adherents of the traditional purchasing system, even as soldiers died for lack of the vehicles in Iraq and Afghanistan, sounds disturbingly familiar to anyone who has tried to encourage the local adoption of new HS frameworks for Risk Management, Response, and Recovery by the thousands of local jurisdictions in the United States.

Gates names six causes for this bureaucratic malaise: elected officials, political interests, operating budgets; the uneven quality of individuals elected/appointed; job security (which weighs heavily against reform); and interference by retirees or alumni. I will leave the rest of the book for your detailed study (which I highly recommend). But this would be a great place to begin serious graduate inquiry into how to lead bureaucracies (made up of well-meaning practitioners) to understand the new challenges of Security MOMs and make the changes required to meet them.

Other experts whose theories about improving bureaucratic function might become the basis for HS theory include:

- John P. Kotter whose work on *Leading Change* (especially with bureaucracies) has been a staple of the business world for decades;
- Donald Kettl, a leader in Public Administration theory, who rejects thinking in terms of organizational structure and management and instead offers a framework to integrate *government* (the collection of institutions that act with authority and create formal obligations) with *governance* (the set of processes and institutions, formal and informal, through which social action occurs);
- Graham Allison, author of *Essence of Decision*, whose bureaucratic analysis of decision-making during the Cuban Missile Crisis set the standard for three generations of scholars and theories in the subject;
- Edward Deming, whose global success in aligning managerial objectives with bureaucratic performance through Quality Systems Management has changed the destiny of corporations and of countries.

Once the higher education community realizes that a major aspect of academic theory missing from the homeland security discipline is to be found in the applied study of bureaucracy, I am confident that many more names will be added to this list.

FIXING THE IMPERFECT INTERSECTION BY LISTENING TO OUR SECURITY MOMS

To summarize, we are not going to find anytime soon a theoretical structure for homeland security like those that drive political science, security studies, economics, public administration, and similar academic disciplines. There are simply too many variables, actors, jurisdictions, perspectives and political considerations involved. So we will have to look somewhere else for a "true north" to guide our thinking if we want to move beyond ever better training on ever more numerous lessons learned.[16]

MOMs are important to thinking about homeland security for two reasons.

1. They help us focus on the dangers that caused us to create homeland security in the first place: events that not only threaten lives, property, and the environment (the arena of traditional public safety and emergency management), but national security—the ability to collect, protect, and project power to advance national interests.
2. They help define the federal role in homeland security, which in traditional hazards and disasters is subordinated to state and local leadership.[17]

---

[16] My thanks to Dr. Bert Tussing of the Army War College for this insightful turn of phrase.

[17] And my thanks to Dr. Mike Dunaway of the University of Louisiana at Lafayette for helping me encapsulate my summary points in this way.

Addressing Security MOMs requires us to find solutions to problems that might threaten the very life of the nation but will be left unaddressed if we allow those who specialize in the Old Normal to drive all preparedness.

As MOMs require us to think differently about the New Normal, we will come to realize that all homeland security agents and agencies share one characteristic in common: their bureaucracy is the source of, and the solution to, their most difficult challenges.

This is not to suggest that we turn our education and training systems upside down and rebuild them with an entirely new focus. Our homeland security practitioners have improved their ability to deal with threats—even big threats—to lives and property that we face on a routine basis. We do not want to lose that hard-won success. You need to read and learn about those routine challenges and the exceptional people who meet them.

But MOMs force us to face a new set of major challenges at the imperfect intersection of two things we know how to do separately: national security and public safety. Can sustained inquiry—asking the right questions—help us to meet those new challenges in some new ways?

- With a bit of federal emphasis, can we revise our exercise programs to focus on the high-consequence missions first, applying lessons learned to lesser threats accordingly?
- Can we expand the focus of educational programs from describing what individual homeland security disciplines are doing now to analyzing how they should be integrated to meet the MOMs and the barriers that prevent their adapting to change?
- In almost every case, that barrier is the same: the bureaucracy that runs the show. Can we think anew about those theories and concepts that already work well in other disciplines? Might we find ways to apply them here?
- The unifying factor in homeland security education is not the policy process as it is with national security: it is the bureaucratic process—including the life cycle of the bureaucracy and how to keep it under the control of management instead of the other way round. Can we find new insights that will help us master the New Normal in threats?

I will explain in a later volume why policy dominates national security while bureaucracy dominates homeland security. But for now, let me leave you with these departure points for thinking anew about our subject.

- Homeland security is about using the tools of public safety to protect both our citizens and our national power against national security threats.

- Doing that requires some major changes in the way we integrate the various jurisdictions and agencies that ensure public safety.
- The goal is not just new capabilities or technology but new perspectives that encourage practitioners to look beyond their own tasks and responsibilities and rice bowls, to ask how they can better contribute to the safety and security of the nation as a whole.
- We have the training and exercise base we need to make the changes at the practitioner level, if we will fund these programs more robustly.
- We have the education base necessary to guide the training base in its integration—but not yet the proper educational focus.
- We can provide that focus by addressing Security MOMs first. Collect and refine the subdisciplines that comprise homeland security into a set of essential skills.[18] Then integrate them through the improved study of the bureaucracies and perspectives that make up the flesh and blood of our homeland security effort.

We should set as our goal the establishment of a new common homeland security culture across agencies. That culture should see sustaining domestic national power in the face of a new thinking enemy as the mission and regard narrow parochial bureaucratic attitudes as the primary foe.

★ ★ ★

And so we reach the end of Volume 1 of *How to Think about Homeland Security* not with a solution but with a challenge. Can the practitioners, academics, leaders, and students of HS mount a campaign of inquiry adequate to fill an existential need for our society—the need for a way to think about HS in its most extreme cases?

The next volumes in this series will provide the context (risk, threat, vulnerabilities, consequences, and some of the major structures and organizations) required for such thinking. Whether the challenge is accepted and solutions developed before calamity befalls us depends largely upon you, the reader. It is after all, your homeland. And your security.

---

[18] See the reference in chapter 15 to work done along these lines by James Ramsey, Paul Stockton, and others on the standards committee on INSPRS, as described in *Development of Competency Based Education Standards for Homeland Security Academic Programs: Report for Undergraduate Degree Programs.*

REFERENCES

Adalja A. A., M. Watson, S. Wollner, and E. Toner. 2011. "A Possible Approach to Large-Scale Laboratory Testing for Acute Radiation Sickness after A Nuclear Detonation." *Biosecurity Bioterrorism Journal* 9 (4): 345–50.

Barry, John M. 2004. *The Great Influenza*. New York: Penguin Group.

Buddemeier, B. R. et al. 2011. *Key Response Planning Factors for the Aftermath of Nuclear Terrorism, LLNL-TR-512111/01049.* Lawrence Livermore National Labs and others. Accessed December 18, 2018. https://fas.org/irp/agency/dhs/fema/ncr.pdf.

Center for Biosecurity. 2011. *Advancing U.S. Resilience to a Nuclear Catastrophe.* Baltimore, MD: University of Pittsburg Medical Center. Accessed December 18, 2018. http://www.centerforhealthsecurity.org/our-work/events/2011_resilience_nuc_catastrophe/nuke-res_cnf_rpt.pdf.

Center for Biosecurity. 2011. *Rad Resilient City*. Baltimore, MD: UPMC. Accessed December 18, 2018. http://www.radresilientcity.org/index.

Center for Disease Control and Prevention. *Radiation Emergencies*. http://www.bt.cdc.gov/radiation/.

Center for Disease Control and Prevention. *Radiation Emergencies*. Accessed February 22, 2019. https://emergency.cdc.gov/radiation/.

Center for Terrorism Risk Management Board. 2006. *Considering the Effects of a Catastrophic Terrorist Attack*. Santa Monica, CA: RAND. Accessed December 18, 2018. https://www.rand.org/content/dam/rand/pubs/technical_reports/2006/RAND_TR391.pdf?

Coleman, C. N., A. Knebel, and J. L. Hick. 2011. "Scarce Resources for Nuclear Detonation: Executive Summary." *Disaster Med Public Health Prep* 5 (Suppl 1): S13–S19.

Coleman, C. Norman, et al. 2012. "Medical Planning and Response for a Nuclear Detonation: A Practical Guide." *Biosecurity and Bioterrorism: Biodefense Strategy, Practice, and Science* 10 (4): 346–71.

Coleman, C. Norman, et al. 2013. *Medical Planning and Response Manual for a Nuclear Detonation Incident*. Washington, DC: U.S. Department of Health and Human Services, Office of the Assistant Secretary for Preparedness and Response (ASPR). Accessed December 18, 2018. http://www.phe.gov/Preparedness/planning/nuclearresponsemanual/Documents/medplanresmannucdet-guide-final.pdf.

Coleman, C. N., A. R. Knebel, and J. L. Hick. 2011. "Scarce Resources for Nuclear Detonation: Project Overview and Challenges." *Disaster Med Public Health Prep* 5 (Suppl 1): S13–S19.

DHS. 2018. *National Preparedness System*. Accessed December 18, 2018. https://www.fema.gov/national-preparedness-system.

Executive Office of the President, et al. 2010. *Planning Guidance for Response to a Nuclear Detonation, 2d ed*. Washington, DC: FEMA. 2nd ed updated 2012. Accessed May 19, 2018. https://www.fema.gov/media-library-data/20130726-1821-25045-3023/planning_guidance_for_response_to_a_nuclear_detonation___2nd_edition_final.pdf.

Federal Emergency Management Agency, US Department of Homeland Security. 2008. *National Response Framework. Emergency Support Function #8—Public Health and Medical Services Annex*. Accessed December 18, 2018. http://www.fema.gov/pdf/emergency/nrf/nrf-esf-08.pdf.

Gates, Robert. 2016. *A Passion for Leadership: Lessons on Change and Reform from Fifty Years of Public Service*. New York: Vintage.

Global Security. July 2004. "Executive Summaries of 15 National Planning Scenarios." Accessed December 18, 2018. https://www.globalsecurity.org/security/library/report/2004/hsc-planning-scenarios-jul04_exec-sum.pdf.

Graham, David. September 2, 2015. "The Mothers of All Disasters." *The Atlantic.* Accessed December 18, 2018. https://www.theatlantic.com/national/archive/2015/09/the-disaster-next-time/403063/.

Helfand, Ira, et al. 2006. *The U.S. and Nuclear Terrorism: Still Dangerously Unprepared.* Washington, DC: Physicians for Social Responsibility. Accessed December 18, 2018. http://action.psr.org/site/DocServer/PSR_NuclearTerr_rpt_full.pdf?docID=781.

Howe, David. 2004. *Planning Scenarios: Executive Summaries Created for Use in National, Federal, State, and Local Homeland Security Preparedness Activities.* Washington, DC: The Homeland Security Council. Accessed February 22, 2019. https://www.globalsecurity.org/security/library/report/2004/hsc-planning-scenarios-jul04_exec-sum.pdf.

Laffan, Alison M., et al. 2011. *Medical Planning and Response Manual for a Nuclear Detonation Incident: A Practical Guide.* Washington, DC: Office of the Assistant Secretary for Preparedness and Response (ASPR), Department of Health and Human Services. Accessed December 18, 2018. http://www.phe.gov/Preparedness/planning/nuclearresponsemanual/Documents/medplanresmannucdet-guide-final.pdf.

Lieberman, Senator Joseph. December 13, 2017. "Safeguarding American Agriculture in a Globalized World." Hearing of the Senate Committee on Agriculture, Nutrition, and Forestry: Washington, DC: US Senate. Accessed December 18, 2018. https://www.agriculture.senate.gov/imo/media/doc/Testimony_Lieberman.pdf.

McKinney, Kelly. 2018. *Moment of Truth: The Nature of Catastrophes and How to Prepare for Them.* New York: Savio Republic.

Mead, Charles, and Roger Molander. 2006. *Considering the Effects of a Catastrophic Terrorist Attack.* Santa Monica, CA: Center for Terrorism Risk Management Policy, RAND. Accessed December 18, 2018. https://www.rand.org/content/dam/rand/pubs/technical_reports/2006/RAND_TR391.pdf?

Murrain-Hill P, C. N. Coleman, and J. L. Hick, et al. 2011. "Medical Response to a Nuclear Detonation: Creating a Playbook for State and Local Planners and Responders." *Disaster Med Public Health Prep.* 5 (Suppl 1): S89–S97. Accessed December 18, 2018. https://www.cambridge.org/core/journals/disaster-medicine-and-public-health-preparedness/article/medical-response-to-a-nuclear-detonation-creating-a-playbook-for-state-and-local-planners-and-responders/A6A01B35902F5E8822CB8E0BF4FC0ED7.

National Hurricane Center. "Storm Surge Maximum of Maximums." Accessed December 18, 2018. http://www.nhc.noaa.gov/surge/momOverview.php.

Rad Resilient City. n.d. Accessed December 18, 2018. http://www.radresilientcity.org/index.

Radiation Emergency Medical Management. n.d. Accessed December 18, 2018. http://www.remm.nlm.gov/.

Sebelius, Kathleen. 2009. *National Health Security Strategy.* Washington, DC: Office of Assistant Secretary for Preparedness and Response (ASPR), Department of Health and Human Services. Accessed December 18, 2018. http://www.phe.gov/preparedness/planning/authority/nhss/strategy/documents/nhss-final.pdf.

Taylor, Alan. December 2, 2014. "Bhopal: The World's Worst Industrial Disaster, 30 Years Later." *The Atlantic.* Accessed December 18, 2018. https://www.theatlantic.com/photo/2014/12/bhopal-the-worlds-worst-industrial-disaster-30-years-later/100864/.

Index

About the Author

DR. DAVID H. McINTYRE has been writing, teaching, and presenting on National Security and Homeland Security issues for thirty years. He has taught for twenty semesters at the Bush School of Government and Public Service at Texas A&M University. Before that he was deputy director of the *ANSER Institute for Homeland Security* in Washington, DC (the first think tank focused on homeland security). Colonel McIntyre (USA, Retired) began those duties after a thirty-year career in the United States Army, where he served in airborne and armored cavalry units, wrote and taught strategy, and retired as the Dean of Faculty and Academics at the National War College.

Dr. McIntyre was appointed to the *National Security Education Board* by President George W. Bush in June 2008, confirmed by the Senate, and served until 2012. From 2010 until 2014, he was a Distinguished Visiting Fellow at the *Homeland Security Studies & Analysis Institute (HSSAI)* in Washington, DC, and he was twice a nonresident Fellow at the *Center for Cyber and Homeland Security* at George Washington University He has also served on the National Board of Directors of the *InfraGard National Members Alliance* (a public–private partnership with the FBI), as academic advisor to the University and Colleges Committee of the *International Association of Emergency Managers (IAEA)*, board member of the *Homeland Security/Defense Educational Consortium*, and on the 2002–2003 *Defense Science Board Summer Study on Homeland Security*.

Having helped Colonel Randall Larsen (USAF, Retired) develop the first graduate homeland security course in the nation in 1999 and directed the Integrative Center for Homeland Security at Texas A&M for four years, Dr. McIntyre also taught the subject at the Elliott School of George Washington University, the LBJ School at the University of Texas, and the National Graduate School of Falmouth, Massachusetts. He designed homeland security curriculum for Colorado Technical University.

He also helped to design and deliver numerous educational exercises and seminars for senior audiences, including the Department of Agriculture, the Environmental Protection Agency, the Portland and Miami Police Departments, the Association of Retired FBI Agents, Washington, DC, think tanks, the Texas National Guard, and various law enforcement organizations.

Dr. McIntyre's education includes: a BS in Engineering from the US Military Academy, West Point, New York; an MA in English and American Literature from Auburn University, Auburn, Alabama; a PhD in Government and Political Science (Security Studies) from the University of Maryland, College Park, Maryland.

His work in public education includes hundreds of radio and television appearances on FOX, ABC, MSNBC, CNN's Crossfire, CNBC, CSPAN, The History Channel, Voice of America, and the US State Department's "Dialogue" series, as well as WMAL, WTOP, NPR radio, WUSA-TV in Washington, DC, and KBTX in College Station, TX. For four years, he hosted a weekly homeland security radio program, featuring nine hundred guests, and recorded two hundred short essays for radio spots. He also wrote, hosted, and directed four hour-long specials on Homeland Security for national educational television.

Learn more at http://www.davemcintyre.net/.

Lightning Source UK Ltd.
Milton Keynes UK
UKHW030216210919
350133UK00008B/742/P